HE'S HISTORY, YOU'RE NOT

SURVIVING DIVORCE AFTER 40

Erica Manfred
Foreword by Tina Tessina, Ph.D.

gpp
life

Guilford, Connecticut
An imprint of The Globe Pequot Press

life   GPP Life gives women answers they can trust.

GPP Life is an imprint of The Globe Pequot Press.

Text design: Sheryl P. Kober
Layout: Joanna Beyer

Library of Congress Cataloging-in-Publication Data is available on file.

ISBN 978-0-7627-5135-8

Printed in the United States of America

10 9 8 7 6 5 4

To my daughter Freda—who asked me to dedicate this book not only to her, but to "all the divorced kids out there."

CONTENTS

Foreword: Just What You Need viii

Introduction x

Chapter 1: Grieving Is a Full-Time Job:
How to Survive the First—Worst—Year 1

Chapter 2: Before You Give Up:
Reconciliation Strategies That Work 35

Chapter 3: You and Your Divorce Lawyer:
A Love–Hate Relationship 63

Chapter 4: Living Alone and Liking It:
It Is Possible to Be Happy Without a Man 87

Chapter 5: No, You Will Not Become a Bag Lady:
Playing Your Cards Right 112

Chapter 6: Waiting Until the Kids Are Grown:
The Kids Are Never Grown 136

Chapter 7: What the Hell Happened to Your Marriage?:
You *Do* Need to Figure It Out 158

Chapter 8: Reinventing Yourself:
How to Become Who You Really Are 183

Chapter 9: Dating Again: On That Little Screen and Off It . . 203

Chapter 10: But I Love Her: Coping with Betrayal 234

Chapter 11: Forgiving the Bastard and Moving On:
Forgive Yourself First 255

Resources 277

Index 289

Acknowledgments 295

FOREWORD

Just What You Need

I'm so glad Erica wrote this book. As a therapist, I work with couples trying to save their marriages, and with individuals whose marriages dissolved. I think both groups will benefit from reading *He's History, You're Not.*

Finding out that your dream come true was a nightmare waiting to happen, that your Prince Charming has turned into an ugly, rapacious troll, and that everything you built your life on has crumbled around you is a shattering experience. Not only has your whole life changed, but your self-esteem tends to dissolve with the rest of your cherished ideals of love and marriage. After such devastation, how do you pick up the pieces?

Even women who initiated the divorce usually find they don't know how to get a grip on the new life they must create for themselves, and they're often devastated to find out that they're grieving for the same marriage they were so desperate to leave.

Never fear, girlfriend: Here comes Erica to the rescue. Smart, tough, honest, savvy, and funny, she has been through the worst of the carnage and come out wiser and stronger. In the following pages, she gives you what you need to achieve the same success.

I love the way the book is organized, and Erica's broad, thorough coverage of every aspect of going through divorce and coming out the other side intact. As a reader, you'll get support for your initial devastation, denial, and overwhelming grief, as well as very cogent and helpful advice and coaching through all the succeeding stages of recovery.

This book will help you come to grips with how your ex views finances and how to protect yourself, which is crucial to your future well-being. It gives excellent resources and guidelines, punctuated with case histories of those who have gone before you.

Erica deftly guides you through the journey she was thrust into by surprise. She learned from her own mistakes, from good and bad advice, and from thorough research, all of which she shares here with you. In the following pages you'll feel supported, encouraged, forewarned, and fully armed for the battles to come. She will point you toward the helpful Web sites, books, and experts, and help you choose what's right for you.

You'll even benefit from what Erica didn't do, because she researched how couples who are faltering can find effective therapy to avoid getting divorced. She has clearly outlined each mode of therapy to help you find what's right for you, and how to reach the practitioners.

If counseling doesn't work for you, or it's too late, she shows you why you need a lawyer and how to find one.

As you grow through the stages of divorce and being on your own, she helps you analyze your failed marriage and understand both your own part in the problems and your ex's contribution. In the process, you'll learn a lot about yourself, about how relationships work, and even how to avoid repeating the same old problems.

It's a wise and powerful journal, both prescriptive and instructive. You'll bless the author for writing this, and yourself for reading it. It will make these difficult days just a little easier, and it could help you change the outcome dramatically in your own favor.

Tina Tessina, Ph.D.
Long Beach, California
www.tinatessina.com

INTRODUCTION

The funny thing about divorce is that it doesn't actually kill you.
—FRANCES MAYES, *UNDER THE TUSCAN SUN*

Like September 11 or the Kennedy assassination, you never forget where you were the moment it happened. You never forget how you heard the news, what you were doing, even what you were wearing.

It was Christmas Eve 2000, and I was in a flannel nightie getting ready for bed in the house we had bought in the woods of upstate New York ten years earlier, when we'd left New York City for the adventure of country life. The daughter we had adopted two years earlier was asleep in the next room. I was used to my husband being very attentive, especially sexually, and it occurred to me that he'd been uninterested in sex, or even in conversation, for the past month or so. This wasn't like him. At the very least he was usually angry with me about something, fuming and raging but relating in one way or another. For the past month he'd simply been bland, almost formal. I remember feeling uneasy, and I asked him casually why he'd been so distant lately. I expected to hear some mumbled answer about pressures at work, or lack of sleep due to the constantly active baby I had pressured him into adopting in an unconscious and misguided attempt to save our marriage, or how angry he was at me about something or other.

"I want to leave you," he said.

If you've ever heard these five words—and if you're reading this, I bet you have either heard them or said them—you know the sheer terror that accompanies this particular announcement.

At first I thought he must be kidding. This was the man I'd assumed would never leave me—the man I'd married *because* he'd never leave me, the devoted husband who despite his often explosive behavior seemed totally dependent on me, and totally in love with me. At least he told me constantly that he loved me. That must count. The next day was not only Christmas but also my birthday, and I was expecting a surprise of a different sort.

"There's someone else," he said, naming a co-worker twenty-five years younger than me who'd been his best friend at work for years. "I'm in love with her."

It's strange how clichés that you've heard countless times on soap operas and TV movies stop being clichés when they're spoken to you personally. This was not a cliché I'd ever expected to hear from him.

Like watching jet planes slamming into the World Trade Center, I was in a state of disbelief. Not denial—not yet—just disbelief. Actually, I'd never been told anything before that seemed less likely. The sensation was strange, like some weird crack in reality had occurred; things as I knew them were not what they seemed. I entered a world like Dali's, where watches and worlds, my world, could melt and slither away. It was like being told very matter-of-factly that someone dead had come back to life, or that Copernicus was wrong—the world really was flat.

"But I'm fifty-five years old, we just adopted a kid, we spent my inheritance," I whined piteously. "How am I going to survive alone? I'm too old to find someone else. I don't have a job. It's not fair." More terror. Being dumped at thirty-five is one thing—the world is wide open for thirty-five-year-old women—but fifty-five? Being left when you're past fifty is like falling into a black hole in space. My life—my past life—passed before my eyes, but now there was no future. I'd never envisioned a future without him.

"But, but, I thought we were going to spend our old age together," I spluttered.

He looked at me as if I were speaking Urdu. I know about a million women have had this experience, but it comes as a revelation to all of us. All of a sudden you realize you have no idea who this man you call your husband really is. He certainly isn't who you thought he was. All of a sudden the softhearted guy who cared about my every ache and pain, who ran to comfort me when I cried, who supported my career and loved my mother, became totally invulnerable and hardhearted. This time my tears left him unmoved. His instant withdrawal from caring about me was the worst shock. One minute I had a best friend, a partner, an us-against-the-world mate; the next minute I had an enemy. No matter how bad our marriage got in other areas, sex among them, we'd always been each other's cheering section, each other's mutual admiration society. We didn't have one of those marriages that had deteriorated to hardly speaking. We shared everything, didn't we? Guess not.

Instantaneously losing that special place in your husband's heart after decades of marriage is worse than a slap in the face. It's a knockout punch. Being dumped is so profoundly traumatic and disorienting, it's amazing so many of us live through it.

As I later found out, he'd been planning his exit for a long time, with the support of various family members, his shrink, and, of course, his girlfriend. I, however, hadn't been privy to these plans, and neither has anyone else who's been dumped. That's why we're in such shock when it happens. We're literally "the last to know," for a good reason—no one told us.

This must be worse than your husband dying, I thought. At least then you can remember the good times and know that you were loved.

"I'm searching for authenticity," he explained in a flat tone of voice. "I have to lead an authentic life."

"Authentic? Gimme a break. Oh yeah, it's real authentic to leave your wife and kid just after you adopted her."

"I'm not leaving her," he protested. "I'm just moving. I'll see her all the time."

"But this is your house. You're leaving both of us. What's all this authentic stuff about?"

It's not that I don't believe in authenticity, if that means discovering who you really are and being true to yourself, but if it comes without integrity it's not worth much. To my ears, *authenticity* was the kind of psychobabble word that sounded like it came from his shrink, let's call him Dr. Twofaced, who had once been my shrink and who had counseled us together as well. Double betrayal. I'd always suspected this guy didn't like me.

"I don't know who I really am," he replied waving his hands around. "I feel that I'm always pretending. I need to find my true self."

Yeah, I thought, and you're gonna find your true self with *her*. "What is she going to do, hypnotize you?"

Actually, it seemed she'd already done that. I later found her love letters to him gushing about how much she adored him, desperately wanted to be with him, longed for him. He was going through the old clichéd midlife crisis, with a wife who took him for granted and didn't want to have sex with him, and a younger woman who threw herself at him. I'd gotten him every job he ever had, including his current one as a caseworker where he met the WWW. This does not stand for World Wide Web, but my name for her, the Wicked Witch of the West whom she somewhat resembled—if Margaret Hamilton had taken steroids for the role. All my feminist consciousness went out the window when it came to the WWW. I sneered openly to friends about how ugly she was. I felt vindicated when people would say, "He left *you* for *her*?" There are no lows to which I didn't sink during this time.

Since *The Wizard of Oz* is one of my all-time favorite movies, I'll call the WWW Almira in this book, for Almira Gulch who turned into the Wicked Witch. I'll call my husband Zeke, for the farmhand who played the Cowardly Lion, because he took the cowardly way out. My daughter will be Dorothy, for the innocent child caught up in a tornado not of her making and tossed into a strange and scary land. Like Dorothy in *The Wizard of Oz*, however, she has shown great courage and imagination in navigating that landscape, even though she's suffered more than any of us. My older foster daughter, Tina, will be Tina. She wants her real name used.

"She's my soul mate," he said in an agonized tone. "I can't leave her."

"I thought *we* were soul mates," I sniffled.

I felt like I was on *As the World Turns*, except with worse dialogue.

While they had been best friends for years, it seemed she had been in love with him the whole time. Her behavior when I periodically ran into her at an office function—moving away from me, avoiding eye contact—now made sense. He insisted their affair had just started. I believed that maybe the sex part had, but the emotional affair had been going on for a long time.

"I thought *we* were best friends. Don't we share everything? Don't I support your artistic aspirations? Aren't I your biggest fan?" I whimpered idiotically.

He shrugged, as if that were all in the past and no longer important. "You didn't understand me," he complained, like the proverbial neglected husband. "You never even listened to me."

"What?" I responded. "We talk all the time."

"No we don't," he protested. "You talk, I pretend to agree with you."

Damned if he wasn't right, the sneaky sonofabitch. I realized later, when doing one of many postmortems on our marriage with my therapist, that he got away with it because he never "yes deared" me, a transparent ploy men resort to when they want their wives to think they're paying attention. He was very convincing in his role of communicating husband, and I wanted to believe that we were actually communicating.

"Are you in love with her?" I asked, like an idiot. I was hoping it was just an affair that would maybe go away.

"Yes," he said, unapologetically. He made it clear that this relationship wasn't about sex. Somehow this was supposed to make me feel better. She was his "soul mate." It still makes me nauseous to write that. I was laboring under the illusion all those years that I was his soul mate. Actually I was his cellmate.

If you've been dumped, that pivotal moment when you hear the truth will be stamped on your consciousness forever. A huge chunk of your adult life, maybe all of your adult life, that you considered happy, or at least comfortable, all of a sudden morphs into something else—a fiction. The life you thought you were living seems to be false. Memory changes, reality changes, your world changes. All the clichés of divorce suddenly apply to you: "He became a stranger," "I was the last to know," "How could he do this to me?" "I thought we would grow old together," "I wasted the best years of my life on him." My life, which was chugging along seemingly happy, or at least peacefully, could have instantly turned into an episode of *The Jerry Springer Show* titled, "Younger Husbands Who Dump Their Older Wives for Younger Women After Adopting Babies," or something equally convoluted. If we'd all been on the show, I would have shrieked, lunged at Almira and torn her hair out, slapped him silly and wrung his neck, then dissolved into tears and begged him to come back for the sake of our little girl. Break for commercial as security guards storm the stage. Luckily there were no guns in the house.

I was fifty-five years old, about to be left for a younger woman, living in the middle of nowhere, in a house on a dirt road that got snowed in during the winter, with a hyperactive two-year-old, no job, no family, a future ex who didn't make enough to support us both, and no prospects of finding anyone else because I was too old and had a little kid. I could go on but I'll spare you. I just want you to know that I speak from experience when I say that if I could survive, anyone can.

I ran out of the house that night, left my husband with our child, and took off for my friend Kathy. Kathy lived in a luxurious Tudor in a ritzy suburb of New York City. Her squishy leather couches and sparkly clean kitchen were reassuring. My house, like my life, was a mess. Kathy had been divorced for a few years and knew the ropes intimately. She listened to me sob, hugged me, and dragged me out to eat Chinese food. We then saw the only movie in the area, *Quills,* a weird, gruesomely fascinating movie about the Marquis de Sade—the movie least likely to comfort someone who's just been told her husband is dumping her for another woman. But it took my mind off my misery for a few hours.

She also lectured me about the reality of divorce.

"You're not going to believe this, Erica, but Zeke is going to become a different person. That sweet, nice guy you counted on to take care of you is going to try to screw you to the wall. He will become someone you totally won't recognize. Remember, he's got someone else now, and she's pulling the strings. She's going to control him and your child. He's going to try to screw you when it comes to money and everything else. You'd better call a lawyer—today."

A lawyer. Omigod, how could I need a lawyer? We had always prided ourselves on not fighting about money. Even if we did fight about everything else, including sex and our daughter, how could I need a lawyer so soon?

I didn't believe Kathy. I knew my own husband, didn't I? He wasn't like that, he wouldn't treat me that way; we'd lived together for eighteen years, been married for fifteen of them. Even if we'd always fought, he'd been my defender when it came to the outside world; he was my champion, my best friend, and my shoulder to cry on. I was sure I knew what he was and wasn't capable of. Leaving me for someone else wasn't in his lexicon. I just couldn't absorb what had happened. Zeke had a leg up on me because he'd wanted a divorce for years. He'd occasionally threatened me with divorce, but I never believed him. I never considered the other-woman scenario.

Of course everything Kathy warned me about came true, but luckily she was around to shepherd me through it. That night Kathy listened to me weep and moan. She got irate on my behalf and even called Zeke and told him not to leave me, which was really going the extra mile. She became my divorce guru and later my Internet dating guru. She saved my life many times, starting that night. The idea for this book was born a few years later, when I realized that to survive a messy divorce you need at least one girlfriend like Kathy. This book is that girlfriend.

I wish I could say I was so outraged by Zeke's infidelity that I went home and tossed him out in a rage like any self-respecting cheated-on wife would do. No way. I was so terrified at the prospect of losing him and going through years of feeling like I felt then—as if someone had set me adrift in a small rowboat on the open ocean with no oars—that when I got home, I launched a major campaign to get him to stay. I tried desperately to hang on to him. I found to my surprise that I really didn't care that he'd slept with someone else. He could have slept with half of upstate New York and I could have dealt with it. What I cared about was that he was in *love* with someone else. I found that unacceptable.

I used all the powers of persuasion I possessed, and I'm a world-class arguer. He agreed with everything I said, like he always had, but kept on saying he wanted to leave. He protested that Dorothy would be better off if he was happy. Somehow he overlooked how her mother being close to a nervous breakdown was bound to affect her. He told me he'd seen *The Bridges of Madison County* and didn't want to wind up like Meryl Streep. Personally I thought it was pretty noble of Meryl to stay for the kids, but it's no wonder the film was set in the 1930s—people don't do that much anymore.

For a year we seesawed back and forth. He was too guilty to actually leave, waiting for me to give him his walking papers while trying to make me as miserable as humanly possible so I'd throw him out. He skulked around the house barely speaking to me and blew up regularly for minor offenses. At times he'd claim he'd stopped seeing Almira and we'd go back to pretending to be comfortably, if not happily, married. At least I was pretending. He just went around looking miserable. Other times he'd go back to the authenticity argument and talk about leaving again. I even tried to be seductive and have regular sex with him, but it never lasted. I just couldn't keep it up. In my crazed jealousy I'd drive by Almira's house regularly to see if his car was outside. When I caught him there one day, I acted like Erica in *All My Children* and made a huge scene, which ended with her running out to my car yelling at the top of her lungs, "I didn't want to fall in love with a married man, but I luuuuuv him, I luuuuv him." How could he resist such adoration? I'd never felt that way about him, nor had anyone else.

We went to a succession of clueless marriage counselors. It's not surprising that so many marriages break up after counseling.

Our marriage dragged on for more months while I continued to be in denial. When he was in one of his "I'm not seeing her anymore" modes I'd go back into married-couple mode and feel like we were a family again. Despite our constant fights, being married was a warm, safe place. The thought of being cast out of that place was so frightening that I felt I'd do anything, put up with anything, to keep him. Then he'd go back to "I want to leave you," and I'd beg him to stay. One sunny summer day, he threw his jacket in my lap as he got out of the car to get our daughter from day care. A love letter from *her* just about fell out of his pocket. Talk about Freudian slips. Finally fed up, I told him to leave. He couldn't get out the door fast enough.

Later he told me he hung around to assuage his guilt, went to the marriage counseling to pay lip service to saving the marriage. I asked why he didn't leave before he found a girlfriend. He said—and I believe this is true for the majority of middle-aged men who can't function without a woman—"I couldn't have done it any other way."

I'm glad he took so long to leave, because it gave me time to prepare for his final departure. Like having a spouse die after a long illness rather than in a sudden accident, it's less of a shock. I had moved us to Woodstock, a community where I had friends, my synagogue, and a chance of surviving alone. His move into the guest room prepared me for his final exit. By the time he actually left, it was a relief, like the windows being flung open. Nonetheless, the grieving process had only just begun.

Why This Book

Even though divorce is a rite of passage that large numbers of women go through every year, its aftermath is impossible to understand unless you've been through it—especially the impact of divorce on older women. In some ways widowhood is easier. There is a support system for widows; there are rituals in place to help them grieve. When you get divorced, friends may shun you as though divorce were catching. You may even be blamed for driving him away. Real sympathy and understanding are in short supply. Instead of leaving you his assets, your ex, who is far from dearly departed, may be busy stashing them in the Bahamas. While you are asking friends to fix you up, your ex, who has become that rarity, an eligible single man over fifty, is probably fending off dinner invitations. It just ain't fair, in fact it's incredibly galling—a discrepancy that takes some time and understanding to get used to.

Alone at fifty-eight, broke, traumatized, depressed, convinced I'd never find a decent job, another man, or another life, made me think about how many other women were in the same boat as me, or an even worse one. It also made me think about who women turn to when they get divorced no matter how old they are: their girlfriends, of course. I was lucky enough to have Kathy to sit me down and warn me about how I'd better get over being part of a couple and start taking care of myself. She told me what to read, insisted I see a lawyer when I was sure I didn't need one, told me what to expect from my soon-to-be-ex and his new girlfriend, answered my desperate calls at 3:00 a.m., reassured me that I wasn't going to end up a bag lady, tutored me in the bizarre etiquette of Internet dating, and eventually let me know when it was time to can the self-pity and get on with life. Divorced women, especially if they're women of a "certain age," need advice not just from experts but also from a wise girlfriend who's been there, done that. If you don't have a Kathy, or even if you do, I intend to be that girlfriend. I've done a lot of research, and I can tell you what you need to know.

Boomer Divorce

We boomers are the ones who feel it's our God-given right to find fulfillment. Those of us who make it through our children's childhoods often pack it in when those kids are out of the house, or even when they're still in high school. According to the *Christian Science Monitor*, "Divorce is rising. In 1960, just 1.6 percent of older men and 1.5 percent of older women were divorced. By 2003, those figures had risen to 7 percent of men and 8.6 percent of women."

According to the February 2006 issue of *Newsweek*, "The 77,702,865 Americans born between 1946 and 1964 came of age in the era of sex, drugs, and rock and roll. And while the last two may have lost some appeal over the years, sex and relationships remain front and center as the oldest boomers turn 60 this year. That's largely because more boomers are single than any previous cohort of forty to sixtysomethings." According to the US Census Bureau, 28.6 percent of adults age forty-five to fifty-nine were unattached in 2003, compared with only 18.8 percent in 1980. (Of those, 16.6 percent were divorced, 2.9 percent were widowed, and 9.1 percent had never been married.)

According to a 2001 census report, even though there's been a slight decline in the overall divorce rate, the highest rate of divorce was for older people, an average of 40 percent for men and women between fifty and fifty-nine. "Gray divorce" (age fifty-five to eighty-plus) has increased as well. From 1970 to 1990 the divorce rate for women between forty and fifty increased 62 percent, according to an article in *More* magazine. As more and more and more of us older women enter our later years divorced, we will need a lot of help. From a financial perspective alone, late-life divorce is much worse than late-life widowhood. Among women sixty-five and older, widows have a 50 percent higher average income than do divorcées.

There are a lot of books about divorce for women out there, mostly for younger women who are dealing with young children and child support and custody issues. However, there's nothing available about the effect of divorce on grown-ups whose kids are grown-ups—and certainly nothing targeted specifically to older women. Women who wait until the kids are grown to split aren't even on the radar.

Being the bookish sort, I read a lot of books about divorce after my husband left, searching for answers. None were targeted to women my age who had been in long-term marriages. None actually told me how to get through the experience alive. They all mentioned the rage, pain, grief, damaged self-esteem, and other varieties of misery you will experience, but weren't a lot of help when it came to dealing with those feelings—especially at my age. I found a lot of wisdom about why marriages end, but nothing about what to do when you must bear the most unbearable feelings of your lifetime, *and* be in your late forties or older.

He's History, You're Not will tell you how to deal with issues specific to you as a midlife or older woman, including dealing with teen and grown children, finances, dating, loneliness, and more.

To gather material for the book, I interviewed experts in all the subject areas, including divorce lawyers, mediators, therapists, career counselors, and divorce workshop leaders. I also interviewed a large variety of older divorced women—both those who were left and those who did the leaving—exploring their experiences as well. The divorcées I interviewed were all forty-five and older, divorced within the last ten years, and married at least ten years. Most were married for twenty or more. There is useful advice categorized by age in most chapters.

Who Initiates Divorce?

As it happens, women initiate a majority of the midlife divorces. According to an AARP survey of older divorced people, 66 percent of women reported that they asked for the divorce, compared with 41 percent of men. However, the same survey reported that most women in their fifties or older said the top killers of their marriages were physical or emotional abuse, infidelity, and drug or alcohol abuse—and they put almost all of the blame on their ex-husbands. On the flip side, most fifty-plus men said they simply "fell out of love" or had "different values or lifestyles." This belies the myth that at midlife women get bored with their husbands and leave them to find fulfillment elsewhere.

Although I was the one dumped, *He's History, You're Not* is relevant to older divorced women no matter how their marriages ended. Even women who finally realized how alone they were in their marriages and left with no regrets still have to deal with devastated kids, financial woes, loneliness, dating again, figuring out past mistakes, self-reflection, and forgiveness. Women cheat too, and suffer enormous guilt because of it. Emotionally, a twenty- or thirty-year marriage that occupied most of a lifetime must be mourned.

I eventually learned to both survive and thrive, overcoming daunting obstacles, including learning to live contentedly alone. I've educated myself in a lot of areas women have barely even thought of when the prospect of divorce looms. I'm the kind of girlfriend a woman needs when she's facing both menopause *and* the trauma of divorce. I am writing the book I wish I had when I got divorced. I would have devoured it whole.

So no matter which camp you're in, the dumpers or dumpees, stick with me girlfriend. I'm going to save you a lot of anguish . . . and a lot of cash.

CHAPTER ONE

GRIEVING IS A FULL-TIME JOB

How To Survive the
First—Worst—Year

I fly to New York to see my shrink, I walk into her office and burst into tears. I tell her what my husband has done to me. I tell her my heart is broken. I tell her I'm a total mess and I will never be the same. I can't stop crying. She looks at me and says, "You were going to leave him anyway."

—NORA EPHRON

The days, weeks, months after he or you leaves may well be the worst time of your life. Unless you've suffered the death of a child, or something equally horrific, make no mistake, girlfriend: Divorce is way up there on the scale of traumatic life events. Some therapists think it's worse than the death of a spouse. A friend of mine who was recently widowed agreed. She had thirty happy years with her husband and now has the memory of those years to sustain her. She doesn't have to suffer the pain of betrayal or the crushing of self-esteem that comes with divorce, and feels sorry for me because I do. Unlike grief after the death of a spouse, there are no acceptable ways to grieve the end of a marriage. You can't sit shivah or hold a wake, no one will bring casseroles (although my gourmet-cook friend Mitch brought me *coq au vin,* which lifted my spirits immeasurably), and—worst of all—no one who hasn't been there will really understand what you're going through. Grieving the death of your marriage can be extremely messy, since the object of the grief is still alive—more's the pity. Nonetheless, no matter how your marriage ended you must grieve it. If you don't grieve you can't move on, and moving on has to be your ultimate goal.

I wish grief weren't so damned melodramatic, because I've never been a fan of melodrama, but there is no escaping the complete collapse I experienced when my husband left. I really wasn't good for anything during that period. I vacillated between extreme grief and extreme rage. I wanted to commit either suicide or homicide. If you feel like your life is over, that you will never survive this trauma, you're not alone. But I'm here to tell you, you will survive. Almost everyone does, and so will you.

As older women who've been married longer, our grieving takes longer and hits us harder. For one thing, our losses are greater. We've lost both our happy memories of times past *and* the expectation of a secure, comfortable future; in addition, we lack the resilience of youth to help us bounce back. After twenty or thirty years of a coupled life—where your mate probably took care of the traditional guy things plus provided economic security—you're suddenly cast out into the cold cruel world of struggling to pay the bills and figuring out how to locate a plumber at 3:00 a.m. when a pipe bursts, plus trying to find both a job and another man at an age when you're supposed to be winding down, not gearing up.

The good news is that eventually you *will* come out of this a happier woman. According to an AARP study on late-life divorce, we divorcées cope fairly well with life after divorce. Seventy-five percent feel divorce was the right decision for them. "Their buzzwords are 'freedom,' 'self-identity,' and 'fulfillment.'" It's hard to believe that this, too, shall pass, but the human organism is pro-grammed to survive.

Levels of grief and rage vary tremendously depending on how a marriage ended. I actually know girlfriends whose marriages ended amicably with a handshake and no hard feelings. Both spouses realized they'd fallen out of love and it was time to part. If money and children were involved, they even managed to sort those issues out in mediation, without a legal battle. These girl-friends not only are lucky, but have undoubtedly reached a level of maturity to which I can only aspire. Or maybe they're just not Jewish, Italian, or any other ethnic group given to histrionics and high drama.

LEAVER VERSUS LEFT

Things are not equal when it comes to ending a marriage. One of the reasons it's so devastating to be suddenly dumped is not just the rejection, but the shock. You have been planning your retire-ment in Maui, not how to fit your furniture into a small condo near the airport. He has his exit strategy laid out, and you, girlfriend, are in blissful denial. Even though studies of divorced couples five years after their breakup show that the one who was left has often made peace with the divorce, realizing that it was best for both, the one who leaves has the benefit of having prepared for the exit for a long time.

In *Uncoupling: Turning Points in Intimate Relationships,* soci-ologist Diane Vaughn explains how it happens. The leaver spends a long time, often years, gathering ammunition and supporters to justify departure. In my case my husband had his brother, his girl-friend, her friends, and his therapist supporting him. He had built a case—with their agreement and support—that our marriage had been moribund for years, that our earlier counseling efforts were unsuccessful, and that our daughter would be better off in the long run if we divorced. His therapist pointed out that he'd been mired in depression for years and wasn't getting anywhere in therapy until he started an affair. I, on the other hand, was in la-la land, determined to maintain the fiction that things were okay, even though they clearly weren't.

If you were the leaver, you probably had your exit strategy planned in advance—and your husband was totally shocked when you announced your decision. Men, who are usually less tuned in to emotions, tend to be even more shocked than women when it comes to being left. When you tell them you want an emotional connection, they're mystified. They don't understand why you can't just accept a life of silence, TV, and the occasional roll in the hay.

IT'S RARELY A CLEAN BREAK

The ending of a long-term marriage is rarely neat and clean. Often the one who wants to leave is ambivalent, not sure if he or she is doing the right thing. There's frequently a wrenching period of leaving, returning, and leaving again before the marriage finally ends. Or, as in my case, the one who's having the affair refuses to stop seeing the girlfriend until his wife finally gets fed up. The leaver may vacillate for years before finally making the move. This period can be more agonizing than the actual end of the marriage because, if you're being left, you get your hopes up repeatedly, only to have them dashed again and again. If you're deciding whether or not to leave, the guilt and fear can be paralyzing. But there is a benefit to the waffling. Just as it's easier to have a spouse die after a long illness because you've had some time to get ready emotionally, it's probably easier to have some preparation time before your marriage ends. A clean break might be the best way to end an affair, but not a long marriage.

Comic Kathy Griffin, describing how she tried desperately to hold on to her husband, dragging him to one marriage counselor after another, wisecracked on *The View* about the end of her marriage: "I thought I'd beat it until it was dead."

Here are some strategies to help you get through that hellish first year.

DON'T MINIMIZE YOUR GRIEF

After my husband left I understood for the first time how someone could actually die of a broken heart. If you, like me, were unceremoniously dumped, don't be surprised if you go through pain more severe than you've ever felt before. I heard this over and over from women who were left, especially if it was for another woman. Men had left me before I got married, but this was different. Those men were only passing through—on some level I knew that—and there was a voluptuousness to mourning their loss, sobbing loudly while sprawled on the couch, drinking wine, listening to torch songs, and feeling desperately sorry for myself. Those breakups lent drama to my otherwise boring single life. The death of my marriage was *real* drama—the kind I'd never experienced before—the kind that breaks you down, tears you up, and can land you in a mental hospital or with slit wrists.

Just in case you think that this level of extreme grief is excessive or abnormal, I'm here to reassure you that it isn't. The pain you're experiencing is very real according to anthropologist Helen Fisher, author of *Why We Love: The Nature and Chemistry of Romantic Love.* Fisher reports that brain scans of people who were dumped show the areas associated with "physical pain, obsessive thinking and extreme rage becoming active. During this time, we're willing to take enormous risks for big gains and big losses." The intense romantic-love center of the brain also cranks up to try to win the person back. It's a profound form of suffering, Fisher says, adding that the drive to love is stronger than the sex drive. No one kills himself or herself over being sexually rejected. People do kill themselves or others over getting dumped. In one study of people who were dumped, 40 percent went into clinical depression.

Whether you're the leaver or the left, divorce, like death, leads you through the five stages of grief originally outlined by Elisabeth Kübler-Ross about those facing terminal illness. If you're the one leaving, you may have experienced some of these stages before you announced your departure.

- Denial. "This can't be happening to me." Or "I can't actually be doing this."
- Anger. "It isn't fair. What did I do to deserve this?"
- Bargaining. "How do I get him to come back?" Or "Maybe I should stick this out and try to make it work."
- Depression. "I feel hopeless. Nothing matters anymore."
- Acceptance. "This relationship is over. I'll be okay now."

You may go in and out of all of these stages—for years. Recovery is an agonizingly slow process of two steps forward and one step back. Abigail Trafford, my divorce guru and author of *Crazy Time: Surviving Divorce and Building a New Life*, estimates that it takes one year to recover for every five years of marriage. From my experience she's right on the money.

Although it may not feel that way for a long time, the reality is that no matter how devastated you are, and no matter how long it takes—and recovery time varies widely depending on individual temperament—you *can* get through this and move on as long as you honor your own grieving process. Don't try to short-circuit it before you're ready. You don't want to be that divorcée still carrying on about how her ex ruined her life ten years after the divorce.

Getting through that time will be an exercise in reaching into yourself and finding survival strategies you never needed before. The first few months to a year is the hardest part. After that it really does get easier.

FIND A GOOD SHRINK

No, it's not enough to talk to girlfriends. Yes, you do need a therapist to shepherd you through the transition. Whether you're consumed with pain, anger, guilt, or all three, a wise therapist can help you turn a trauma into a turning point.

Our final marriage counselor was the tall, slim, beautiful Kali. She was fifty but looked forty, dressed in smart tailored casual clothes that, unlike my wardrobe, definitely didn't come from Wal-Mart or Goodwill, and had the tall, slim body I'd always longed for. I would have preferred a plump, cushiony, grandmotherly type with a reassuring number of wrinkles, but despite her fashion-model looks, Kali exuded such warm, nurturing motherliness that I bonded with her instantly. You should look for the kind of therapist who, like Kali, makes you feel taken care of and hopeful about the future.

I desperately needed to fall into the arms of a mom—any mom. My own mother had died five years earlier, thank God, because she adored my husband so much that news of our split-up would have certainly killed her. I didn't have a sister or any other family, and I didn't want to burden my long-suffering girlfriends with nonstop kvetching. If you are lucky enough to still have a mom to comfort you, don't be ashamed to cry on her shoulder. No matter how old you are, or Mom is, that's what moms are for . . . as long as she's not more devastated by the divorce than you are.

I cried pretty much 24/7 after being left. This is another common pattern. If you can't stop crying, don't try. Just let the tears flow. The more tears you get out at the beginning, the fewer you will have to cry in years to come. Although life's pleasures held little appeal at this time, every week I'd look forward to my session with Kali. Sometimes I could barely wait. I would flop on her soft brown couch and moan about how miserable I felt, how pitiful I was, what a disaster my life had become, that I couldn't stop crying, how I was in such intense pain I could barely move. I raged bitterly against Zeke and his wretched Jezebel of a girlfriend. Kali always congratulated me for doing such a great job of mourning. She said some people were afraid to let it all hang out—they blocked out the pain and anger, made believe everything was okay—and those people were bound to suffer much more in the long run. She thought it was terribly brave of me to allow myself to feel my pain and express my anger. Wow! I could actually feel proud of myself for the very loss of control I was so ashamed of. I was vying for the championship of the grief Olympics. It seemed I was on fast-forward when it came to recovery. Slowly, my self-esteem, which was at rock bottom, started to inch upward. If you're feeling like a loser for weeping a geyser of tears or dissolving into rage and self-pity . . . don't. Kali was right: Allowing yourself to feel all those feelings is part of the process. You need to go through them all to come out the other side.

I always left her office feeling better than when I'd walked in. Every week I told her how worthless I felt, how I wanted to crawl under a rock—being dumped is hell on a girl's self-esteem. Every week she reminded me how smart, funny, compassionate, and downright wonderful I was. I didn't believe her, of course, but I sure liked to hear her say it.

Kali also helped me deconstruct what went wrong in my marriage. I went over my lonely childhood, realizing that in my marriage I'd re-created my relationship to my depressed, angry, helpless father. We talked about how I was trying to repair the wounds of my childhood through my marriage. We all do this to one extent or another, but often don't come to terms with it until we get divorced. Figuring out what went wrong is a major part of recovery. You need a shrink who is wise and understanding of the dynamics of relationships, and who can guide you through the confusing maze of what actually happened in your marriage while gently helping you sort out why and where you lost your way.

HOW DO YOU FIND A GOOD SHRINK?

You're exquisitely vulnerable at this time, and it's easy to wind up with someone who's either clueless or critical. I found Kali through another therapist whom I'd gone to for compulsive eating problems. If you have a friend who has been helped by someone, and you like what she says about the person, go to her. Interview a few therapists and choose someone who makes you feel better about yourself, who makes it clear that she respects *you*—what you believe, who you are, and what you have to say. Avoid the arrogant ones who make you feel like they know the way and you are a dolt who has no idea which end is up. They're all too common in the world of therapy. You'll know you're in the right place if you feel better when you walk out of your therapist's office than when you went in. You should be busy mulling . over all the insights you gained during your session.

When it gets really bad—if you can't stop crying or get out of bed or have suicidal thoughts—go to a psychiatrist and ask for medication. There's no shame in popping some Zoloft in your time of need. SSRIs have rescued stronger souls than you. I'm still taking my Wellbutrin regularly.

THE PHOENIX PROCESS

Divorce is a trauma that breaks us open, as Elizabeth Lesser, cofounder of the Omega Institute, explains in *Broken Open: How Difficult Times Can Help Us Grow* (Villard, 2005). She talks about the Phoenix Process, which she defines as an experience of going through the fire and rising from the ashes of your former life to reinvent yourself. Her book gave me hope. It made me feel that what I was going through could actually mean something, could make me a better, or at least different, person. The one advantage—and it's a big advantage—of getting divorced later in life is that we've reached a time when we're pretty much "cooked." We are who we've become. At this point we have enough perspective to look back and reflect on the past. Self-reflection comes more naturally with age, when the kids are grown and it's time for you to work on you. Divorce can be used to look at the past, to reflect on what you've lost, what you may have gained from that loss, and who you want to be from now on. If you do it right, divorce pushes you to change and grow.

The Phoenix Process is the gift of divorce, so don't look a gift horse—or in this case a gift phoenix—in the mouth. Do the work *now*. Remember, you're not getting any younger. This may be your last chance to reinvent yourself, so take advantage of it.

DON'T BE AFRAID
TO SHOW YOUR FEELINGS

My husband and I had been going to services at the Woodstock Jewish Congregation for a long time. It was one of the only times during the week that we were at peace with each other. I loved sitting there, holding his hand, and experiencing the power of the prayers we sang together. After he left I had to force myself to go and sit there alone, with no hand to hold. I kept going because it was somewhere to take my daughter on a Friday night and because our rabbi is charismatic and inspiring.

I'd never felt a part of the community before, but after I started attending alone my experience started to change. My husband was not a sociable man, and after the services we both had stood awkwardly on the sidelines, feeling left out, wondering who to talk with. I like people, but I tend to get shy in a group. In my first months without him, I felt naked. When people would ask how I was doing, I'd smile woodenly and reply, "Fine." I didn't know what to say. I assumed no one wanted to hear my tale of woe, so I made believe I was okay.

Finally I couldn't hold it together anymore. At High Holy Day services a few months after our separation, I was so profoundly moved that I started weeping. And once I started crying, I couldn't stop. It felt really weird and embarrassing. I felt like an idiot, but people I'd known for years, whom I'd always thought were standoffish and cliquish, came up to me, hugged me, told me that they cared about me. The woman sitting next to me, a total stranger, hugged me and held my hand. I was stunned.

Maybe you, like me, need to be in control and are afraid of showing vulnerability. Unfortunately, this kind of stiff-upper-lip approach to life has the effect of keeping people at a distance. But if you practice telling people how you actually feel when they ask, you may find, as I did, that instead of driving them away you'll get all kinds of positive responses. These may well include outpourings of sympathy from other women who've been through divorce and want to share their experiences with you.

You can't cry absolutely everywhere, of course. Breaking down at a sales meeting will not result in a promotion. Weeping at the supermarket is probably going to create a wide berth around your cart. But crying with friends will separate the genuine from the fair-weather ones in a flash. Try sniffling at your desk and see who comes over with a tissue. If the teller at the bank has a sympathetic face and asks how you're doing, tell her. Don't be afraid to let a few tears roll down your face anywhere around middle-aged women. Guaranteed one of them will come over, ask you what's wrong, and share her own divorce story. We are everywhere and we feel for you. Right now you need all the sympathy you can get. Don't feel bad about letting it all hang out.

Warning! Spread the tears around. If you constantly call the same person with the same tale of woe, even a good friend will—understandably—get worn out.

DEPEND ON YOUR GIRLFRIENDS

I could not have survived my divorce without my friends. If you don't have supportive friends, you'd better go find some. It's okay for a sister or cousin or other family member to be a girlfriend, but don't try to dump all your troubles on a family member—and especially not on your kids, a route that can be very tempting if you're lonely. It's too much of a burden for a child, whether that child is five or thirty-five.

I talked to many divorced women for this book, and just about all of them mentioned the importance of girlfriends in surviving divorce. For instance, Melissa Tanner, a fellow Woodstocker whose husband left her at sixty-one after twenty-seven years of marriage, told me, "I opened my heart to other people to feel better. I let other people in. I had done it before but not as much because I was so involved in our life. I had a friend say to me 'I've been waiting for you.' I found that my friends really wanted to be with me."

Girlfriends You Will Need for Support

These are a few of my closest girlfriends. They all played different roles in my recovery. You will also need a bunch of girlfriends who, hopefully, have different outlooks on life and a variety of viewpoints to offer. When I complained to Kali about how lonely I was, she asked me to list all my friends. By the time I finished, I felt a lot better.

KATHY: THE BEEN-THERE-DONE-THAT GIRLFRIEND

I have been lucky enough to have Kathy, whom I described in the introduction, as my been-through-it girlfriend. We had both struggled with rigid, argumentative, angry exes with whom we had to co-parent, and we both had kids with problems. Whatever I was going through, Kathy had usually gone through already. As the queen of Match.com, she also shepherded me through Internet dating. I helped her down the line when she had legal problems with her ex-husband because I'd done so much research for my own settlement. Most importantly, Kathy is funny as all hell and could turn my worst moments of post-separation angst into the kind of black humor that never failed to crack me up. You will need a girlfriend with a great sense of humor to lighten you up during your inevitable bouts of self-pity. You will also need a girl-friend who has been through a divorce and come out the other side healthier and happier. She will provide a role model for your recovery.

MINDA: THE DEVIL'S-ADVOCATE GIRLFRIEND

You will also need a Minda. Your Minda has to be willing to tell you the truth even when you don't want to hear it. You might want all your girlfriends to mindlessly agree that your ex is a rat and you are a saint, but you need someone to play devil's advocate. My Minda is happily married and got me off the pity pot on many occasions.

"Erica, we weren't surprised at all when he left," Minda would say. "We thought he should have done it long ago. You were always putting him down and bullying him. You two were misera-ble together. I hope you don't get offended by my telling you this," she'd always add apologetically. Even though I tried to defend myself by explaining how Zeke was Dr. Jekyll in front of her and Mr. Hyde alone with me, I realized that it took a lot of guts to tell the truth to a woman as opinionated as me.

Whenever you get stuck totally in victim mode, have the pres-ence of mind to call your Minda to force you into a reality check. The more she helps you look at the interlocking neurotic LEGOs that you've built into a shaky marriage, the more inevitable the breakup will seem. That inevitability is comforting. Being a vic-tim has its rewards—hey, you get a lot of sympathy—but it also feels crappy being so helpless over your own fate. You need a girl-friend who will force you to look at yourself straight-on and take responsibility. If you're smart, you won't defend yourself, you'll just listen. It may sting, but in the long run it will help.

Roz: The Moral-Compass Girlfriend

Roz, who like me loved dining out and the movies, was my regular Saturday-night date after the breakup. Single at fifty-five, she'd had many torrid affairs and was a riveting storyteller, especially when it came to her own love life. Like Aesop's fables, all her tales had morals, which were very instructive, though not always in ways you would expect.

My favorite was Roz's story about a man she'd been seeing who was seemingly the perfect guy. She adored him and they were planning to marry. Then during one Thanksgiving dinner at his home, he blew up at his teenage daughter for a trivial incident, becoming so enraged that he threw the turkey on the floor. Roz had never seen him that angry before. She broke up with him on the spot, refusing to ever see him again, despite his desperate pleas for forgiveness. No way was she going to keep seeing a man who had that kind of rage bottled up inside, especially one who bullied his own child.

I was blown away by this story. My ex-husband had gone into rages repeatedly before I married him—always for insignificant reasons. Why didn't I dump him the first, the second, or even the fifteenth time he blew up at me? Why did I marry the guy? I was incredibly impressed with Roz's ability to make that kind of decision and never look back. If, like many of us, you didn't have much of a role model in your mother, who may have put up with all kinds of mistreatment, it helps to have a girlfriend who knows how to set limits with men, especially once you start dating again. Roz was also adamant in her outrage about Zeke's affair. A strong-minded girlfriend with an old-fashioned sense of right and wrong can help you sort out the moral and ethical dilemmas of divorce and dating.

WENDY: THE LIVING-ALONE-AND-LOVING-IT GIRLFRIEND

You would be extremely lucky to also have a Wendy. My Wendy lives a few minutes away from me and was there when I really needed her, which was often. Like Peter Pan's Wendy, she is sensible and down to earth and gives great advice. In addition to being a therapist who has a great deal of insight into people, Wendy is a role model for living alone and loving it. At fifty-seven she's perfectly happy with her dogs, her books, and her imagination. Whenever I start feeling really lonely, she reminds me how miserable I was when I was married and how desperate I was to get away from my husband and hang out with her. You will need some single girlfriends who live alone and like it to remind you that that's possible.

JOANIE AND AVIGAIL: THE HOW-TO-DEAL-WITH-YOUR-KIDS GIRLFRIENDS

My girlfriend Joan is Supermom. A foster mother who has taken in a few children with major problems and turned them around, she can deal with just about any issue involving kids. When I bemoaned my inability to deal with my daughter, she reassured me that it wasn't my fault; that it was an impossible job to deal with a child with Dorothy's problems alone at my age. Then she'd give me a few helpful tips in a nonjudgmental way. She supported me, guided me, alleviated my guilt. Because she was supermom, I believed her. If you have kids at home who are troubled by your divorce, it really helps to have an expert mom like Joan to give you advice, not to mention a single mom like Avigail who went through a similar scenario with her kids after her divorce. Avigail's tales of her experiences with her kids made me feel I wasn't alone.

WRITING WELL IS THE BEST REVENGE

The anger after a separation or divorce can eat you alive. The rage is much worse than the pain. You can cry to relieve the pain, but rage just sits there and festers, making your life hell. The worst thing about rage is that it tends to transmute into other, more destructive emotions and behaviors. Rage turned inward becomes self-hate. Women tend to turn their anger on themselves and sink into depression, a truly self-destructive way to deal with divorce. Rage turned outward becomes nastiness to those around you who did nothing to deserve it, such as your co-workers or children. Rage acted out is dangerous. Think *O. J. Simpson.* It becomes stalking and sometimes murder, which is mostly male behavior, but women scorned also stalk and are not immune from homicidal action.

So what to do with all that rage? Because I'm a writer, I wrote long, vituperative e-mails to my ex. Everyone will tell you not to send them, and maybe you won't need to. But if you don't, you won't get the satisfaction of knowing that you've finally said the very thing to him that you've wanted to say all these years and he's read it (unless he hits the delete key when he sees your e-mail address).

I did have one rule: Never hit the send key after midnight. Those wee-hours e-mails are likely to get you in trouble. I have sent many over-the-top e-mails late at night that I later regretted when I read them the next morning. Wait until the next day, read the e-mail, and then send it if it still sounds rational. Also make sure you delete anything that can be used against you in court. Other than that, fire away.

Here are some other ideas.

Keep a *How Do I Hate Thee, Let Me Count the Ways* Journal

Don't hesitate to get really ridiculous.

Write a "Letter to Harry"

Susan Becker, a contributor to *Cut Loose: (Mostly) Older Women Talk About the End of (Mostly) Long-Term Relationships*, edited by Nan Bauer-Maglin, wrote a series of e-mails to her ex, which she called the X-files. (She didn't send them, however.) These are models of rapier-sharp wit that cracked me up.

> *These e-mails are dedicated to Harry, my partner and mentor of thirty years, who taught me everything about life I would rather not have known. First there is nothing more important than money and power. (I'm not so clear about the order here. I think Harry would find this a tough call.) Second, there is nothing so sacred we can't joke about it. Third, and more important, you should aim with great precision, right below the belt. Thanks, honey.*
>
> *Dear Harry,*
>
> *I know that this thank-you note is a little belated, but I was just looking down at the bracelet you bought me only a few months before you dumped me. It was rather amusing, because a close friend (whose name will go unmentioned because you know how I hate gossip) received a similar bracelet from Tiffany's from her husband when he was having an affair a few years back. What can I say? Great minds think alike. Anyway I was*

thinking to myself how much I adore this bracelet. You always did have excellent taste. And I want you to know that I wear it every day, even though some of my friends think it's a bit weird since you later confided that you bought the same bracelet for your "twinkie." Did you get a bulk discount? Since it is the only piece of jewelry that you didn't ask to have returned, I also like to think it has some sentimental value. My booby prize, so to speak . . . However, the real reason I love wearing this bracelet is that it reminds me I am a survivor, one of the walking wounded, a dumped, middle-aged woman, cut loose in the prime of life. And although you always found me pretty hard to take in this regard, I believe in calling a spade a spade. So tell me Harry, does your twinkie wear her bracelet every day like I do? I hope she appreciates your elegant taste as much as I always did. By the by, does she know you bought one for me? I am worried that we might wind up at some family function like our kid's wedding wearing our matching bracelets, and it could be embarrassing for everyone.

Sensitively yours, as always, Susie

Anita Liberty wrote a book about her ex titled *How to Heal the Hurt by Hating (Villard, 2006)*. This poem gave me a good laugh.

Smile
"Lighten up."
"Be happy."
"Why the frown?"

"Smile! It's a beautiful day!"
OH SHUT UP
I worked hard to find the darkest mood I could.
I won't give it up that easy.
And you—with your cheer-ups
smiles
behappies
you just gave me another reason to stay there

The letters to Harry and this poem by Anita Liberty are pretty juvenile stuff for mature women like us, but hey, anything that gives you a chuckle at this stage of divorce recovery is permissible. Black humor was invented for occasions like divorce—anyone who's seen *War of the Roses* can appreciate that observation (rent this movie if you haven't seen it).

Write a Good-Bye Letter

This letter is for your own benefit. It's extremely cathartic to write down every little—and big—thing about your husband and your marriage that you're saying good-bye to, good things as well as bad. Mail it or not, however the spirit moves you. Here's mine, for an example:

Good-bye to:

The vegetable garden you planted just before you left. You must have known you wouldn't be here to harvest the veggies.

The lawn mower you managed to break and refused to replace when you came over to mow the lawn after you left. Now I have to pay someone to mow the lawn.

Good-bye to:

My best friend. Despite everything that was missing from our marriage, we were a family, and you cared about me—or I thought you did.

Good-bye to:

Talking about the things we both enjoyed, like *Northern Exposure, Citizen Kane,* folk music, and MGM musicals.

Bob Dylan, your favorite singer who you got me to appreciate. It's too painful for me to listen to him anymore.

Good-bye to:

Someone to worry when I'm sick or in the hospital, to bring me chicken soup when I have a cold, to take me to doctor's appointments and bring me home.

Being the most important person in someone else's life.

Sharing my day-to-day life with someone who cared.

Good-bye to:

Having to walk on eggshells for fear you would blow up at me.

Your constant criticism of things like my talking too loud, or embarrassing you, or wanting to move to a better table in a restaurant.

Your backseat driving—God, did I hate that.

Your passive-aggressive way of promising you would do things and then "forgetting." Or doing them so badly that I'd do them myself.

The way you'd lie to me just to get off the hook.

Your need to be taken care of, your inability to do anything for yourself.

Your lack of integrity in cheating on me and leaving me for another, younger mommy.

Your insistence on drawing me into your obsessive-compulsive worrying.

Having to turn out the light in bed when you wanted to go to sleep.

Having sex when I didn't feel like it.

My inheritance, which we managed to spend, and which I would have saved if I knew you were going to leave.

Good-bye to the future we were making for us and our daughter.

Good-bye to my future as a married woman—part of a couple. I really liked being married.

Good-bye to loving you. I needed you to not feel lonely, even though I felt lonely a lot of the time we were together. I loved you because you really were my best friend. That is the worst loss.

Start Journaling

The journaling technique that works for me involves sitting in a quiet place and just writing your feelings without stopping for at least twenty minutes. The secret to journaling as a way to heal is to write unself-consciously, letting your feelings flow on the page without re-reading what you've written or worrying about anyone else reading it. You will find when you finish that you have uncovered feelings you never knew you had and will experience a sense of relief. If you want to keep an online journal and get comments and input from other divorced folks, post it at www.divorce360.com. It's a great site for divorce support as well.

SELF-REFLECTION—
THE ANGER ANTIDOTE

This is the hard part. After you've finished spewing vitriol in his direction, take a long look at yourself and your role in the failure of your marriage. It helps to write down a list of your contributions to its demise, and to reflect on it when you're in full victim mode. Well-meaning friends may tell you that forgiveness is the antidote to anger, but forgiveness is not even a possibility for a long while, if then. Initially, the only real antidote to rage is self-reflection, taking responsibility for your part in the failure of your marriage.

It's extremely seductive to wrap yourself in the cloak of victimhood when you've been dumped—or even when you've done the dumping for a good reason—because, of course, you *are* a victim. But you are not an innocent victim, girlfriend. On some level you participated in the end of your marriage, even if you weren't conscious of it. It's paradoxical, but the more responsibility you take for the death of your marriage, the better you will feel.

For instance Stella, sixty-two, whose husband left her for another women after thirty-three years of marriage, reflected back ruefully on the start of their own relationship—an affair when he left his wife for her. She realizes now that she should have known the same thing would happen to her someday.

As for me, I took my husband totally for granted and was in complete denial about how unhappy we both were. Anything that was threatening I pushed under the rug. I lied to myself about the marriage working. I was the proverbial ostrich with my head in the sand. Looking at my own role in the death of my marriage was, paradoxically, comforting.

Take a few steps back and look at your marriage as if you were an outsider, someone analyzing it who didn't know either you or him. What do you think that person would see? What would she see about your role in the marriage?

GET YOUR ASS MOVING

Your usual sources of relaxation may not work during this period. I have always turned to food for comfort, but it held no appeal for me after being dumped. Okay, I'll admit that a box of chocolates would not have gone begging during this period. Still, like just about all recent divorcées, I lost weight. That is possibly the only immediate benefit of splitting up—loss of appetite is almost universal. Music grated on my nerves. Talk radio, one of my favorite distractions, didn't hold my attention. I couldn't concentrate on books or movies.

Physical activity is the best remedy for depression. It stimulates your natural endorphins—and if you do it outdoors, just moving your body and breathing fresh air will help. Find a physical activity that you enjoy. Lifting weights at the gym generally won't do the trick. Seek something exhilarating that you actually like or you're punishing yourself further. You need to get those serotonin levels up. Try any sport that provides speed, like bicycling or skating. Judith, a fifty-year-old writer from Houston, rides a motorcycle. "Biking is a metaphor for life. You have to swallow your fear and do it anyway."

Your exercise regime should restore not only your body but your soul in some way. For some women it's yoga; for others, ballroom dancing. For me it was swimming. I was lucky that my husband left at the end of June—the start of the summer. I'm a long-distance lake swimmer, and when I'm in the middle of a lake I am somehow able to leave my troubles ashore. The movement of my body in the silky water makes me feel alive and soothed at the same time. I do the backstroke and look up at the blue sky and feel that my troubles are an insignificant blip in the magnificence of the natural world. When I get out of the water I'm pleasantly spent and can sit in the shade reading a book and relaxing. Swimming never fails to lift my spirits. Hopefully, you will find a physical activity that makes you feel that way—or that at least gives you a break from the pain.

The divorced girlfriends I talked to *all* mentioned exercise as a survival tactic. Many of them did yoga, which they found particularly healing. Stella, who had never done any exercise before, started going to yoga sessions four times a week. Lydia, who suffered terribly in an abusive marriage, wound up teaching yoga. Its spiritual aspect helped her deal with the long-term trauma from abuse.

Dancing is also a very popular outlet for many divorcées. "You can ask anyone to dance. If you're the new kid they all want to dance with you," says Lola, fifty-eight, who goes swing dancing and zydeco dancing. There's usually a lesson before the dance, and you can learn enough to get by. Moving to music uses a totally different part of the brain, and a lively rhythm lifts spirits. Swing, tango, and salsa have become very popular, and you don't need a male partner to participate. I was a big Lindy Hopper once upon a time, and to my surprise the first time I tried swing, the steps all came back to me. I had a blast.

GET LOST IN ANOTHER WORLD

Find something that you can get lost in, that takes your mind away from your misery and sweeps you into another reality. My lifesaver was the TV series *Sex and the City*, which allowed me to get lost in the fantasy of being young and single in New York, which once *was* my reality. Each episode reminded me of my life before marriage, a life that at the time seemed empty and lonely, but in retrospect was just as fabulous as the life Carrie and the girls led—minus the Manolo Blahniks and miniskirts. My girlfriends and I picked up guys, had a lot of sex, and traded stories about it. Little did I know that those were the best years of my life—they beat marriage by a long shot.

I rationed my *Sex and the City* videotapes, only allowing myself to watch one episode at a time, at night when I couldn't sleep. Like gorging on sweets, I could have watched a whole season in one viewing orgy . . . but then I wouldn't have enough new

Best escapist TV shows:
FYI: If you're a subscriber, you can now watch hundreds of hours of old shows instantly on Netflix on your computer; you don't even have to rent the DVD.

I Love Lucy
Your Show of Shows
I, Claudius
Upstairs, Downstairs
Arrested Development
Monty Python
Everybody Loves Raymond
The Twilight Zone (the old ones)
Honeymooners
Seinfeld
Mary Tyler Moore Show
Heroes
Lost
The Sopranos

Best escapist movies:
anything with Audrey Hepburn
anything with Danny Kaye
anything directed by Preston Sturges
any MGM musical
anything with the Marx Brothers
The Wizard of Oz

Movies for a good laugh about divorce:
War of the Roses
The First Wives Club
Heartburn

She-Devil
The Squid and the Whale (not so funny but oh so true)

Best escapist books:
During one bad breakup when I was young, I read the whole Sherlock Holmes series. A series mystery that engages you can be a great escape.
The Poldark Saga
Childhood favorites like *Mary Poppins, Charlotte's Web, Winnie-the-Pooh*
Agatha Christie mysteries
Anything by Anita Shreve or Anne Tyler
The *Bridget Jones* series

Best books about divorce:
If you are comforted by reading about and gaining insight into your own experience (and if you're reading this book, you're probably in this category), here are my favorite divorce books.
Crazy Time: Surviving Divorce and Building a New Life by Abigail Trafford
Getting the Love You Want; A Guide for Couples by Harville Hendrix (not specifically about divorce but contains insights about relationships)
Uncoupling: Turning Points in Intimate Relationships by Diane Vaughn
Cut Loose: (Mostly) Older Women Talk About the End of (Mostly) Long-Term Relationships, edited by Nan Bauer-Maglin
Broken Open: How Difficult Times Can Help Us Grow by Elizabeth Lesser

*Coming Apart: Why Relationships End and How to Live
   Through the Ending of Yours* by Daphne Rose Kingma
Private Lies: Infidelity and the Betrayal of Intimacy by Frank
   Pittman
Rebuilding: When Your Relationship Ends by Dr. Bruce Fisher
   and Robert Alberti

episodes left to tide me over during other dark nights of the soul. Like Carrie, I fell in love with Big. Like her I was devastated when I was left for a younger woman. I burst into tears during the episode when he turns up at her door and tells her he's sorry, he made a mistake, he never should have left her. Of course that was my fantasy as well.

I'm not the only woman to get lost in a television series.

Karen, a forty-nine-year-old librarian who was devastated when her husband left her right after her mother's funeral, hunkered down with her thirteen-year-old son in their empty house (their home had burned down a few years earlier, and they had just moved into the new one) and watched the DVD of the first few seasons of the TV show *24*. "I had bought that DVD to give to someone for a birthday, but I kept it and we watched it," she told me. "We survived the first week that way. It's very dramatic—you can't think of anything else. We'd watch a show, eat or sleep, then watch another one. We also took turns every night reading a book about brave people. It made us feel we could be brave."

Whatever it is that allows you some relief from grieving, go for it. You have my permission to try retail therapy. Shop till you drop if that helps, but take cash only. Leave your debit cards, credit cards, and checkbook home. Or shop at Goodwill. It's guilt free.

Avoid alcohol, drugs, gambling, and sex, however—at least until you're thinking straight. You don't want to wind up penniless and in rehab with an STD.

SEEK GUIDANCE FROM THE STARS

Have you ever longed to know what the future holds? Do you want to know whether or not he'll come back? When your life is turned upside down, when you lose the anchor that marriage provides, you, like me, may be inexorably drawn to storefronts with crystal balls in the window. Actually, that's how psychics survive, by preying on the man troubles that afflict so many women like us. Don't be embarrassed about this not-uncommon female addiction. Despite a lifelong skepticism about anything even hinting at hype or charlatanism, I long ago became hooked on psychic readings. It is a guilty pleasure that I am loath to admit to my more cynical friends. When I'm under stress and no one is watching, I skulk into storefronts with tarot cards in the window, seeking a psychic fix.

If you pursue your psychic fixes for fun, and don't actually depend on the predictions coming true, go ahead and indulge. In fact, if you find anything harmless that alleviates your pain, go for it! After I was dumped, I went back on the psychic circuit. Florence, a local reader whose predictions had come true in the past, told me with total confidence that Zeke would break up with Almira and want to come back to me, but by that time I would have moved on. Well, that hasn't happened, but by the time he married Almira, I had managed to move on anyway. Even so, the prediction made me feel better during those desperate moments when I just wasn't ready to accept reality. If you look around, you'll find a wise psychic who will give you a good pep talk or a bit of cheap psychotherapy in addition to her reading. Florence, a motherly type who is my age, would give me a lecture about how us older women have to stop depending on men. The lecture helped more than the reading.

DON'T BE ASHAMED TO ACT CRAZY

As the title *Crazy Time* implies, you will not act like yourself during this time, and you may do very weird things.

Kay, who was left for her sister-in-law and whose amazing forgiveness story I relate in the last chapter of this book, didn't start out that way: "I am no saint. I was hateful," she says. "I ordered dogshit and had it sent to her house. I did some terrible things. I was executive director of our church and while she was visiting one day I said to the maintenance man, 'There's garbage in the hall, please get rid of it.'"

I would regularly drive past Almira's house to see if Zeke was there. One day I barged in and tried to drag him out. I even went through her mailbox when she wasn't home, looking for letters from him. When he and Almira insisted on taking my daughter to class on her first day of school, even though it was my parenting day, I started shrieking at them in the parking lot. I'm still pretty ashamed about that outburst but hey, I wasn't in my right mind, and neither are any of us when we go through this kind of trauma. The important thing is to forgive yourself for acting "witchy." Just don't resort to extreme measures like Clara Harris, forty-five, a Houston housewife who ran over her cheating orthodontist husband three times with her Mercedes-Benz when she caught him at a hotel with another woman. (Though I'll admit that I said "you go girl" to myself when I heard the news.)

HELP OTHERS

Volunteering was mentioned by many divorced girlfriends as a way to get through the worst times during a divorce. Helping others takes you away from focusing on your own misery, and gives you the opportunity to take care of others who are needier than you. Volunteering also gets you out of the house, which can be a major battle when struggling with the paralyzing depression that strikes so many of us after the breakup.

Deborah, forty-nine, became the moderator of the divorce support forum on *About.com.* "I like helping people through the early stages of divorce," she says. "It breaks my heart when I see a woman feeling scared and desperate, and run to anyone who'll have her, or even take her ex back because of it. I like letting women know it's not the end of the world if you don't have a man."

Melissa, sixty-one, whose husband left her for another woman, started volunteering at a nursing home and then a hospital. "I live more of a reclusive life and it was hard for me to go into a nursing home or hospital, but I find it rewarding. I don't know why but it feels like I'm doing something for me."

BECOME A GROUPIE

If you've gone to the typical divorce support group, you may find a bunch of people intent on trashing their exes and whining about their victimhood. That kind of group can be helpful in a paradoxical way—there's nothing like a good look in the mirror to see what you could turn into if you don't watch yourself. You may discover, however, that you really want to meet people who've survived nasty divorces and lived to tell the tale. Not all divorce support groups are pity pot sessions, as fifty-six-year-old Mae found when she signed up for one at her local Jewish community center. "I needed support to make another life, I needed support to get off my butt. I needed support to go out and look for someone else." She wound up doing all those things successfully. If the first or second group you attend isn't helpful, keep looking. Here are some other ideas:

Try some of the 12-step groups. If your ex was a drinker, go to Al-Anon, or AA if you've got a drinking problem. There's CODA (Co-dependents Anonymous) for the wives who enabled their mates to mistreat them. You can even find Love and Relationship Addicts Anonymous. There are uplifting divorce support groups based on the 12-step model.

Join a grief group. You'll find support for getting through the grieving process rather than the affirmation of your victimhood. You might also get some perspective from people who have suffered losses greater than yours.

Treat yourself to a divorce retreat. I went to a luxurious spa in Austin, Texas, for a retreat called Ariadne's Thread: Spa for the Soul. It was wonderful. (You can find it on the Web at www .aspaforthesoul.com.)

Join an online support group. I've already mentioned www .divorce360.com. It has a very strong support component—and my blog! Also visit www.firstwivesworld.com, an active community of women who are going through divorce.

Get a pet. The healing effects of pet ownership have been well documented. My little doggy Shadow is my constant companion, a warm body to hug at night, and an eager face to wake up to in the morning. Walking him gives me a reason to get out of the house and exercise. He helps me socialize and meet new people because he's so cute that everyone stops to pet him. I don't know how I ever lived without him. Even if you've never considered owning a pet, give it a try. There are groups that will allow you to foster a pet while it's waiting for a home. This way you can give a dog or cat a tryout, and keep it if you like it.

IF YOU'RE IN YOUR . . .

Forties . . .

You may not have the luxury to focus totally on yourself during this rough time. Your kids may need you to be there for them. Even if you're depressed, spend time with your kids—play sports, go to movies, play Monopoly if that's what they enjoy. Putting yourself and your feelings aside for a while can be therapeutic in itself. Sparing your kids some of the trauma of divorce by being there for them is a long-term investment that will pay off.

Keep your head high. No matter how common divorce is these days, there is still shame attached to it, especially when there are school-aged kids in the family. It's tough to be the only single mom at the soccer game, or at the school barbecue. Seek out other single moms to sit with at events where both parents usually attend. I was an older mom who was forced to hang out with the happily married young moms in their twenties and thirties—and I hated it. If you don't know any single moms, bring a friend to couples events.

Take advantage of your kid-free time. The upside of divorce is that your ex (hopefully) will have the kids part of the time, leaving you the luxury of time on your own. Keep reminding yourself that this is time to do whatever you want, whatever will make you feel better—even if it's spending the day in bed with a book and a box of chocolates.

Fifties . . .

You may have teens at home or young adults in college. Don't rely on them to help you through. There is an unfortunate tendency for moms to reverse roles during a divorce, turning their kids into parents or peers. Don't pour your heart out to your teenage or college kids—that's what your friends are for.

Do something you've always dreamed about. Take a trip to Paris or go rafting down the Colorado or spend a week at a spa. If you've spent your life taking care of kids *and* your husband, which most women in their fifties have, it's now time for *you*.

Sixties or older . . .

Spend time with your grandchildren. There's nothing like seeing life from a child's perspective to lift your spirits. Your grandkids will remind you that your marriage wasn't a total loss—anything that produced these wonderful little beings couldn't have been all bad.

Focus on yourself. You may have spent your entire life focusing on others—your kids, your husband, your aging parents, his aging parents. This is *your* time. Do whatever makes you feel good, as long as it's not self-destructive. Evelyn Kaye, sixty-nine, went back to school to become a teacher of English as a second language and traveled abroad. Her attitude toward aging helped: "Aging post-divorce is no more difficult than aging while married. Why would it be different? Which sounds better to you: Living with someone you can't stand and getting older, or being free and getting older? Need I say more?"

CHAPTER TWO
BEFORE YOU GIVE UP

Reconciliation Strategies
That Work

A dirty little secret in the therapy field is that couples therapy may be the hardest form of therapy, and most therapists aren't good at it. Of course, this wouldn't be a public health problem if most therapists stayed away from couples work, but they don't. Surveys indicate that about 80 percent of therapists in private practice do couples therapy. Where they got their training is a mystery, because most therapists practicing today never took a course in couples therapy and never did their internships under supervision from someone who'd mastered the art. From a consumer's point of view, going in for couples therapy is like having your broken leg set by a doctor who skipped orthopedics in medical school.
—WILLIAM DOHERTY, FAMILY THERAPY NETWORKER

Before giving up and calling a lawyer, many of you may still be on the fence, learning about divorce but still trying to save your marriage. You may live in a state that mandates marriage counseling before a divorce is granted; or you simply may not be ready to give up on twenty or thirty years of your life without a fight. If you're still in the game, still making some effort—no matter how last-ditch—to save your marriage, you need to have some solid information about marriage counseling: what works, what doesn't, and what to try before you give up.

If you've already been to marriage counseling that didn't work, you're not alone. Before ending a marriage there's a social expectation that you should try counseling, if only to fend off the disapproval when your friends and family ask if you tried it before splitting up. Unless alcohol or abuse is involved, they *will* ask, guaranteed. If the answer is no, you'll get more than a few raised eyebrows, the implication being that you're a quitter. Unfortunately, few couples get to counseling in time to actually save their marriages. Often it's more like the last rites for the marriage. Even fewer people find the right kind of marriage counseling—the kind that actually saves marriages.

I am still wrestling with the what-ifs when it comes to my marriage. What if I had known about Harville Hendrix's Imago therapy, or Emotionally Focused Therapy, or John Gottman's workshops before my marriage wound up on the rocks? Maybe we could have rescued it. Unfortunately, I learned what works too late. I hope to give you the information I didn't have. When it comes to a long marriage, there are so many good reasons to save it rather than ditch it.

All marriage counselors agree that the earlier the better when it comes to counseling. Although my husband and I did try counseling many years before we broke up, we wound up with Caroline, a new-agey flake. She said I had too much male energy and Zeke, too much female energy. Her remedy was an assignment to gaze into each other's eyes and try to connect with each other's souls. We did try it a few times, but while my husband dutifully stared at me I kept wishing I could flee the room.

After his announcement about his affair, I dragged Zeke to a succession of marriage counselors. But since he was continuing the affair and lying about it, there wasn't much point. However, I truly believe some marriages can be brought back from the brink of death if there is some motivation left on both sides and you and he are willing to make a good-faith effort. Sometimes, even if there is an affair going on, certain approaches might work.

WHAT IS GOOD MARRIAGE COUNSELING?

Unfortunately, most couples in trouble just haul themselves off to the local mental health clinic and see a counselor who may or may not have a degree or training in marriage counseling. The reality is that marriage counseling is very different from psychotherapy—the therapist should have certain skills. Those without this training often take a mechanistic approach. They think couples are having a communication problem, or a particular conflict that needs to be resolved, instead of addressing the deep-seated, underlying issues that have to be uncovered first for counseling to work.

"Most counselors miss the intention," my friend and couples therapist Wendy Wynberg, M.S.W., told me. "The counselor first needs to establish what each member of the couple expects from the marriage. You can't just work on the details. First you need to see the forest and then work on the trees." Wendy asks couples to relate what their marriage would be like if it were a movie, to discover what their fantasy marriage is. She often finds that couples are in two separate marriages. After each describes their ideal vision this way, she asks why they want the marriage to work. Only at that point does she explore what's non-negotiable and what each can compromise on. None of the counselors we visited ever asked those kinds of questions.

My experience was, I'm afraid, typical. Our first counselor was a very sweet, jolly fat guy at the local counseling center. We told our tale of woe, including Zeke's affair. When the counselor asked him if he'd stopped seeing *her*, I could tell by Zeke's sullen tone that he was lying. The counselor bought his story without question. He seemed to want to believe him.

First he asked us what we didn't like about each other. This seems to be a typical marriage counseling technique. We gave him laundry lists of our complaints. Then he commanded us to tell each other what we loved about each other. We dutifully came up with nice things to say.

"I see a problem in communication here," he said. "You two need to let each other know more often how you feel in a positive way. I want you to do something nice for each other every day and come back and tell me how it feels." This is another typical "exercise" marriage counselors assign that is useless without examining what's really going on between the two of you.

He jabbered on about his theories of what constituted a happy marriage, which had nothing to do with us. At one point he said with a self-satisfied air, "I can see that you two are really in love with each other. You'll never break up."

I somehow felt better when he said this. After all, how could a marriage counselor be dead wrong? Then he left to have surgery, and we never went back.

Our next attempt was an elderly, stern-looking lady with iron-gray hair in a church-lady outfit who, after asking us for a long history of our lives and marriage, told us our problem was that we were angry at each other. Duh! We spent a hundred dollars to discover that? She said that at the next session she'd help us express our anger and that would help. We'd been expressing our anger for eighteen years without getting anywhere. I didn't see how paying a hundred bucks a session to express anger would get us anywhere. There never was a next session.

Zeke lied again to our third counselor, Kali, who wound up being my individual therapist. If there's an affair suspected, some therapists will insist on seeing the members of the couple separately before proceeding with counseling and ask straight-out about the affair. That might have worked with Zeke and saved us a lot of trouble, but none of the counselors we visited suggested it.

Seek counseling if:
You actually still love the guy and he loves you.
You think he is willing to work with you in therapy.
You think his affair will blow over and you're willing to wait.
He has remorse for what he's put you through.
You want to give it one last try.

Split if:
He's abusive, verbally or otherwise.
He's in love with the girlfriend and plans to marry her.
He doesn't care about your feelings.
He's willing to go to counseling only because you drag him.

HOW TO FIND THE RIGHT COUNSELOR

A *New York Times* study of the outcomes of marital therapy showed that 25 percent of couples are worse off after ending two years of marital counseling than they were when they started; and after four years 38 percent are divorced.

These grim statistics are actually not set in stone if the couple finds an experienced therapist with an effective approach. Some

SOME QUESTIONS TO ASK

- *Are you trained in marital therapy? Where did you get your training?*
- *What approach do you use? A seasoned clinician should be able to explain what his or her model is all about.*
- *What's your rate of success?*
- *Can you give us an assessment of our marriage and the chances of saving it?*

Pay attention to whether or not the therapist has shown any insight into what makes the two of you tick. The counselors we went to all seemed clueless about the dynamics between us.

approaches, such as Emotionally Focused Therapy, claim a success rate as high as 75 percent.

How do you find a good marriage counselor? "Shop around," says Dr. Michael Zentman, director of New York's Adelphi University post-graduate program for marriage and couples therapy. "Ask if the person is trained in marital therapy. Meet them. Ask about the approach they use. A seasoned clinician should be able to explain what his or her model is all about. Then think about the fit. Are you and your husband comfortable with this person, do you both feel a connection?"

Zentman explains that most counselors who aren't trained in marital therapy don't come up with a diagnosis, but work on the symptoms, such as communication. They tell the couple to do things like go out together one night a week, give each other more compliments, listen without arguing. This might work for a few weeks or months, but if the underlying issues aren't addressed, the problems will reemerge. He also explains that therapists miss dealing with what has changed in a relationship that caused it to fall apart. If a couple got along relatively well for twenty years, but things have gone downhill for the last ten, the therapist has to find out what happened ten years ago in order to discover why there is a problem now.

Granted, it's not easy to bare your soul to more than one shrink, but remember that you are the consumer—and this may be one of the most important decisions you ever make. Unfortunately, shopping around is easier said than done when you're in crisis. It's hard to make a good choice when your marriage is falling apart and you may be falling apart with it. How do you go about this search? When I was looking for a marriage counselor, I asked other therapists whose opinion I respected; they referred me to people they thought highly of. Unfortunately, they didn't seem to notice that these particular colleagues had no specialized expertise in marriage counseling. Don't just ask other therapists for referrals. Ask other couples, preferably one or two whose marriages were actually saved through counseling with a particular therapist. When it comes to finding a competent marriage counselor, there's nothing like a recommendation from a satisfied customer.

There are several types of couples therapy that have good track records and specific theories that underlie their particular method. Therapists who use these approaches don't just work haphazardly, but have a specific set of tools they use with all couples. A few have books written by their founders that you can read to find out about the approach before you try it. Even more importantly, they all have Web sites where you can find lists of therapists all over the country trained in the particular method. Instead of searching the Yellow Pages, call the therapists in your community who are trained in one of the specific types of therapy that appeals to you and your husband. If there's more than one, talk to a few and pick whomever seems the most personally compatible.

Even though all this information is widely available, it would never occur to most people to search for a counselor this way. It didn't to me, and I'm fairly savvy about therapy, having been in private therapy for years, plus having a journalism background in psychology and self-help.

Which approach to pick? According to Dr. Zentman, different theories are like swimming strokes: None is right or wrong, better or worse. The only question is, Does the clinician fit the couple? As long as the therapist is well trained it may be a good fit.

MARRIAGE COUNSELING WITH A TRACK RECORD

Retrouvaille

The name means "rediscovery," or "return again," in French. Although the Catholic Church runs it, Retrouvaille is nondenominational and involves one intense weekend and six follow-up sessions in a classroom setting. It's inexpensive, which is why I sought it out. After spending a ton of money on counseling, it was a last-ditch attempt. The program is run by volunteers, peer couples who have saved their own marriages through Retrouvaille. The stories they tell about their own marriages are riveting, and when you hear them, you believe the program can work. Listening to actual people who've experienced all the pain you have and have managed to get through it has an immediacy that professional marriage counseling lacks. Although it didn't save my marriage, I learned a lot about what a good marriage was supposed to look like.

There is no preaching of religion during Retrouvaille, but it does have a spiritual aspect. Retrouvaille believes that there is a higher power working within the couple. Serious Catholics, of course, see marriage as a sacrament and don't believe in divorce in the first place, which gives them a leg up when it comes to saving their marriages. What scares people away from Retrouvaille is the fear that they're going to be preached to. However, it's considered a peer ministry since it's led by couples, not clergy and there's no preaching.

It's also very effective when one member of a couple, usually the man, feels uncomfortable opening up to a marriage counselor. In Retrouvaille, the couple communicate only with each other, and there's no need to reveal anything to the group.

How It Works

The workshops are held at Catholic retreat centers or hotels around the country. We got to go to a lovely retreat center in Queens, New York, formerly a monastery. The peaceful atmosphere resonated with the participants, most of whom were in turmoil emotionally. We also enjoyed food that could have been served at a four-star restaurant. After long, grueling sessions of revealing our feelings, we ate pasta so delicious it replenished soul as well as body. I will warn you that Retrouvaille is a marathon, a draining, tiring process. It's no quick fix. You have to be willing to look at yourself openly, honestly, and objectively, and reveal yourself to your spouse.

You sit in a large room with about twenty to thirty other couples, most of whom look pretty grim. The first exercise is to introduce your spouse, including his or her best quality. I said something like, "My husband has a good sense of humor." Other couples couldn't think of anything.

The workshop leaders give talks on various topics and then assign the couples to write for ten minutes on a particular question, such as "How do I feel when we have a fight?" or "What is my reason to go on living?" Then husband and wife go to their room and read their answers to each other. There is no interrupting or arguing allowed. After the wife reads an answer, the husband tells her what he has heard, repeating it in his own words, and vice versa. Each spouse also is supposed to ask the other a lot of questions to clarify what the other has written, and come up with other ways to express it. Metaphors and similes are encouraged. This process is called dialoguing, and it's at the heart of the Retrouvaille experience. A lot of other programs advocate this type of active listening, but the power of Retrouvaille is that it's not just an exercise led by a therapist. The couples who lead the groups share their own stories—how they came to the brink of divorce and found each other again. They are actively walking their talk. Couples are supposed to do one of these exercises every night for twenty minutes for the rest of their married lives. That's quite a commitment.

One of the Retrouvaille rules is that if you're having an affair, don't do the weekend—but some couples do it anyway, and sometimes it even works. Jane Kirsch, who with her husband, Bill, leads workshops in Buffalo, told me about one such couple. The husband came reluctantly, just to satisfy his wife. He'd told his girlfriend to meet him in the parking lot Sunday night when it was over. The weekend was so moving that on Sunday he went out to his girlfriend's car and told her it was over.

Jane, now sixty-six, went to Retrouvaille when she and Bill were in their early fifties. Their oldest child had left for college and "I couldn't face the rest of my life with a man I didn't like. He had a gambling problem, he stole from the family business. I had problems as well, including a drinking problem—however, I blamed it all on him. I was considering divorce. I had a career and could take care of myself. What made me have second thoughts was not wanting to live alone. My mother, who was widowed, told me how lonely she was. I was afraid I'd lose all my friends as well since all of them were couples."

Retrouvaille was the beginning of a new start to their marriage. Bill learned that Jane couldn't stand dishonesty. No matter what he'd done, she wanted him to be honest about it. He let her know that he couldn't stand her anger. She's pretty fiery and tends to lose her temper. Even though the weekend didn't cure their problems—he still gambled, albeit sporadically, and she still drank—it helped them air their differences. They did all the follow-ups, helped in the organization, and things improved over time. Retrouvaille opened their eyes to the fact that they could have a discussion on sensitive issues without going into rage and anger. "The Retrouvaille technique helped because you don't approach the most serious problems immediately," Jane told me. The process of taking a topic, writing about how you are affected by it for ten minutes, exchanging your writing, and having your spouse read back his or her interpretation of what you wrote defuses the anger. By the time you discuss what you've written, you quickly learn that feelings are neither right nor wrong, they're just feelings, and by sharing them you get closer.

We went to New York City for Retrouvaille right after 9/11. I will never forget one young couple who were leading our group. The husband was a fireman who had been at Ground Zero when the Twin Towers collapsed. The dialogue involved his wife helping him explore his feelings about the event, which included his terror, pain at seeing his fallen colleagues, guilt that he had survived, relief, and many other emotions. It occurred to me that many people who had been there may never have expressed to anyone, even their spouses, how it really made them feel. This tragedy was an opportunity to bring these two people closer together. This kind of intense communication is usually reserved for the "honeymoon" period of a relationship, where you stay up all night sharing your deep inner secrets. As life and kids take over, growing apart is inevitable unless you make a conscious effort.

After twenty or thirty years of marriage, we assume we know everything about our mates, but we don't—it's an illusion. We are all hiding who we are to some extent, fearing there's a part of ourselves that's unlovable. Exposing those fears and vulnerabilities can bring you and your husband closer and ultimately save your marriage.

Imago Relationship Therapy

Imago was started by Harville Hendrix, Ph.D., author of *Getting the Love You Want: A Guide for Couples*. The premise underlying it is deceptively simple. Basically Hendrix believes we all suffer from childhood wounds. Even those of us with the happiest childhoods had many needs that went unmet by our caretakers. Parents simply aren't perfect and are often unwilling or unable to meet our infant needs. Every unmet need makes us feel scared. As small children we have no idea how to make ourselves feel safe. We might cry a lot to get attention, or withdraw, denying that we even have needs.

Attachment is a basic human need, one of the first to emerge as we grow. Then the need to explore evolves, then the impulse to establish a sense of identity, competence, concern, and intimacy. Each stage builds on the last, but any impairment interrupts our ability to move on to the next stage. We are simultaneously being socialized by society, told what to do, what to say, and how to behave by teachers, parents, friends, even TV characters. Socialization teaches us that in one way or another we're not acceptable;

we're too fat, too shy, not smart enough, not dressed right—myriad aspects of ourselves that we have to then disown or deny. We stop feeling good and start feeling flawed and incomplete.

Luckily, if most of us had "good enough" parenting, we survive and prosper. However, some of us are handicapped by deep hurts. No matter how well we do as adults, we were *all* wounded in childhood to some extent and now cope as well as possible with the world, using defenses we developed when we were very young.

Then we fall in love. All of a sudden everything feels perfect, including ourselves. The sun is sunnier, the sky is brighter, even the annoying boss doesn't get on our nerves anymore. Our lover is what we've been looking for all our lives; we tell him everything; we melt when he kisses us; we can be who we really are with him. Most of all we can relax and feel safe. Inevitably, however, things go wrong. The traits that seemed so endearing in the first place become the most annoying. The strong, silent man who made us feel protected now seems distant and aloof. The boyish, carefree man whom we could mother becomes a millstone around our neck. Once we come out of the love trance, we may wind up in shock when we notice that Mr. Adorable has become Mr. Incredibly Annoying.

Congratulations, Hendrix would tell you, you've found your Imago. Despite all your best intentions, your unconscious has spotted him across a crowded room: the very man who most resembles Daddy or Mommy or both, whoever failed to give you what you needed in childhood. Since in order to feel okay, you need to repair the damage inflicted on you as a child, your unconscious need is not to find Mr. Right, who will give you everything you never got as a child, but Mr. Not-So-Right and sometimes Mr. Totally Wrong, because you can only get your feelings of aliveness and wholeness restored by someone who reminds you of that inadequate caretaker. We look for someone who has the same faults and who will inflict the same pain. Only he can repair the hurt. Even worse, we seek the qualities in our Imago missing in ourselves—if we're shy we seek someone outgoing, if we're messy we want someone neat, if we're repressing anger we seek someone angry to express that anger for us. Eventually, however, those very qualities will be the ones that annoy us the most, because they're the ones we've repressed in ourselves.

It's uncanny. It solves the mystery of why women with alcoholic fathers fall in love with one alcoholic after another, or women who were abused by their fathers fall in love with abusive men. This is too simplistic, however. The Imago often consists of a complex mixed bag of qualities formed in reaction to our caretakers' responses—both father and mother. These collective impressions form an unconscious portrait of Mr. Right. Luckily, most of us were deprived or hurt in more subtle ways and fall in love with men who are merely flawed, not dangerous or damaged beyond repair. The good news is that with Imago therapy, you actually can heal those childhood hurts by making them conscious and following the Imago process—which, like Retrouvaille, involves dialoguing.

Long after my marriage ended, I read Hendrix and had a field day analyzing how Zeke was my perfect Imago. Try it with your own relationship. You will learn a lot from this exercise. Although I convinced myself that Zeke was totally different from my parents when I married him, he actually fit the bill down to the tiniest details—scarily so. He was both of my parents—good qualities and bad—rolled into one extremely flawed human being. I was supposed to be his "good mother" who would care for him and love him in ways his mother never did. He was supposed to be my "good father" who understood me and was comforting in ways my father never was. We both fell down on the job.

Zeke's anger, which he displayed on our first date, should have driven me away, but even though I found it repellent, I also found it somehow mesmerizing, especially the apology that inevitably came after an outburst. I got hooked on those apologies, which I'd never gotten from my father—who was also angry, but unrepentant. If you're wondering why you picked an angry mate, as so many women do, Hendrix makes a really interesting point when he says, "The anger we repressed because it was punished in our home, and which we unconsciously hate ourselves for feeling, we 'annex' in our partner." Often as women we're not allowed to express anger, though we may feel it, so we choose mates who will express it for us.

The power struggles that ensue after the romance ends are perfectly normal—they are "supposed" to happen, they're signs that we are trying to get our needs met. The paradox is that our mates can actually "heal" us, but only if we become conscious of the patterns that are ruling our relationship. This is what Imago therapy aims to do: to bring those childhood scenarios to consciousness and actually use them to heal ourselves and each other. It's a tall order, and a task that can be extremely painful and difficult because it involves bringing to consciousness parts of yourself that you may have denied for your entire life. The conscious part consists of actually giving your partner what he needs in order to heal, and vice versa. You have to stretch a whole lot to do this, but it works, and it's a powerful technique. The goal is for you and your husband to become passionate friends, with a love based on reality, not on childhood needs. It helps to have an experienced practitioner.

How It Works

Kristin Harrington, an Imago therapist in Kingston, New York, explains: "I serve as a coach to help the couple communicate effectively, to actually hear each other rather than just reacting in the same old ways."

Her therapeutic process consists of the couple talking mostly to each other, not to her. How often does it save the marriage? "It depends on the level of commitment, " she says. She asks couples where they are on the commitment scale—totally out to totally in. For couples who are frustrated but still in the marriage, Imago Relationship Therapy works most of the time. If one spouse is way far out, it works less often. Kristin takes the temperature of the relationship. If the couple are engaged, expressing emotion, and talking about the marriage, even if it's about separating, the prognosis is better. If they don't talk at all, or if they're overinvolved with other things, the prognosis is worse.

Wendy Capella, fifty-four, credits Imago Relationship Therapy with Kristin for saving her marriage of thirty years when it was on the rocks a few years ago. Wendy says learning to communicate was key. "It was very hard to reach my husband, Carl. He was an abused child who had trouble confiding in people. I was brought up to stay married no matter what happened. We developed separate lives, and he became so distant and withdrawn it was unbearable. At one time we had a lot in common; we had a lot of the same interests, and we enjoyed doing things together. Then he stopped wanting to be with me. Everything I said sparked an outburst. I couldn't do anything right."

They saw Kristin in a last-ditch attempt to save the marriage. Carl, who was having an affair but told Wendy it was over, quit after three sessions when Wendy found out he was still seeing the girlfriend and confronted him. At that point he attempted suicide, and Wendy found she simply couldn't walk away. Although friends and family were telling her he was a monster, in her gut she knew there was something else going on, which turned out to be a mood disorder—he was bipolar. They started seeing Kristin again together, and continued with her for nine months once a week. After his diagnosis, and going on medication, Carl started working hard at putting himself together.

"We [each] wrote down a list of things that were important in our marriage, then compared the lists to see if we had the same goals. We pretty much wanted the same things. Because we'd been married so long and had so many similar interests, we found we really did love each other deep down. I found the mirroring approach—where you paraphrase and then listen to what your partner is saying—to be really helpful. Formerly we'd say things and have explosive battles. I had to learn to back off. We also had to ask permission to talk about certain things. He was able to tell me when it wasn't a good time for him. The Imago communication exercises really helped. Once you start talking and listening, it makes a huge difference. We hadn't had any real communication in a long time. He never let on about his depression. I never knew the extent of the abuse he suffered as a child. I could go to my parents. He was the complete opposite. His mother had abandoned him and his brother when he was very young, and he had a big problem trusting women. The therapy we got with Kristin made a huge difference. The reason I have my marriage today is that I have a really good therapist."

John Gottman

If your husband, like a lot of (especially older) men, thinks marriage counseling won't help, that it's unproven or softheaded, try a Gottman workshop or therapist. "Gottman's approach works well with guys because it's logical, research-driven, and backed up by statistics," says Mike McNulty, Ph.D., a Chicago psychotherapist, couples counselor, and consultant with the Gottman Institute. "Men love facts and figures."

A Gottman workshop, like Retrouvaille, also involves the couple talking only to each other, so there is no need for your husband to feel threatened about having to reveal his feelings to strangers.

John Gottman takes nothing about marriage for granted. He started as a researcher and studied couples for fifteen years, including some 700 couples whom he followed over time to find out who were what he calls the *masters of marriage* and who were the *disasters of marriage*. The research involved everything from interviews and surveys to videotaping couples interacting over a weekend, analyzing every little interaction between them. Based on this research Gottman came up with the concept of the seven principles that make relationships work. He trains therapists all over the country in his methods, and runs workshops for couples as well.

After studying how newlywed couples interact, Dr. Gottman claims to have developed a method that predicts, with 90 percent accuracy, which will remain married and which will divorce four to six years later. It is also 81 percent accurate in predicting which marriages will survive after seven to nine years. Unsurprisingly, Gottman discovered that the foundation of a happy marriage is friendship with your spouse, which he thinks is overlooked by a lot of marriage counselors, who tend to focus on resolving conflict rather than focusing on the positives. Using what he learned from observing marriages that work, Gottman came up with the concept of the sound relationship house and the seven principles that make marriages work.

According to Gottman, happily married couples have certain characteristics. They know each other really well; they regularly express appreciation to each other; and they regularly turn toward each other, instead of turning away, by making comments and sharing small things. To encourage couples to get to know each other better, Gottman asks them to complete detailed questionnaires about their lives, past experiences, emotions, family background, and more and share them with each other. This is a powerful first step to healing.

Contempt is a major killer of marriages, so part of his method is to teach couples to regularly express fondness and admiration for each other. He recommends the couple focus on the past to see if they can dredge up good memories that might resurrect some positive feelings.

Another Gottman discovery is that men in happy marriages allow their wives to influence them. The vast majority of wives already do that, but older men in particular come from an era when they were considered "henpecked" if they consulted their wives about decision making.

Gottman found through his research that 69 percent of a couple's problems are perpetual and only 31 percent are solvable. If people realize which problems can't be solved, they'll stop beating their heads against the wall and try to find the solvable problems. The gridlocked conflict will probably always be an issue, but couples need to learn to talk about it without hurting each other.

Shared meaning is also key. "Developing shared meaning occurs naturally if you are open to each other's perspectives," Gottman says in *The Seven Principles for Making Marriage Work.* "The more you can speak candidly and respectfully to each other, the more likely there is to be a blending of your sense of meaning."

How It Works

"With couples in midlife or older, the most common issue is the wife's complaint about lack of emotional connection," says Gottman couples counselor Virginia M. Boney, PhD, located in Jacksonville, Florida. This goes along with the AARP survey findings that women initiate 66 percent of midlife divorces. As their children become more self-sufficient, women in their forties start looking at their marriages more critically and really notice what's missing.

Gottman's research actually shows that there are two crucial periods for divorce—during the first seven years of marriage, and in midlife, when couples often have young teenage children. Couples in the early divorce group are openly contesting and fighting with each other; in the later divorce group they're alienated and avoidant. They are the people you see in a restaurant who are not talking to each other. They raise kids together, but there is not much going on together and they realize their marriage is empty. These couples stifle things and do not raise issues with their partner. Their marriages are a suppression of negative emotions and a lack of positive emotions—passive and distant relationships with no laughing, love, or interest in each other. This style of suppression can cause intense loneliness that's almost like dying. The end of this type of marriage often coincides with a midlife crisis when one partner realizes his or her marriage, life, and/or job are empty and begins looking for something better.

Such couples have what Gottman calls "the four horses of the apocalypse" galloping through their marriage: contempt, criticism, defensiveness, and stonewalling. According to Gottman's statistics, 85 percent of couples who demonstrate such behaviors will split up. However, such marriages can be saved if at least one member of the couple has some motivation.

Virginia Boney told me about her work with Carol and Doug. Carol was a nurse and office manager; Doug, a floor manager in a manufacturing plant. Both were in their midforties. Carol started treatment with Dr. Boney because she felt a lack of emotional intimacy in her marriage, claiming "I feel like we're roommates." While Doug complained that she had no interest in sex, she said she wasn't interested because there was no emotional connection and he made her feel like a piece of meat.

It was the second marriage for both; all their kids were grown and out of the house. Carol complained about him being irritable, describing him as like a "gray cloud" because he'd become so negative. She felt he wasn't interested in her world. They didn't talk.

One underlying conflict had developed over years about his daughter by a first marriage. She was resentful that she had reached out to his daughter, who ended up blowing her off. He didn't want to hear how painful it was for her because he felt so bad that he couldn't fix it. She felt dismissed as a result.

They were in Gottman-oriented therapy with Dr. Boney for about four months. They worked hard, doing exercises to enhance their friendship outside the office—which is how Gottman therapy works. Dr. Boney told them to spend time doing what they enjoyed when they were dating, to tell each other about their day, to express appreciation. Most importantly, they learned how to talk about their perpetual issues with the goal of revealing the dream, hope, or longing beneath the problem. In Gottman therapy, if there's a perpetual issue, there's always a dream, or hope, or longing underneath. When the conflict becomes gridlocked, it's not safe for the dream, hope, or longing to emerge.

Most of the time people are unaware of what the dream or hope is. They just know they feel strongly about something that is causing conflict in the marriage. The dream underneath Carol's complaint was that she wanted to make a difference in her stepdaughter's life because she herself had been a child of a divorced family. Carol had a huge sense of failure. Her husband's dream was to be a good dad—but that wasn't possible, either.

When Carol talked about her pain, Doug would get defensive because of his own sense of failure. The hardest thing is for a spouse to stop defending his or her position and just listen and understand. Finally, through asking open-ended questions and listening, they were able to hear each other. One day they had a breakthrough—and cried together. They finally managed to hear each other instead of each promoting their own agenda.

Emotionally Focused Therapy

A relatively new entrant into the couples' therapy arena, EFT claims a very high success rate. It was developed in Canada by Dr. Sue Johnson, director of the Ottawa Couples and Family Institute. Its research shows that 70 percent of couples become satisfied with their marriage for at least three years after EFT, including the most at-risk couples, such as those who had been through extramarital affairs and other major breaches in trust. EFT is short-term therapy that should take about twenty sessions. If you agree, as I do, that marriage counseling has been too focused on just changing behavior rather than discovering the underlying causes of it, EFT may be for you. It's a very psychoanalytic approach that concentrates on discovering what's going on underneath the negative emotional cycles that destroy marriages.

EFT is based on attachment theory, which explains how infants need a secure attachment with a parent to develop into whole, independent human beings. So far attachment theory has been applied solely to the mother–child bond. However, as Dr. Allison

Lee, an EFT couples therapist with the Ottawa Institute, explains, "We are hardwired to need to hook up with someone throughout our lifetimes. We once had tribes, then extended families, but now the emphasis is on our primary relationship. Being in love is about being securely attached. When you don't feel secure you protest, complain, nag, yell, scream, or withdraw. It's normal to need to be understood, to need to know you're in your partner's heart."

There are a number of different attachment styles. Some people are securely attached and may take their partners for granted. Others are insecurely attached and quick to jump to the conclusion that their partner isn't there. Some are avoidantly attached with a restricted range of emotions and tend to pull away. Others, the crazy makers, are fearfully avoidant—they're the push, pull types. Most of us have been involved with at least one of those in our lifetime. Understanding attachment styles helps the EFT therapist get to the primary vulnerable emotions in a couple. For example, the nagging, complaining, pursuing wife who is very emotional, demanding, and suspicious may be terrified underneath that she doesn't count.

In EFT the key is to break through the repetitive fights that couples have and make them feel safe enough to reveal their feelings. Dr. Lee gives the example of a wife who's always telling her husband she's disappointed and angry with him. He hears he's not measuring up, feels hurt, and withdraws, saying nothing. She sees him saying nothing and thinks he doesn't care.

When a partner is angry, that's a threat, and the other partner's alarm bell signals danger. Both react in their usual, predictable ways. The EFT therapist tries to understand that cycle and find out what's under it, which is usually poignant insecurities such as, *Do you love me? Can I count on you? Am I on the top of your list? Am I enough for you?*

How It Works

In EFT the therapist asks the couple open-ended questions such as, "Tell me about your relationship." EFT doesn't have a whole program of specific exercises like Imago and Gottman; it's more like "sitting down and having a nice cuppa tea together," says Dr. Lee. EFT therapists call themselves process consultants rather than therapists because their approach is to collaborate with clients rather than telling them what to do. The couple teach the therapist about their relationship, rather than the therapist being the expert behind the desk.

Harry, sixty-eight, and Martha, sixty-three, were on the brink of divorce when they consulted Dr. Allison Lee for EFT. Harry was brought up by a depressed mother and learned that if he said anything, it would set his mother off. So he said very little. Martha felt she didn't have any value because of the way she'd been belittled by her parents as a child.

Their marriage started going downhill thirty years earlier, when Martha got pregnant. Harry, angry about the pregnancy because he was afraid he couldn't make enough money to support the family, was afraid to say anything to Martha. She felt he didn't value her and became resentful; he pulled away from her. Of course they never expressed these feelings to each other. Over time she gave up trying to engage him and made her own friends, getting what she needed from them. He tried to please her with gestures like buying her a sports car for her fiftieth birthday. She rejected the gift because she hated sports cars and thought he was just showing off. Eventually she had an affair because of the lack of connection with Harry.

In therapy he talked about how the affair broke his heart, how precious she was to him. She had a hard time believing it, but eventually he opened up and helped her understand his childhood, how afraid he was to speak up. Dr. Lee asked what Harry needed from Martha to feel safe. He asked her to reach out and hold his hand. At this point they were able to reengage.

I would choose EFT if I had it to do over again. I am always more drawn to the softer, gentler approach that promises to dig underneath the facade. If Zeke and I had ever been able to get to the root of our mutual anger and disappointment, be honest with each other, cry together, admit our insecurities, hopes, and dreams, who knows, we might have been able to save our marriage.

WHERE TO FIND A THERAPIST OR WORKSHOP

Retrouvaille: www.retrouvaille.org. You will find a schedule of workshops all over the country, with the home phone number of the couple leading it. These couples are extremely friendly and will be happy to chat with you about Retrouvaille and your personal situation.

Imago: www.gettingtheloveyouwant.com. There are hundreds of Imago therapists in every state, and many offer Imago workshops as well as private therapy. The Web site is very detailed, with videos and lots of information.

Gottman: www.gottman.com. Since the training to become a Gottman therapist is extremely rigorous and time consuming, there aren't as many Gottman therapists as Imago or EFT therapists. Still, Gottman workshops are held regularly in many areas, and you may be able to attend.

EFT: www.eft.ca. There are EFT therapists all over Canada and the United States. To find a therapist in your area, visit the Web site.

IF YOU'RE IN YOUR . . .

Forties . . .

If you still have children at home, it's worth going the extra mile to reconcile if at all possible. Financially, maintaining two homes when there are kids is an extreme stretch unless you're rich. Kids, teens as well as little ones, suffer lasting damage from divorce no matter how many reassuring books and articles are written. A recent study of 1,500 divorced adults by Elizabeth Marquart, a scholar with the Institute for American Values, found that divorce causes lasting psychological damage to children no matter how amicable it is and no matter how successful the child of divorce eventually becomes. In her book about the study, *Between Two Worlds: The Inner Lives of Children of Divorce,* she found that there is a residue of pain, which remains for a lifetime. Divorce turns children into "little adults" who anxiously protect their fragile parents, instead of being protected, the way they are in "intact" families.

My friend and neighbor Jeri, now fifty, has three kids and has been staying in her marriage for their sake even though she would dearly like to escape from her raging, controlling husband. They've gone to counseling for the middle child, a teenage girl who is rebellious, depressed, and has a learning disorder. As a result her husband has become somewhat less angry and is trying to treat her—and especially their daughter—with more respect. She doesn't know if she'll want to stay in the marriage once the kids are grown, but it's clear that her children have benefited from having an intact family even with parents who fight a lot.

Fifties . . .

Older women with grown children should recognize that finding another partner won't be easy. If this is of prime importance to you, it's worth sticking it out if there's enough positive energy left in the marriage to save.

Teresa, a dynamic, energetic girlfriend of mine, now in her late sixties, was fed up with her husband, Fred, who was a total couch potato, a depressive who refused to go anywhere with her or get involved in anything but sitting around and watching TV. Teresa dreamed of a partner to travel with, to go to plays, workshops, and dancing. In her fifties after the kids were grown, she seriously contemplated leaving Fred because she desperately wanted to be active in the world and lead a more exciting life. However, she realized that she was unlikely to find Mr. Dynamic at this stage. After thirty-seven years together, she and Fred had a lifetime of shared memories that she valued—and he still made her laugh. Even though he was overly passive and dependent, there was no reason she couldn't do her own thing, on her own, and stay married. Fred was willing to go along with Teresa having a life of her own outside the house, and they both accommodated a different kind of marriage until he died in his late sixties.

Teresa is still going strong, and she's glad she stayed with Fred as long as possible. She never realized how much she'd miss him—how comforting it was to have him to come home to. His companionship, though limited, was worth staying married for. He refused to go to marriage counseling, but she went to therapy herself, which benefited both of them.

Sixties or older . . .

Not only is finding another mate at this age unlikely—though it is possible—but growing old with a partner rather than alone can be a powerful incentive. Even if you've grown apart, you share a history and family. You may need each other's support if there are health issues. I recently ran into a woman in her seventies at a local woman's event. She expressed her dissatisfaction with her marriage to me, saying that she and her husband had nothing in common and she didn't enjoy socializing with him. In fact, she thought he was pretty obnoxious. However, she was sticking it out because they still took care of each other and she couldn't imagine life without him. They were each other's support system despite their lack of compatibility.

CHAPTER THREE

YOU AND YOUR DIVORCE LAWYER

A Love–Hate Relationship

*I don't think I'll get married again. I'll just find a woman I don't like
and give her a house.*

—LEWIS GRIZZARD

What went through your mind when your husband told you he was leaving or you first considered divorce? Chances are it was money. Like most middle-class couples, Zeke and I couldn't afford a divorce. My husband had a job, but it didn't pay much. I no longer had a steady job; the inheritance my mom left me was gone, and we had an adopted child to support. Luckily for me I lived in the state with the most regressive divorce laws in the country—New York, which still has "at-fault" divorce. This worked in my favor.

I've since come to believe that no-fault divorce makes it too easy to dump a spouse, and much too easy to impoverish an older woman who doesn't have the earning power of her husband. Divorce rates have skyrocketed since no-fault divorce swept through the nation in the 1960s and '70s. In most states you can divorce your spouse without any reason, and although there are laws mandating "equitable distribution," men are much more likely to get more than is equitable because they start off after divorce with better jobs, more money, and more financial savvy. Even though I got my terms met in my divorce, including the house, there just wasn't enough to split up. Like most older divorced women, I'm looking forward to a very precarious old age financially. Still, I'm better off than many women, because I have an education and worked as a freelance writer throughout my marriage. So many older women have no education and no work history.

Arlene never thought poverty could happen to her. At fifty, she'd been married for thirty years to a man who had a good union job. The only work she'd ever done was driving a school bus. Their three children were grown and out on their own, and Arlene was looking forward to a comfortable retirement with a husband she still adored.

Today, at fifty-eight, she's living in a tiny, shabby apartment in Kingston, New York, struggling to pay the rent. She doesn't even have the money for gas to get to her divorce support group, which she desperately needs because she's terribly depressed. Meanwhile her husband is taking cruises with the girlfriend he left her for, a woman fifteen years younger than Arlene. Like so many older men, he went through a midlife crisis when facing retirement, and ran off with a co-worker. Arlene, predictably devastated, didn't understand she'd wind up financially as well as emotionally destitute. She stayed in the house but couldn't afford the mortgage payments. He helped with the payments for a while but then stopped. He hasn't given her any support since they don't have a separation agreement yet. They went to mediation, but it went nowhere. She consulted a lawyer initially, but can't afford one anymore. She still drives a school bus for eight dollars an hour—the only job she could get with no skills, no work background, and no college degree. She will eventually get a cut of her husband's pension plus Social Security, but not until she's sixty-five.

Arlene's scenario is all too common for an older divorced woman from the days when women were expected to stay home and raise the kids. Even women who worked on and off during their marriages are at a major disadvantage when it comes to divorce. The statistics show it. Women fifty and older experience a 39 percent drop in income immediately following divorce, while men undergo only a 14 percent decline. One year after divorce only 21 percent of women have regained their pre-divorce income while 40 percent of men are back on their feet. Eighty-eight percent of the women had money worries in the first year, and five years later money was still a major concern for seven out of ten.

The reality is that many of us older women have spent our prime career-building years home with the kids, and have no way of supporting ourselves after divorce. For most middle-class families, marriage is the way we create wealth, according to Nancy Dailey, Ph.D., author of the book *When Baby Boom Women Retire*. When the marriage ends, so does our comfortable standard of living. According to Dailey, the legal system assumes that women are in the labor force, so men shouldn't have to support them. Alimony, which used to be given for life after a long-term marriage, is now considered "rehabilitative"—just enough to get you on your feet. The reality is that a woman in her fifties or sixties is not about to find a lucrative source of income. The courts simply don't see all those years raising kids and taking care of a home as a marital contribution that should be taken into account when a divorce settlement is being negotiated.

The bottom line is that unless you started out rich—and have millions to split up—you are going to be substantially poorer after your divorce. However, that does *not* mean you should just roll over and take whatever he offers. Women who fight for more get more, so be prepared to look out for yourself, girlfriend.

WHY SO MANY WOMEN GET SCREWED

"Most women are not comfortable with the adversarial atmosphere of the judicial system," writes psychotherapist Donna F. Ferber on www.divorcesource.com. "They are more comfortable in resolution and nurturance than in being the aggressor. The idea of being able to advocate for one's self is difficult and emotionally draining." Ferber explains that women find they must be the strongest at the worst time of their life, a task that is difficult under any circumstances. It is especially difficult when your enemy was once your best friend. "Even women in the throes of a horrific divorce, still find themselves seeking counsel, or wanting to comfort their estranged husbands. The idea that their partner is no longer available to them leaves them feeling frightened, alone, abandoned, and worthless."

Additionally, settlements are made according to who is the better negotiator, and women are usually worse at negotiation than men, adds Dailey. She tells her clients to run the numbers, because if you are thinking emotionally rather than with your pocketbook, you will get screwed.

Older women who were raised to be "nice" girls don't play hardball with men. After my husband left I was torn between giving him what he wanted and putting myself first. I played tough because I knew I had to survive, but I felt guilty the entire time. Looking back I have absolutely no regrets and am proud of myself for holding out for what I needed, even though it made him furious. I recommend you do the same, or get yourself a lawyer who can do it for you. How many men do you know who are concerned with being "nice"? No matter how horrible you feel, no matter how big a hit your self-esteem has taken, get yourself together, girl, and fight for your rights. Here are the worst mistakes women make. Avoid them and you'll come out okay.

Mistake #1: Failure to Plan Ahead

As well-known Philadelphia feminist lawyer Lynne Gold-Biken says, "The most sensitive part of a man's body is his pocketbook. When he decides to leave, he's been to a lawyer and has already removed all the financial documents from the house." Men who are planning to leave tend to clean out bank accounts and hide assets, which are extremely difficult to recover. Gold-Biken emphasizes that women have to pre-plan for divorce just like men do. "When the marriage starts to go bad, when he stops having sex with you or stops coming home at night, don't make excuses, go to a lawyer and find out how to protect yourself."

The reaction of Cheryl, who was fifty-six when her husband of twenty-four years left her for another woman, is typical. "Financially, I got screwed," she told me. "Legally I went along with what he offered me. He'd been thinking about it for a long time and had planned it out down to who got what piece of furniture. I went along with it because I was in shock and pain and didn't want to fight. I thought my life was over. I lost my mom's diamonds; we sold the house to liquidate our debt. I walked away

FIGURE OUT YOUR FINANCES

Web sites to visit:

www.urbanext.uiuc.edu/ww1: Working Woman's Guide to Financial Security. This is a terrific financial planning resources for women, pre- and post-divorce.

www.divorceandfinance.org and www.idfa.com. Listings of divorce financial planners plus resources for divorce financial planning.

www.womensmoney.com. A helpful site to figure out your future income needs.

with my furniture and clothes. He'd taken out a second mortgage on the house, and I had to assume the debt. He had assets that he hid from me. I'd put away a little money for my kids' college out of what I'd inherited when my parents died and that was all I got back."

This was only one of the many second-mortgage debacles I heard about. Men borrow on the house, take the money, and stash it or spend it. When the divorce then happens, there are no assets, since many married couples' only asset is the house. When women are the ones who leave, they fail to think of cleaning out the bank account. My girlfriend Kim left her husband of twenty-five years when she was forty-five for an old boyfriend. A week or so later, she tried to cash a check, but her husband had already cleaned out their joint bank account and canceled all the credit cards. It had never occurred to her to protect herself financially. She also basically walked away from the marriage with nothing but guilt. Very few men who dump their wives do the same.

I advised my girlfriend Jeri, fifty, who is now contemplating divorce, that she'd better figure out what's going on with the family finances before she even tells her husband she wants out. He has always handled everything, and she realizes she knows nothing about what they have. Most women don't think this far in advance. If you are planning to leave, visit a divorce lawyer and a financial planner (preferably one who specializes in divorce planning) *first*—before you even ask for a divorce. Get your financial ducks in a row before announcing your imminent departure.

Mistake #2: Assuming Your Lawyer Will Take Care of Everything

We older women are from the generation where getting taken care of was the norm. We assumed our husbands would take care of the leaky roof, mowing the lawn, and the family finances. We were responsible for the kids and the household. We're simply not used to taking total—and I mean *total*—responsibility for ourselves. So when divorce strikes, our first inclination is to put our fate in the hands of a white knight, another protector, our lawyer.

Yes, you do need a lawyer, and you should consult a lawyer immediately when divorce is imminent. But before you walk into that lawyer's office, you must educate yourself about divorce law in general and your state's laws in particular. I cannot emphasize this enough. You don't want to waste your precious money getting an education about divorce law in your lawyer's office. He or she is probably a lousy teacher and will be throwing around terms that are totally mysterious to you: *equitable distribution, financial disclosure, alimony, fault versus no-fault divorce, marital property,* and so on.

If you don't know what all these terms mean, you will be at a big disadvantage. Get on the Internet or buy a book and start researching. Find out what your state's divorce laws are—laws can vary enormously from state to state. Write down a chronology

HOW TO FIND OUT ABOUT DIVORCE LAW

www.about.com. This Web site's divorce support area has links for each state explaining its divorce laws and also provides extremely helpful, simplified explanation of the divorce process.

What Every Woman Should Know About Divorce and Custody by Gayle Rosenwald Smith and Sally Abrahms. The legal process is explained in detailed but easy-to-understand terms.

of events of your case, and also provide the attorney with *copies* (never originals) of everything related to your case: contracts, receipts, bills, whatever. When you go for your consultation, keep your description of the problem to the facts and don't wander onto tangents. You may consult a few lawyers before you choose whom to hire, and you need to know what you're talking about in order to make an educated decision.

WHERE TO GO IF YOU CAN'T AFFORD A LAWYER

Federally funded programs. There is a national network of legal services offices receiving federal funds to provide free legal help to low-income people in civil (not criminal) cases. Services are generally provided by staff attorneys and sometimes paralegals with experience in certain areas, such as divorce.

Pro bono programs. Many state, local, and county bar associations have pro bono ("for the good" in Latin) programs operated by local attorneys who've agreed to provide free legal representation to those who qualify thanks to either income or circumstances, such as AIDS, a battering husband, being over sixty-five, or the like. As with legal services offices, you may have to prove your income level as well as the value of your assets.

Self-help clinics. Some local and county bar associations put on free self-help clinics in which volunteer lawyers answer questions and help with forms. These often occur weekly or monthly. You may get to talk with an attorney individually, or you may be part of a large group, asking questions within earshot of others.

Courthouse facilitators. Increasingly, county courthouses have facilitators to help people process their legal claims. Check with your local bar association or courthouse to see what's available. At a minimum, a courthouse facilitator can help you figure out where you should file your paperwork and walk you through the process of getting your paperwork to the right people within the court system. Don't be afraid to walk into the courtroom without a lawyer, especially if you have few or no assets. Judges are likely to sympathize with an indigent older woman who can't afford legal representation.

Public defender organizations. All states have networks of criminal public defenders who provide free or low-cost legal help to defendants in criminal cases. People have to meet income eligibility requirements, so must document their income (or lack thereof). If there is abuse involved, particularly if you have an Order of Protection, you should be eligible for legal aid.

Low-cost legal programs. More and more programs are available for people who earn too much to qualify for legal services or pro bono programs, but don't make enough to hire an attorney at traditional rates. If you fall in this category, which a lot of us do, there are telephone hotlines that charge by the minute and sliding-fee programs to get you the advice and representation you need at the lowest price possible.

Prepaid Legal Services (www.prepaidlegal.com). Prepaid Legal costs twenty-five dollars to join and fourteen a month; it gives you unlimited phone consultation with a divorce (or other) attorney. If you need local representation, it will recommend a participating local divorce attorney who will give you a discount. Prepaid Legal is not for everyone, but if you're really financially strapped it offers a lot of help for very little money. Prepaid Legal seems to have a larger network of participating lawyers than any other non-employer-related legal insurance plan.

The American Bar Association. The ABA has a Web site that provides information on obtaining pro bono or free legal help state by state at www.abanet.org/legalservices/findlegalhelp/home.cfm.

During the divorce proceedings you need to rely on yourself as well as your lawyer to make decisions and come up with options. Think about it. Unless you're Ivana Trump and are paying a top law firm $500 an hour, you are not going to have a lawyer whose main concern is your welfare. Your lawyer has lots of clients and will be juggling his or her time among them. You have only one client—yourself—and no one can protect your interests as well as you can. If, like most middle-class women, you only have a few thousand to spend, you're going to run out of money quickly and your lawyer may stop returning your phone calls. If you're not fully educated and proactive, you will wind up with a settlement you'll regret for the rest of your life. That's why there are so many horror stories about divorce lawyers.

Mistake #3: Choosing the Wrong Lawyer

Desperate women will often settle for the first lawyer they consult. The wrong lawyer can be a disaster for your case. Here's what you should consider:

What is his or her experience? Does he or she specialize in divorce law? Does he or she know the players in the local court system, especially if there are custody issues? You don't want a divorce attorney from a neighboring city. You do want an attorney who specializes in divorce in your jurisdiction.

Is he or she recommended? The best way to get a good divorce attorney is through a recommendation from a satisfied customer, preferably another older woman. So many women wind up hating their attorneys that a satisfied divorcée is your best source of recommendation.

My girlfriend Norma, who at age fifty-eight was being dumped for a forty-year-old, told me my favorite divorce lawyer story. She found her attorney through her friend Magda, who had a ten-year-old child and an ex who drank, used drugs, and was abusive. A year before Norma even knew she was being dumped, Magda had complained to her about how her divorce lawyer—let's call her Sherry Smith, a local attorney with a reputation for being "tough"—had totally screwed her. "All she does is settle, she doesn't fight for me," Magda told Norma. "She agreed to let him have weekend visitation without even asking me. And she refuses to return my phone calls. She's lazy, nasty, and a total bitch." Magda was getting Legal Aid because her income was so low, and Sherry Smith did as little as she could for her, because, in Magda's opinion, "She's not gonna make the big bucks on my case."

A year later, while looking for a divorce attorney, Norma ran into Magda again. This time she glowed about her current lawyer, Bill Eisenberg. "He's a doll. I managed to get rid of the bitch and got Bill from the Legal Aid panel. He feels for me and my kid and has managed to limit visitation with my ex and get my child support payments. He even returns phone calls." Norma retained Bill and never regretted it. She felt he sympathized with her situation and went the extra mile on her case, plus he was sharp. He promptly returned e-mails and phone calls. Norma wasn't taking Legal Aid, but she was hardly paying him the big bucks.

Meantime her ex wound up with Sherry Smith because of that "tough" reputation. Needless to say Norma came out on top in the settlement. One more case of the Universe working for us older women in strange ways.

Mistake #4: Failure to Consult a Lawyer at All

If you can't afford a lawyer, but your husband has substantial assets, you can ask the court to order that he pay your legal fees, which is not unusual in cases of extreme inequality of assets. Again, if there is a possibility that you may get a substantial settlement from a wealthy husband but can't pay your lawyer a retainer up front, an attorney may agree to accept payment on contingency, as with an a personal injury case.

Mistake #5: Relying on a Meditator

It may sound counterintuitive—because mediators are supposed to resolve issues without conflict and save legal fees—but savvy divorce lawyers are adamant that you *should not* go to mediation unless the playing field is totally level between you and your husband. If there are any contested financial issues, you may lose out big-time in mediation.

Mediators are trained to do exactly that—mediate, to help the two parties come to an agreement. At that point the mediation agreement is presented to the judge, who finalizes the divorce. The downside is that in order to get a settlement they push the person most likely to agree, and that's usually the woman. Mediators are supposed to be impartial and also inform both parties of their rights, but mediators are also human and sometimes inadequately trained. "Mediation is terrible for women," says Elizabeth Bennett, a specialist in divorce and alimony law with Bennett and Associates in Wayne, Pennsylvania, who is also involved in family court reform. "Men know they can con mediators, they go in with everything all set up in advance; I've seen more fraud and rip-offs. I rarely do mediations and never recommend them."

Arlene, whom I described at the beginning of this section, still isn't divorced after three years and has no settlement in sight after fifteen sessions with a mediator at over $200 per hour. She thought she and her husband had come to agreement on various issues, but got nothing in writing. She may have gone to someone who called herself a mediator but wasn't trained or a certified by the county. Now Arlene is going to court without a lawyer because she can't afford one.

Initially I suggested mediation to my husband to divide up our assets because I had some mistaken notion that lawyers would cost too much. Thank God he said no, he didn't want to pay for a mediator since we'd still have to pay for a lawyer to finalize the agreement anyway. At the time I had no idea what my rights were and might have lost major assets in mediation, such as half my equity in the house. I would also have been making one of the big mistakes I now warn women against— moving too quickly. In the end I delayed divorce for years, during which time I stayed on my husband's medical insurance, and eventually got the house.

Mediation *can* work, but only when both spouses have relatively equal assets, and just need help in dividing them up. For example, Jamie—a guy I dated after my divorce—successfully mediated a property division with his wife. They had both worked as teachers for thirty years and were both retired with equal pensions. The only issue was the house, the contents of the house, and payment of their daughter's college tuition. Since he was the one who left while she stayed in the house, she agreed to buy out his share at the current assessed value, and he agreed to let her have the contents of the house in exchange for paying their daughter's tuition. He took the canoe and that was about it.

When there are contested issues, you might consider a new alternative to litigation: collaborative divorce. This involves each side hiring a lawyer to represent him or her, but with a commitment in advance to work out an agreement without going to court. Collaboration requires that both spouses provide all pertinent documents and information. In the event that experts are necessary, it encourages the use of jointly retained experts. Both spouses and attorneys are required to work together toward a shared resolution that is geared toward the future well-being of the family. The upside of collaborative divorce is that you have an attorney to represent you; you're not on your own with just a mediator. The downside is that the lawyers retained for the collaborative process can't represent you if you go to litigation. If you can't reach settlement through the collaborative process, these lawyers withdraw. You have to retain trial attorneys to pursue the matter in court, which involves a lot of extra expense.

Some lawyers, however, are opposed to collaborative divorce. My own divorce lawyer feels that the job of an attorney is to protect the interests of his or her client, not to recognize joint interests and collaborate. He doesn't think you should pay your lawyer his billable hourly rate to sit around pretending to be a therapist. To be fair, though, many collaborative attorneys work with therapists who charge a lot less than attorneys and submit their reports to the lawyers.

Mistake #6: Failure to Ask for Enough Alimony

In the good old days, homemaking spouses got alimony for life after a long marriage ended. Feminism pretty much did away with that system, because we women advocated that we were able to support ourselves and didn't need men to open doors, pay for dinner, or pay the rent. Men jumped all over that: *Well then, we don't have to support you after divorce, do we?* We feminists basically committed economic hari-kari and are still paying the tab all these years later. Even today, for women twenty-five and older the earning gap has remained nearly seventy-six cents on the dollar earned by men. For feminists, tossing out alimony was definitely tossing the baby out with the bathwater.

The statistics tell the story. Women in midlife and older who work full-time year-round earn less than two-thirds the income of men in the same age group. The average income for women fifty-five to sixty-four is $21,388, while men in that group earn $37,469. Women in this age range are mostly employed in the female "ghettos" of sales, service, and clerical jobs. Even in female-dominated professions, older men are more likely to work in supervisory and higher-paying positions. One reason so many older women work in female ghetto professions is that we came of age and started working before the women's movement in the 1970s encouraged women to have careers. As a result, we often do not have the training or education for higher-paying jobs, not to speak of a huge experience gap while we stayed home taking care of children.

Legally marriage is a partnership, but the courts don't treat it that way. You may assume that getting a divorce means you'll be independent. But the reality of divorce later in life is that you'll still be dependent. Women have a tendency to say, "I don't need you, I can take care of myself." Not true. You and your husband are interdependent. Marriage is an economic partnership and has to be viewed in the same way as a business partnership. For example, a woman who stayed home has invested in the skills of her husband for twenty years. Instead of putting money in the bank, she put it into a person. Women need to calculate what that investment was and negotiate from that.

"You need to run the numbers," Nancy Dailey emphasizes. She gives an example of a husband who made an average of $50,000 per year over twenty years. Now, $50,000 times 20 is essentially $1 million. What was his wife's investment in that? Did she take care of the children, clean the house, cook the meals, and facilitate her husband's ability to work overtime or get better training? How much would all of that have cost if he had paid someone to do it? You've got to think like that going into a negotiation. You have to think of yourself as valuable. It's really hard for women to grasp that notion.

There are signs that the tide is turning when it comes to alimony, however. A number of states have changed their alimony laws to allow longer awards to women. "One reason is the 'nationwide effort to trim the welfare rolls,'" according to the *Christian Science Monitor* in November 1999. "Spouses who don't provide for exes often leave the state holding the tab." Also keep in mind that states may have alimony rules, but judges also have a lot of leeway when it comes to awarding alimony. Judges don't like to leave ex-spouses destitute.

This means you have to make sure you ask your lawyer what the law is in your state before you go to court, or negotiate, and find out if you have grounds to ask for more. Run the numbers for him or her as well; this includes projecting the numbers outward so you know what your income is likely to be in the future, before and after you start collecting Social Security and/or your husband's pension. Many divorce lawyers don't know much about economics. They're like real estate agents: The faster they get the divorce done, the better. You need to educate your lawyer about the reality of your economic situation. Lifetime alimony is still being granted in some states in some circumstances.

If you can't run the numbers yourself, don't beat yourself up about it; see a certified financial planner who specializes in divorce. "However, be careful not to get sucked into long-term money management," warns Elizabeth Bennett. "Check that fees are competitive and the financial planner isn't trying to sell you products." Bennett has a financial planner on her staff who charges by the hour to give advice. If you don't know anyone who does this, ask your lawyer for a referral.

Mistake #7: Insisting on Keeping the House

Arlene's scenario at the beginning of this chapter is all too common. Residences with mortgages, high real estate taxes, and high maintenance costs can be more of a liability than an asset. Many divorcées, of all ages, do not want to move and wind up house-poor. They may have a nice place to live, but they're eating peanut butter sandwiches for dinner. Older divorcées, without children at home, need to run the numbers again before deciding to stay in the house. How much is that place going to cost you every month? How are you going to pay those expenses? You may well be better off selling the house and splitting the proceeds with your husband, rather than keeping it. Emotionally, it may also make a lot of sense to get out of the place you've lived in with him for twenty years and start fresh in an apartment or condo, where the maintenance is taken care of.

Evelyn, a freelance journalist who finally left her philandering husband at age sixty-nine after putting up with his infidelities for thirty years, found it freeing to get rid of their house. "During the first year, I couldn't believe it was over. I was going to hang on to the house, but then we sold the house and I moved into a town house. That was exhilarating. I put my own stuff in it and got a dog, which he never wanted. It was intoxicating to be free."

Mistake #8: Getting Bogged Down in the Tchotchke Wars

Too many older women get obsessed with fighting over furniture, antiques, knickknacks, photographs, televisions, and other possessions, losing the big picture in the process. A lifetime of memories may be bound up in stuff, and we don't want to let go of any of it. However, it's easy to waste your time, and worse, your attorney's time, in petty battles. At an attorney's average $200 to $500 an hour, those *tchotchkes* better be pretty valuable. ·

I was lucky. My husband walked out and took nothing. I guess he felt guilty for cheating—plus his girlfriend had set up an apartment for him, fully furnished. In many cases couples have lawyers on the clock fighting over the Lalique vase.

The not-so-hidden agenda behind the *tchotchke* wars is bitterness and desire for revenge. "I'll be damned if I let that bastard have a set of dishes so he can set up housekeeping with that bitch." Sound familiar? Keep in mind that fighting over possessions, unless they have strong sentimental or financial value, will just make other negotiations on the important issues, like the house and support, more difficult. Follow the usual rule for splitting possessions—you both get what you came to the marriage with, and split the rest. As for things you acquired jointly that you really want, be a savvy negotiator. Make a list of your must-haves, making sure to include some less important items that you're willing to let go. Then "compromise" on the nonessentials. This is what smart negotiators do. As a woman facing divorce, you need to become one—fast.

Mistake #9: Being Overly Anxious to Get Closure

Timing is a crucial aspect of divorce negotiations. As attorney Elizabeth Bennett says, "Lawyers can be insensitive and push women into divorce too fast. If the woman hasn't expected the divorce, she has a three-year learning process to deal with the three major issues: relationship and identity; home; and career. It can't be done in six months and she can't be pushed."

Too many women rush into divorce settlements that might be ill advised because they're seeking "closure." Somehow, just as we feel marriage is a guarantee of commitment, we mistakenly feel divorce will allow us to move on from that commitment. Unfortunately, especially if you have children, marriage is forever and divorce is just a piece of paper. No matter what you sign, you're going to have to deal with your ex over and over again. Even if your children are on their own and you may only run into him at weddings and funerals, seeking premature closure will wed you to him forever because you'll always regret those ill-advised, too-early decisions.

Sometimes the desire for closure can mean the difference between a comfortable retirement and a marginal one. Stella, whose husband dumped her for another woman, wanted to get a quick divorce, so she gave him half of everything although, because she lived in New York State, she didn't have to. Right now she's still working, but she may well regret it down the line when she is facing retirement without the kind of income she was counting on.

Remember, a piece of paper does not give you closure. Only time and working on yourself can do that.

Mistake #10: Believing Your Husband About His Assets

Women who have let their husbands handle the finances for twenty-five years have enormous resistance to finding out what the family's assets really are. It may seem easier to just believe what your husband tells you, but as attorney Lynn Gold-Biken says, "When he decides to leave, he's been to a lawyer and taken the financial documents out of the house." She recommends not signing anything you don't have a copy of—ever. Don't sign anything without legal representation, either. If you suspect your husband is hiding assets, talk to your lawyer about your options. You may be able to order him to produce financial documents in court. Or you may have to consult a forensic accountant to uncover his assets.

My accountant, Michael Torchia, in Hudson, New York, conducts a lot of forensic accounting work and described to me how it's done. It's not rocket science—any savvy woman can find evidence of hidden assets. A lot of it just involves sifting through paperwork, looking at credit cards, debt payments, finding out facts like what's being paid out monthly for car and house payments versus what he claims his income is. You can see how much money is being spent—and if he's spending more than he says he makes, you've got a case. If he does a lot of business in cash, threatening to report him to the IRS can give you leverage. If you filed a joint return, you can get copies from the IRS. The returns will show any bank accounts that generate interest, all dividends from stocks, and any other assets. Any good accountant can look at a tax return and tell you if something's out of whack.

Don't forget your husband's retirement account. Debra Speyer, a Philadelphia-based elder law attorney and former accountant says, "Often one of the largest assets is the husband's retirement account. The husband might have a 401(k), Keogh, or employee stock option plan, deferred compensation plan, and accounts wives aren't aware of. These plans may be worth a lot but you might not understand anything about them. You need to get a letter of authorization from your husband, which the court may have to order, and contact his employer to find out exactly what's in there."

IF YOU'RE IN YOUR . . .

Forties . . .

Make provisions for the future in your settlement. If you have young children and a high-powered job or a business where you're currently making a lot of money, it might not occur to you that things could, and probably will, change after your divorce. Very few women—or their lawyers—take into account the increase in mommying you have to do as a single mom. You could easily lose that job or business due to child care responsibilities, and be screwed because you didn't get child support. Going back to court to change a divorce agreement can be extremely difficult.

Charlene, forty-five, made a disastrous settlement with her ex because she never considered the future. At the time of the divorce, Charlene was making about $400,000 a year in her own business as a high-powered real estate salesperson to the stars, and her husband was making about $100,000 as a lawyer. Because her income was greater than his, she agreed to give him $50,000 to make up for the value of her business, in addition to agreeing to joint custody and splitting their daughter's expenses down the middle. Her lawyer told her she was getting a good deal, that her husband could have asked her for alimony or child support. Somehow it never occurred either to her or her lawyer that her "business" was basically worthless. It had no value independent of her personality, energy, enthusiasm, and ability to get on the phone and sell the multimillion-dollar homes her one-woman agency listed. Her husband, on the other hand, had a law degree, which enabled him to make more money in the future. Charlene had no degree, no corporate experience, nothing but her own personality and smarts.

After the divorce their daughter became seriously ill. Charlene was distraught, lost her passion for real estate, and had to expend what little energy she had to take care of her child. She was no longer a brilliant saleswoman, but an overwhelmed mother, struggling with her own depression over divorce and despair about her daughter's illness. Her ex took no responsibility for the work of caring for a sick child. Her business totally tanked, she went deeply into debt; she had to borrow to pay off her ex-husband. Eight years later she went back to court to try to get child support, but she had no money to pay a good lawyer, and by that time it was her ex who was making the $300,000 per year—and as a lawyer himself he had a big advantage. (Warning: The worst divorcée stories of financial disaster that I heard were from women married to lawyers.) Ten years later Charlene is still digging herself out of the hole. She would like to change careers to something more creative, but has to stay in sales to make enough money to pay her debts. Her ex has been relentless in his refusal to help, to the extent of insisting that she pay half of their daughter's prep school bill, which she can't afford. If provision had been made in the settlement for change in the future, she might have been able to get child support.

Fifties . . .

You will need to protect the financial future of your children, who may be teenagers or in college. According to E. Mavis Hetherington, who wrote *For Better or for Worse: Divorce Reconsidered,* "Teenagers fear not only emotional security but financial. Young people are thinking about college and they worry about finances in the wake of divorce." When negotiating a settlement, be sure to include ironclad terms about who pays for college, including ways to enforce them, such as that the money will come out of his pension if he doesn't pay up.

You may want to keep the house for the sake of the children. Divorce disrupts children's lives enough without having to move out of their home and possibly change schools. If you do decide you want the house, make sure there are provisions for your ex to help with the mortgage, taxes, and maintenance.

This is a precarious time of life, when you may be too old to start a new career but are still too young to collect Social Security and Medicare. If you need training or education to pursue your career, have provisions for your schooling included in the settlement. However, if your ex is unreliable, you may be better off with a lump sum for tuition rather than alimony, which he may or may not actually pay.

Make sure to project outward what you will need to survive, before and after Social Security kicks in. Don't forget health insurance costs. If he's been covering them, you need to include them in any settlement. Figure out how many years you stayed home with the kids, and what it would have cost to hire someone to do that. If your ex isn't rich, get as much support for as many years as you possibly can.

Unless you still have kids at home, if there's substantial equity in your residence you will probably be better off selling it and splitting the profits. However, if you can turn your house into an income property by renting out part or all of it, especially in a weak housing market, it might make sense to try to get it in the divorce.

If you are interested in going back to school, negotiate for that in your settlement.

Make sure you investigate what his assets are before agreeing to anything.

Sixties or older . . .

You are entitled to half your husband's pension benefits, so make sure you know what they are before you sign anything. As mentioned above, if he won't give you the information, get your lawyer to ask for a court order to obtain it.

If you have no source of income aside from what your ex has been providing, project outward what you will need to survive for the rest of your life and give your lawyer that figure. You may be able to make a case for lifetime alimony or a very large settlement if your lifestyle was comfortable, your ex still makes a good living, and you have no way to maintain anywhere near that on Social Security. There's no way a judge can tell a woman in her sixties to go out and get a job if she has no skills or experience—or even if she does. Age discrimination alone makes finding a decent job a long shot for a woman your age.

Again, make sure you know what his true assets are before negotiating your settlement.

CHAPTER FOUR

LIVING ALONE AND LIKING IT

It Is Possible to Be Happy Without a Man

The initial trauma of being alone is difficult because you assume that you are going to live the rest of your life with someone. And I suppose that none of us feels that our own company is good enough for a lifetime. Yet, in reality, the most important person to learn to live with is ourselves. We invest so much time in the comfort of others that we often ignore the nurturing we need for ourselves.
—ANN RICHARDS, FORMER GOVERNOR OF TEXAS,
AFTER HER THIRTY-YEAR MARRIAGE

The bad news is that past a certain age, there aren't enough men to go around. The good news is—you don't really need a man to be happy. In fact, it's a lot easier to be happy alone the older you are. Your need for sex has declined along with your hormones, while your need for your own space has surged. The older you get, the harder it becomes both to find a mate and to make the compromises necessary to sustain a relationship.

This doesn't mean that being on your own will be easy, at least initially. Even though you may wind up loving it eventually, the prospect of being alone—possibly for the first time—can strike terror into the heart of the bravest of older women, no matter how miserable the marriage. Even if you're one of those wives who had a marriage where you and your husband never shared an intimate word, where you long ago gave up hope of real companionship, where you felt lonely even when he was in the room, living by yourself can be a big adjustment. Luckily, after the mourning period, the majority of older divorced women make this adjustment pretty easily, especially if they have inner resources.

Unfortunately, I lacked those inner resources, even though I'd lived alone as a single woman in New York City for twenty years before meeting and moving in with my husband. I had lots of friends and many boyfriends; I had easily survived breakups with men before I got married (although I might have indulged in some melodramatic weeping and moaning afterward). I considered myself a self-sufficient, independent woman unafraid of taking risks. Nonetheless I clung to my marriage like a drowning woman holding on to a sinking ship, absolutely terrified of being alone. At the time I was mystified about where that fear came from. What exactly was I so afraid of? I thought I was a tough cookie. More of a crumbling cookie as it turned out.

WHAT THE HELL IS SO SCARY ABOUT BEING ALONE ANYWAY?

Fear of being alone is not just about loneliness—although that's a big part of it—it's more like fear of being parachuted into a foreign land, behind enemy lines, where you don't know the landscape, don't speak the language, have no idea how to find the nearest convenience store, and are afraid of noncombatants taking potshots at you. It's damned scary for any woman, and for us older women—especially those of us who have been married our entire adult lives—it can be downright terrifying.

We women make the mistake of assuming that being alone is bad. Actually, aloneness is a neutral state, says Florence Falk, author of *On My Own: The Art of Being a Woman Alone.* "If you can begin to take away the coloration, which is almost always negative, you won't automatically interchange it with loneliness. Aloneness is part of the human condition. One of the ways we get in touch with ourselves is to really enter aloneness, from there finding our way into solitude. It is frightening at first. You need to reframe it to get over the fear. Think of the experience of peace you get walking on a beach, reading, taking yoga, anywhere there's silence and not a lot of distractions. Our culture is endlessly fueling us to be distracted, to buy more, use that cell phone, turn on the TV or computer, anything to keep us temporarily occupied and temporarily satisfied. That's what you're bucking when you try to experience solitude in a positive way."

This terror of being alone keeps a lot of women, especially older women, in bad marriages.

My girlfriend Frances, a pretty, funny schoolteacher who just turned fifty-five, often fantasizes about leaving her angry, controlling, hypercritical husband who flies into rages when he doesn't get his way. They have nothing in common—they don't even vote for the same political party. She even feels that her children, who are teenagers, would be better off without him micromanaging their lives and exploding at them and at her. She says she'd like to leave when they're all grown, which will be soon. But she admits she may not be able to do it even then. She has a good job, so her worries aren't financial. When she envisions splitting up, she instead worries about who would mow the lawn, or fix the furnace, or take care of the finances. When I point out that I do those things alone, and so could she, I still get a sigh and a "maybe someday." She says she's not afraid of loneliness: She likes her own company and could happily spend her spare time reading. She's not worried about finding another man. Something else is going on here.

Frances has been married since she left college. She's never lived alone; the concept is foreign to her. The fear of entering alien territory, creating a whole new life where she is solely responsible for herself, where she is not being taken care of any longer, trumps being in an unhappy marriage for her and for many women.

You may not believe it when you're going through it, but despite the traumatic first year after divorce when loneliness seems like a black cloud you can't escape, most divorcées eventually treasure living alone. There's nothing like eating whenever the mood strikes you, staying up and watching TV till the wee hours with total control over the remote, throwing books and newspapers on his side of the bed, hanging out with friends whenever you want to, and in general never having to say you're sorry. If your ex was a control freak like so many men, if you always felt you were walking on eggshells to avoid his wrath, being alone can feel like escape from prison. If Frances ever does leave, I'm sure she will feel incredible relief at being able to live her own life in her own way.

To get to that place where being alone feels like liberation rather than a life sentence, you need to take a trip through your own past and your own subconscious fears.

BACK IN THE CAVE

Did you ever wonder why it's so easy for men to leave their children to go off to work while we women agonize over it? Or why it almost never works when a woman supports the family while her husband stays home with the kids? According to Patricia Wall, a teacher of self-mastery in Ottawa, Canada, it all goes back to prehistory. Wall presents a compelling analysis of the tribal basis of marriage and divorce. She shed new light for me on our fear of being alone. According to Wall, back when we lived in caves, women owned the fire. We were the ones who remained in the cave, kept the fire going, took care of the children, cooked the food, kept the tribe together. The male role was to hunt, provide food, and protect the tribe from predators. Men earned their way into the fire by doing a good job of feeding us and keeping us safe.

Our primal role as women is to have a happy, safe family. When our marriages break up, we women judge ourselves harshly, no matter who left, because no matter how liberated and sophisticated we are, we're stuck with those primal instincts. They explain not only why being alone is so frightening, but also why we are the ones who bring the tribe together for holiday dinners, why we keep in touch with the in-laws. "No matter what the reason for the divorce, your tribe is broken; your subconscious tells you that you've failed," Wall explained. "Your primary family tribe had rules and your subconscious wants you to obey those rules because in the cave disobeying the rules was a matter of life and death. Back then if you weren't part of the tribe you were on your own, cast out of the cave, which meant certain death at the mercy of predators or the elements with no male protection." Not only have you failed, but you actually might die because of that failure. No wonder divorce is so scary.

I experienced an aha moment when Wall mentioned the connection between divorce and fear of death. When my husband left, I actually felt as though I wasn't going to survive; the separation might kill me. Even though I'd gone through painful breakups with boyfriends before I got married, this terror was a new experience for me. However, I've since heard the same exact sentiment from many divorcées. The image of being cast out of that warm, cozy, safe cave resonated with me as it might with many of you.

Paradoxically, marriage, even if it's abusive and actually danger-ous, can feel like a safe place. The big, wide world, even though it's much safer, emotionally and physically, can seem scary as all hell.

We women feel this way no matter how successful or accom-plished we are in our own lives, no matter how much money we have, and no matter how much we recognize the necessity for the divorce. Today I look back at that feeling of fear for my survival and know how absurd it was, but it was only too real at the time.

The feeling of failure can be even worse than the fear of being alone. We women take responsibility for marriage, for keeping the tribe together, and if it falls apart, no matter the reason, we feel it's our fault.

THE FREEZE-AND-HIDE SYNDROME

You've probably heard of the fight-or-flight syndrome. There's also the freeze-and-hide syndrome, Wall explains, which is probably what our ancestors did when they were under attack but had no weapons and nowhere to run. Some women tend to freeze and hide after divorce. We isolate ourselves because we feel like we've failed as women, we're punishing ourselves for scattering the tribe, we're terrified of facing the world outside the cave alone. Simple freeze and hide is characterized by becoming forgetful, procrastinating, avoiding activities and people you used to like. Beyond that is depression. I went into a clinical depression after my divorce. Severe depression is common. The extreme reaction is post-traumatic stress disorder (PTSD). Lots of women come out of divorce with PTSD and don't know it.

We may feel lonely even if in reality we're not alone. We may have friends and family reaching out to us, but we still feel abandoned because our tribe is broken. Luckily, the very thing that makes you feel so devastated after a divorce—the loss of your fire, your capacity for belonging—is the very thing that will heal you. The gift of our tribal origins is that we women have the ability to connect with others. We have a talent for belonging. You have to make a conscious decision to change tribes, to take on caring for a different set of people. This is why volunteer work is so healing after a divorce. Creativity is another way that women give to the world. "The fundamental female power is as the creator," according to Patricia Wall. "Creation is our gift to the tribe. We create comfort and beauty, which is nurturing." Friendship is another female gift, and the women who survive divorce most successfully quickly develop a set of close female friends to replace the broken family unit.

Initially there may be exhilaration in finally being alone. Most marriages dissolve slowly and often agonizingly, with fights, recriminations, angry silences, even physical outbursts. My husband went around glowering at me and exploded over every little annoying thing I did, real or imagined. We circled around each other, fuming and snapping. It was a relief when he moved from the bedroom into the guest room, and more of a relief when he finally left. I could come home and flop down on the couch without having to worry about what he was going to say to needle me, or demand from me, or insist I was wrong about. Whew!

During that stage I would say to myself, *Wow, this is easy. Being alone isn't bad at all.* Then the existential loneliness came crashing down on me. My house began to feel more like a tomb than a refuge. I didn't know what to do with myself except weep uncontrollably.

The intense loneliness you suffer when separating from your lifelong partner can be more overwhelming than anything you've felt before. In fact, it's disorienting. When you start coming come home to that empty house, with no one cook for, eat with, go out on Saturday nights with—the list goes on—you may experience a frightening sense of emptiness. The silence takes on physical qualities; it becomes a "thing" you have to grapple with. At the same time, you may be suffering from depression and feel too miserable to leave the house. This freeze-and-hide stage may be scary, but it's perfectly normal. You are not going crazy—even though you may feel that way at times; you are simply adjusting to a major, traumatic change in your life where pulling back is an essential part of the grieving process. You have the right to hide in your cave for as long as you need to and come out only when you're ready. In fact you may need to be alone to process what has happened to you. That processing, being honest with yourself, is the long-term remedy for loneliness.

BEING HONEST WITH YOURSELF

After my husband left I consulted my wise former psychotherapist Jim Walters, whom I'd seen in my thirties when I was still single and lived in Manhattan. Jim has the gift of knowing just what to say when you most need to hear it. "Living alone is awesomely difficult," he told me reassuringly. He explained that we're never really prepared to be alone. It doesn't feel natural, it doesn't feel appropriate, especially if you're tuned in to the culture. After all, you've been married for many years and he didn't die, he left you (or you left him). No matter how many people you have supporting you, they're always at a distance; they don't live with you. Generally no one but your spouse has an intense interest in your day-to-day life. I was used to sharing everything with my husband, and this was one of the highest hurdles for me. I felt a lot better when

Jim reassured me that being alone wasn't easy, that it was going to be a struggle. Whew! I wasn't some kind of weak leech who needed a man to feel okay.

Another hurdle, he said, is the amount of honest self-examination you need to do in order to be alone but not lonely. "Being alone without feeling lonely requires a degree of honesty that a lot of people aren't accustomed to," Jim explained. We had spent many sessions examining the illusions I carefully maintained so I wouldn't have to make life changes that scared me. "If you're alone and unhappy, you're strongly pressured from within to look at yourself—to see who you actually are."

How many couples do you know who reinforce each other's skewed view of the world? How many women do you know who could achieve much more but limit themselves because they don't want to rock the boat of their marriage? They may even buy in to their husband's assessment that they're not smart enough or good enough to accomplish things on their own.

Although it may not feel that way, especially at first, it's perfectly natural to be alone. Leaving aside sex, you have choices about how to share your time and your feelings, and you can be with yourself. Jim says the problem is self-deception. If you insist that the divorce is all his fault, that means you have to relate to someone who isn't there. His presence as the enemy is a fear reaction against being alone. This little insight Jim gave me explains a lot—especially why I, and so many other divorcées, are unwilling to let go of that rage against the husband who did us wrong. The anger is keeping us company. As long as we can feel it, we're not faced with the terror and emptiness of being alone. To me that anger is a warmth in the gut, a way of feeling alive instead of cast adrift. However, you never get to enjoy your life if you're too busy being angry at someone who doesn't matter to you anymore.

Marriage helped you avoid things you needed to do for yourself in order to grow. Your husband provided a way to avoid a big piece of your own life. Once you let go of the anger, you can start finding out how you really want to live.

SPINSTERS, CRONES, HAGS, AND OTHER STEREOTYPES OF WOMEN ALONE

We still think in terms of the archetype of a woman alone as a spinster, which resides in our collective unconscious. The spinster is seen as dried up, desiccated, thrown away. She is very different from the archetype of the desirable, dashing eligible bachelor. Think *Hugh Hefner,* who in his eighties is still bedding twenty-year-olds. Luckily we do have the inimitable Mae West as a role model, who at eighty had a coterie of young male escorts. However, she got away with it partly because she was a comedienne. Funny women get a lot more leeway in our society.

"Until we women grow comfortable with being alone, we carry a lot of shame," Falk explains. Older women especially carry a larger burden of shame when it comes to being alone. After all, a nubile twenty-five-year-old living in her own apartment can be seen as a swinging single. A not-so-nubile fifty- or sixty-five-year-old, however, who's been dumped by her husband for a younger woman, is likely to be seen as a pitiful old lady. Or actually not seen at all. Aging women are invisible in our society.

"We single older women alone are really going up against the burden of history," says Falk. Simone de Beauvoir, author of *The Second Sex,* wrote that throughout recorded history woman has been defined exclusively by her relationship to man. She begins to see herself through his eyes, as an object, an "other." Fear of losing or never attaining social status prevents her from asking "Who am I?" but rather "Who does he want me to be?" Instead of wondering what she wants for herself, she's always asking what he wants from her. No wonder aloneness is so terrifying for women. "How can we feel liberated by being alone when for most women being alone is virtually a euphemism for being flawed—not with a modest flaw, mind you (some relatively superficial and fixable feature like crooked teeth or poor eyesight), but inherently flawed, defective at the core," explains Falk.

Luckily we older women now have feminism to support us. We were the first feminists, and we are still the most fervent. We have Gloria Steinem as a role model, a woman who was never afraid to live alone and who married very late in life. Older feminists these days are even taking on the identity of "crone" willingly, turning it into a positive rather than a negative. In the cave, crones were valued by the tribe for their wisdom and healing abilities. They started getting a bad name during the Spanish Inquisition, when they were called witches and burned at the stake. Dropping the need to be defined as a "wife" and rebelliously defining yourself as a "crone" can be enormously liberating. I call myself an old lady and take a kind of perverse pleasure in the term. Of course the stereotypical crone lives alone. Can you imagine any of the witches in *Macbeth* with husbands? Could they be stirring a cauldron of eye of newt and toe of frog in the middle of the night with kids or a husband waiting at home for dinner? Not on a bet.

Luckily times have changed. We crones don't have to live in huts in the forest anymore and suffer from toothlessness, hideous noses, or a wardrobe of rags. We can benefit from modern dentistry, plastic surgery, and fashionable attire. We can even choose to become Wiccans and cast a few spells without fear of being burned at the stake. If you're feeling somehow flawed because you're alone, embrace your inner witch. Just as witchcraft has become respectable, so have we older women who live alone.

HOW YOUR CHILDHOOD INFLUENCES YOUR ABILITY TO BE ALONE

Just as your childhood influences your ability to do well in school, make friends, have good relationships, feel good about yourself, deal with anxiety and anger, and just about every other aspect of coping with life, it also influences your ability to deal with being alone. When I started doing research for this book, I was struck by how many women were perfectly content after their marriages ended, many of them happier than ever. So many women who were lonely in their marriages felt an enormous sense of relief when they finally were husbandless, plunging into doing things they'd always wanted to do. I, on the other hand, was panicked—and I think a good deal of that panic was left over from childhood.

We learn about how to cope with being alone as children. My psychotherapist friend Wendy explained to me how it works: If we get enough comfort and love as a child, we internalize that, and can comfort and love ourselves when no one else is around to do it. Babies feel they are a part of Mom—they're one and the same. When the mother leaves, the child feels total abandonment. Differentiation occurs when the child starts to realize she's separate. However, the longing for wholeness stays with us, and the more neurotic we are, the worse that longing gets. What is loneliness, after all? What's the difference between sitting in the same room with someone else, and being alone? The difference is feeling that you're not complete in yourself, longing for the emotional connection you felt with your mother, or rather never got. If your mother wasn't there for you, you will need to connect with a man in an unhealthy way. Women who can end a marriage without suffering that kind of loneliness probably had a stronger connection with their mothers or other caregivers during childhood, or had an extended family that took on that role.

I will never forget one of the happiest days of my life—when I was ten years old and got hit by a car. You wouldn't think getting hit by a car would be an occasion for joy, but since I wasn't hurt it was memorable because my mom hugged me tightly and told me how worried she was and how much she loved me. In that moment I felt warm and adored and comforted. I remember wishing I could stay in her embrace forever. Then she went back to being her usual hysterical, critical self, lashing out at me for running across the street against the light. I was cast out of the warmth back into the cold, cruel world where I was alone and terribly lonely. My mom was not a cruel or mean person; she loved me dearly. She just had no idea how to be nurturing. It didn't come naturally to her.

I spent my life trying to make up for that bleak childhood, seeking the feeling I got in that embrace, and Zeke gave that to me—at least part of the time. I became addicted to that sense of caring, security, and comfort he provided. Of course the other part of him was angry, critical, and intrusive, just like Mom.

"Inevitably there's a mourning process," Falk says, "but unless a woman is exceedingly needy she marshals other resources. I find this over and over in my practice. Women who have the most trouble being alone have never developed an inner life and are believers in the myth that someone else will complete them. These women never look within, they're always looking outside themselves to be saved. When we do that we're diminishing our own value and asking someone else to do for us what we can do for ourselves."

HOW SOME DIVORCED GIRLFRIENDS DEAL WITH LONELINESS

I admire Mae, a feisty, ebullient fifty-six-year-old teacher who wasn't the least bit afraid of being lonely when her husband of ten years told her he wanted to leave.

"When we separated, even though he instigated it, I was the one who got the most relief. I couldn't bear listening to him because he talked so slowly. I felt that he was intimidated by me. I talk fast, think fast, process fast. Instead of telling myself that I should accept it, I hated it. It was his processing issue. He'd accuse me of being intolerant and I'd tell him, you're intolerable. When we separated I was so relieved. Now I not only got time to be with my son, but I got time for myself." I just love this story. Mae is the rare woman who doesn't blame herself for not "fixing" her husband, or putting up with him. I'm sure it was no coincidence that Mae found someone else fairly quickly and is now happily living with him. She is the kind of woman who makes things happen.

Sylvia, an accountant, also fifty-six, has a great attitude as well. "I was almost lonelier when I was married," she says. "There are worse things than being alone. You come into the world alone and leave it alone and you might as well like who you are in between."

Contrast these women with Arlene, fifty-eight, the school bus driver I described in a previous chapter, whose husband left her for the woman he was having an affair with. Arlene's misery is etched into her face. "Every day I'd cry," Arlene says. "I couldn't drive. The first year was horrible. I cried all the time, the loneliness was unbearable. It's such a pain in my heart, twenty times worse than losing my dad. I'm afraid to go out with anyone—too scared to go through that again. I was a doormat and let a married man do whatever he wanted. He was living like a single man. I told him when we broke up that he never treated me like a wife or a woman should be treated. He never told me I was pretty. There wasn't a lot of love there toward the end. I miss having somebody, it's so weird—I hate him but I miss him holding me. We did communicate, when I had a bad day I could talk to him." She was willing to settle for crumbs.

It's hard to separate loneliness from mourning at the beginning of the breakup. After all, you're losing not just a man but your dream of family. Younger women have a shot at starting a new family, but for us older women that dream has to die. We may find love, and eventually fulfillment, but we're not walking into the sunset with the father of our children and grandfather of our grandchildren anymore. Mourning the loss of your dream can feel lonelier than actually being alone.

Sharon, a fifty-year-old accountant whose husband left her for another woman, says: "I was lonely, especially at first. I had a fear of being alone for the rest of my life. But I really wasn't alone because I had kids. What really got to me was that the whole picture of my life wasn't what I thought it would be. That's still tough. Other times I say so what, it could be much worse."

However, if you're willing to just sit with the loneliness and find out what it can teach you, you can make some surprising discoveries about yourself.

"Coming into an empty house for the first year was so hard, but I think I revived through the sorrow," says Stella, an ebullient sixty-two-year-old newspaper reporter who was left for a younger woman. "I had been so pressed down by living with a depressed person that my former self bubbled up. I rediscovered my *joie de vivre* even in the sorrow. I certainly found out how loved I was, which was a shock. My friends and family really came through. The support was huge, overwhelming."

CULTIVATING SOLITUDE

Some women fill every moment of their time with stuff—friends, family, work, things to do—when what they really need is to cultivate solitude, which is very different from loneliness. To find out what solitude means for you, close your eyes, relax, and think back to a time when you felt perfectly content alone; when you actually wanted to be alone. This may take you back to girlhood, when you were bicycling, making a sand castle, playing in your tree house. Or it may take you to a time you were walking on a beach picking up shells, or reading a book in bed, or listening to Mozart (okay, forget Mozart . . . maybe the Rolling Stones). For me it's swimming. I have no desire to swim with anyone—I love being in a lake, on a sunny day, swimming all alone.

Solitude is the other side of relationship, explains Florence Falk. "The more you grow into yourself, the more connected you are, the more able you are to be a good friend and lover. Sometimes women need to tiptoe into the experience of aloneness, of solitude. We're afraid we're empty inside, which is terrifying. Then we come up against fear, shame, and guilt—what did I do wrong so this man left me? The solution, after the mourning period is over, is to move into meditation, a more spiritual life, doing things you've never done before."

Even though I consider myself spiritual, I have no idea what a spiritual life is and I can't sit still long enough to meditate. I have a picture of a "spiritual" woman as slim, soft-spoken, and sweet. She wears flowing clothes in natural fabrics, goes to vegetarian retreats, and has absolutely no sense of humor. She is definitely not outspoken, abrasive, sarcastic, and pushy—like me. When I despair of ever being "spiritual" or even being any good at being alone, I think of the least spiritual person I ever knew, an atheist in fact, an old woman who had a gift for solitude—my mother.

Even though she wasn't great at being a mom, she was a champ at living alone. Loyal to her marriage vows, she took care of my dad for his entire life, including the last fifteen years when he had Parkinson's disease. She was miserable; she hated being his caretaker. When he finally died, she felt released. Happy as a clam, she spent the last fifteen years of her life, until her death in her late eighties, doing essentially nothing. I was blessed that during this period we became great friends and got to heal our relationship. Mom lived in a Florida retirement community where she and her bosom buddies, three other widows, would get together daily to go to a movie, concert, museum, mall, the beach, the Everglades, to explore a new neighborhood, or visit someone they knew. They traveled all over the world together. Her friends complained about how my tireless mother dragged them from one museum to another. They had dinner out together every night. For the first time in her life, I could see that my mom was perfectly happy. She didn't like being married to my father, and probably would have been happier never marrying, but that wasn't an option when she was a young woman. When I asked her if she wanted to meet another man, she was absolutely horrified by the prospect. She'd throw up her hands. "What, take care of some *alta cocker* who needs a nurse. No way. Now, maybe if I could find a handsome forty-year-old," she'd laugh with a leer. She was totally happy and complete alone. Maybe that was why she didn't fear death. Even near the end she managed to bask in the simple pleasure of a sunny day surrounded by friends.

Mom, although she loved socializing, also wanted to go back to her own apartment alone every afternoon, to sew, read, nap, relax. She needed her friends and she needed her space. When she got sick she insisted on staying alone in her Florida condo, refusing to come live with me. She might not have been the most nurturing mom when I was a child, but as an adult I was lucky to have her as a role model. They say that the last lesson our parents teach us is how to die. My mother certainly taught me that lesson, but she also taught me that it was possible to live happily alone.

WHO GETS CUSTODY OF THE FRIENDS

Just about all divorcées talk about friends as the antidote to loneliness. As older divorced women we may no longer have our moms to rely on, the way many younger divorcées do. In fact, a lot of younger divorced women take their kids and move back home. We no longer have a home outside of the one we make for ourselves. What we do a have is a gift for friendship, and after a divorce that ability is key to recovery.

When Abigail Trafford wrote *Crazy Time* in the early 1980s, she included a whole chapter about "Public Divorce." In it she talked about how divorcées are excluded from their former social networks, especially if they were the ones who initiated the divorce. At that time women were often dropped after a divorce by former friends; shared friends from the marriage were conflicted about which spouse to call and often terminated the relationship.

Luckily, times have changed since then. It seems we no longer live in an exclusively couples world, and the stigma of divorce has pretty much vanished. Initially I was going to include a chapter in this book about who gets custody of the friends. When I started talking to divorced women, however, I found that it was a non-issue. Almost no one lost friends due to divorce—or if they did the friends clearly belonged to their ex-husbands, and they didn't care. Most women just kept the friends they had before the marriage, as I did, and so did their exes. If they were friends with couples, somehow they just sorted out who got which friends.

Stella's experience was typical. She and her husband pretty much split their friends according to gender, but she was no longer invited to a lot of couples events. "The couples world just closed down on me," she says, "which hurt me for a while. But then I thought, *Screw that, I don't care anyway, I've got plenty on my plate.* No one I was close to stopped calling."

I find I'm not invited to couples events, either. Couples like to socialize with other couples, and as a single woman I really do feel like a third wheel when I'm with a couple. However, I do have women friends who are married. We just hang out together without their husbands coming along. This kind of same-sex socializing is much more accepted than it used to be.

HOW TO BE YOURSELF BY YOURSELF

Do something creative. For me it's writing, but creativity can mean anything from gardening, to cooking, to home decorating— anything that engages the right side of your brain. One divorced girlfriend's version of creativity was giving dinner parties. Creativity puts you in a state of "flow" where your rational mind turns off and you become totally caught up in what you're doing. Children do this naturally when they play. Creativity is play for grown-ups.

Feng Shui your home. Feng Shui is the ancient Chinese practice of placement and arrangement of space to achieve harmony with the environment. Arranging your living space for maximum beauty, calm, and harmony will make you feel those qualities in your life. Go through closets, simplify your life. Cut the clutter. When you throw away, you get rid of mementos of your former life. One divorcée pitched all the pictures of herself and her husband into the fire and found it enormously liberating.

Raise your consciousness. Our culture works to diminish a woman's sense of self unless she's attached to a man. Read some of the early feminists, like Betty Friedan or Germaine Greer, to get in touch with the ways in which you are a product of your culture. We women often feel guilty about allowing ourselves to feel whole and complete alone; somehow it doesn't seem natural. If you can experience your loneliness as political as well as personal, you'll get some perspective.

Do things alone. Go to dinner, or the movies, or a concert alone. It's empowering. There's no shame in being alone. If you look around, you'll see other singles at the event or restaurant. "I still go out alone, even though I'm married now," says Miki McWade, author of *Getting Up, Getting Over, Getting On: A Twelve Step Guide to Divorce Recovery.* "I learned how to do that in my divorce. I don't wait for my husband to make it okay to go somewhere."

Come up with your own affirmations. I'm not a fan of the usual affirmations because they sound sappy, but I have a few that work for me, such as "This, too, shall pass," or "I'm much better off without him," or "If he was here I wouldn't be able to do this." If you think about it, you'll come up with affirmations that work for you.

Get a dog . . . or two, or three. Dogs are better companions than most men. They worship you unconditionally, never talk back, and cuddle on demand without asking for more. My little doggy Shadow has become the great love of my life, which may sound kind of pitiful, but if you love a dog you'll understand. Read *A Three Dog Life* by Abigail Thomas if you have any doubts (her latest book is *Thinking About Memoir*). Here's her take on being alone:

> *I don't always want to answer a question about why I'm coughing if I'm coughing. I like falling into* Return to a Place Lit by a Glass of Milk *without being asked what am I reading. I appreciate not being interrupted in the middle of thinking about nothing. Nobody shoos my dogs off the sofa or objects to the three of them with sardine breath farting under the covers in bed at night. I like moving furniture around without anyone wishing I wouldn't or not noticing that I have. I like cooking or not, making the bed or not, weeding or not. Watching movies until three a.m. and no one the wiser. Watching movies on a spring day and no one the wiser. To say nothing of the naps.*

HOW TO REACH OUT TO OTHERS

Nurture the needy. When you've lost your tribe, you need another outlet for your nurturing instincts. It may not be enough to raise funds for your favorite charity; you may find it more satisfying to do more direct caretaking, such as in a women's shelter, cancer ward, nursing home, hospital with needy children, Meals on Wheels—anything that involves actual contact with others.

Find a community. That community could be your church or synagogue, your neighborhood, your colleagues at work, or a group of friends. Even an online community. Joining a group is another way to become part of a tribe. You might even create your own tribe. One divorcée in Kansas City told me about a *Fete Mardi* a friend started for all her women friends. Every Tuesday night this group of women—both married and divorced—get together for dinner just to eat and hang out. In addition to exchanging gossip, they've become an informal support group. As an unexpected benefit, hearing the details of everyone's marriages and remarriages has convinced her she's better off single.

Join a virtual community. These are just a few. There are hundreds on the Web.

www.divorce360.com

www.firstwivesworld.com

www.divorcesupport/about.com

www.divorcesource.com/wwwboard/bulletin

Make new friends. It's too easy to isolate yourself. Be proactive. You can't expect people to call you, you have to call them. I was impressed with Lola, a fifty-eight-year-old craftsperson with a warm, accessible personality who lived in New York City during her twenty-five-year marriage. After separating from her husband a year ago, she moved to the Hudson Valley, which she feels was a great decision. "Because I moved, I'm meeting new people here. I never had very many friends in New York City anyway; I still have friends from California. I've met a nice group of women friends up here. Some are ex–New Yorkers, divorcées. I met a chiropractor who is divorced with three kids. I met a woman at a garage sale, she's here all week and her husband comes up on weekends. Some know each other, some don't."

Make plans. Make sure you have plans, especially for the weekend, says Miki McWade, who found that keeping busy over weekends was extremely helpful for her support group members. That requires planning and sticking to your plan.

Spend more time with your grandkids. It's impossible to be lonely while hanging out with little kids; they literally force you to see the world through their unjaded eyes. I'm lucky to have a daughter who is still young. She is constantly amazing and delighting me with her sense of wonder, especially about the natural world. I am never lonely when I'm with her. If you don't have grandkids, borrow someone else's, or volunteer to work with children.

Create your own rituals for holidays. When you lose a marriage, celebrating holidays together with family may not be possible anymore. I make Thanksgiving dinner every year and invite anyone I know who doesn't have a place to go. If it's my turn to have my daughter, she comes; otherwise I still cook for my foster daughter and her son. If you're stuck with nothing to do on a holiday, volunteer at the local soup kitchen. In our town we have a community Thanksgiving and Christmas celebration for everyone. Those who can afford it bring food, and those who can't, come and eat. The beauty of it is that everyone who is lonely has a place to go.

Call a friend for a reality check. When I complain to my girlfriend Wendy about how lonely I am, she reminds me how miserable I was when I lived with Zeke and how desperate I was to get away from him and spend an evening with her. Find a friend who does that for you. It's likely that you have more than one.

IF YOU'RE IN YOUR . . .

Forties . . .

Hang out with your teenagers. If you're lucky enough to still have kids at home, enjoy them. Invite their friends over. Become the neighborhood mom whose house all the kids hang out in—be the confidante of the local teens. It's hard to be lonely in a house full of kids. The upside is that you get to keep an eye on your own kids, find out who their friends are and what they're into. The downside is rap music, but hey, you might get to like it. Teens can be great company if they're not in full rebellion mode. Don't lean on them, but do enjoy them.

Fifties . . .

Do something that requires courage—preferably something you wouldn't or couldn't have done when you were married. One divorcée in her fifties whom I talked with forced herself to travel cross-country alone, an experience that taught her how independent she really was. Another started rock climbing, a sport that her husband would never have allowed because it's so dangerous. She's since climbed some tall peaks and wants to try Everest someday. Once you prove to yourself you have the courage to do something really scary, living alone will seem a whole lot less frightening.

Sixties or older . . .

Take a week and spend it totally alone, in a beautiful place where you can really experience solitude. Many women who divorce at this age have *never* been alone, and it's about time. Get to know yourself, find out who you are without distractions. My girlfriend Mara, who is sixty, a nonstop talker with a very intense personality, went to a silent retreat where she literally spent a week meditating without speaking to anyone. Initially I thought she was nuts, but when she got back I noticed how relaxed she was and how she'd been able to get past her anger at someone who had treated her badly, a grudge she'd been carrying for a long time.

CHAPTER FIVE

NO, YOU WILL NOT BECOME A BAG LADY

Playing Your Cards Right

Married women fear that divorce will turn them overnight into bag ladies, toting paper bags of possessions round the streets, sleeping under the bridge, dozing in the library, helplessly poor and useless, unable to work or support themselves if they don't have a husband. Even educated, working, high salary holding, intelligent and competent women feel the icy hand of fear as they look out from what they think is the shelter of married life to the wild woolly jungle of Being Alone.

—EVELYN KAYE ON LATELIFEDIVORCE.BLOGSPOT.COM

It's amazing how many of us older women use the words *bag lady* when contemplating our worst post-divorce fears. According to the AARP study, financial destitution is one of the major fears of older divorcées. Unfortunately, to some extent those fears are realistic—usually not to the extent of homelessness, but many women will fall down the economic ladder precipitously after divorce. Women's incomes drop 27 percent and men's *increase* 10 percent post-divorce. These statistics aren't calculated by age, but chances are the gap becomes larger the older you are at the time of divorce. After all, if you've been staying home taking care of the kids and your husband has been working, he's the one with the career and you're the one who has to get back into the job market in your forties, fifties, or even sixties, or find a career when you should be thinking about retirement. Alone, you are not in a position to create the kind of lifestyle you had with your husband.

MARRIAGE IS A BUSINESS

"Society's promise goes something like this," says Nancy Dailey, author of *When Baby Boom Women Retire.* "If you invest in job skills and/or in your education and work throughout your adult life in the paid labor market, you will be entitled to security and leisure in old age. The catch is, for women, you have to stay married. Marriage is the way we create wealth in our economic system. Marriage is like a business partnership. When you dissolve it, you are dissolving a business. When the business is dissolved, often the wife is the one left holding the bag."

We older women seem to be ashamed to admit that we can develop financial skills and become wealthy in our own right. We feel we ought to give money away, be generous, make people like us by handing out gifts to show them we're not really rich. There is no male corollary to the expression *rich bitch.* However, there is a flexible line between making sure you can support yourself and being generous without bankrupting yourself. Everyone has different values and different interests. Few of us are millionaires. So for the rest of us it is important to find out what we need to live on, how we can earn it, what we can do without, and what we feel is essential.

As a woman's income declines after a divorce, her standard of living may go down as well. But moving from a large fancy house in the suburbs with three cars to a more modest condo with one car is not becoming a bag lady. It's simply being realistic.

After all, for millions of people in the world, our standard of living is luxury—just having running hot and cold water, central heating, and a stove and refrigerator would be enough. So keep the financial picture in perspective. You may have lost something you accepted as normal, but life will go on.

In my case marriage was the way two creative types, neither of whom made a lot of money, could live comfortably. I was freelancing and my husband had a civil service job. We were just getting by with a combined income of about $55,000. Adopting a child had taken a large chunk out of the modest inheritance my mother left me, and like so many financially ignorant folks we spent most of the rest instead of saving it. However, we lived frugally in a rural area where our expenses were low, and with my inheritance we were fairly comfortable, as a married couple. Divorce was going to mean a huge financial hit for both of us. I was totally terrified when Zeke told me he was leaving. I didn't see how I could support myself and my daughter alone.

I have always been a survivor, however, and divorce was no exception. Somehow I managed to put together a life for myself without him by thinking outside the box. I turned my basement into an apartment, and now that my support has ended I may chop off another room and rent it—or I may do doggy day care. I never planned on becoming a landlady, or pet sitter, but when divorce strikes, ya gotta be creative. I didn't have to cut back much on my lifestyle because I've always driven used cars and am a yard sale junkie anyway.

I didn't consider getting a job because I was sixty, hadn't worked outside the home for twenty-five years, and had no marketable skills in a location where there are few professional jobs. I was damned if I was going to work at the local convenience store for eight dollars an hour, which my husband's lawyer actually suggested during the support hearing. So I put together a patchwork of income sources to get by, including freelance writing. Little did I know that I was doing exactly what Dailey recommends for older women: putting together a few different sources of income to survive. As an older divorcée you, too, may need to come up with a combination of career and financial strategies that will enable you to survive and hopefully still live comfortably. Depending on your age, education, work background, financial savvy, and, most of all, self-confidence and resourcefulness, you will be able to survive and even thrive—especially if you start thinking outside the box.

"When I began this divorce process, I had allowed my husband to take over managing our money," says Evelyn Kaye, a resourceful sixty-nine-year-old. "Though we discussed things, he was clearly in charge. After I realized I would no longer go on being his wife, the enabler and the doormat, I was ready to leave and be penniless because I felt so desperate. And I am a woman who has worked as a writer, editor, organizer all my life, earned money, kept my own name for writing, and been as independent as I possibly could be within the confines of marriage. I had contributed to the numerous funds for our retirement through the money I had earned. And yet I imagined I would have to be penniless, a bag lady, if I was on my own. It's *insane* to think that, but I did. In the reality of the past few months, I have learned that I am perfectly capable of managing money as well as him. I can find people to ask for advice. I can look things up on the Internet. I can read books about finance. I can take classes on the subject. I may not manage money in the same way—I don't buy large quantities of whiskey, gin, vodka, and other liquor—but I will do it my way and it will reflect my values, and I prefer books to bottles."

HOW TO THINK SINGLE

In order to make a life for yourself after divorce you need to start thinking single. Single women are used to taking care of themselves; they take control of their finances and don't expect someone else to take care of them. Unless they're making six figures, they are very careful where and how they spend their money, invest prudently, and make the most out of what they have.

Sit down with a divorce financial planner or someone with that kind of background to get organized after the divorce. Don't make any long-term commitment for financial planning, but go for one or two sessions to figure out where to go from here. The planner should project your expenses into the future and set up a budget for you. He or she will help you figure out if you should keep your home or sell it, what kind of investments make the most sense, how to protect the money in your husband's retirement plan so he can't borrow against it or take any out.

Ask your financial planner to help you come up with a budget. Then stick to it. Many divorcées make the mistake of living beyond their means initially—they think they can still buy expensive clothes, travel, and maintain the BMW when they should be downsizing from day one post-divorce. This doesn't mean wearing ratty clothes, eating TV dinners, and driving an old heap. But it does mean being very careful what you spend your money on, eating at home more than out, selling the gas guzzler for a small car that gets good mileage, and visiting your friends in Florida for vacation rather than taking a luxury cruise.

If you're a typical middle-class divorcée, who maybe got a small settlement plus the house and maintenance for a few years, you need to parlay that into a lifetime income. Even though you are not going to run up credit card debt, you need to establish credit on your own. You may have cut up your credit cards pre-divorce so your husband couldn't run up debt that wound up on your credit report, but post-divorce you'll have to establish credit again. Even if you have cash to pay for the car, finance part of it. Make sure you make the payment every month until it's paid off. Then figure out what you're going to do when your current car dies. If your husband screws with your credit, take advantage of the low-rate credit card offers that arrive in the mail. Juggle them, transferring the balance to another low-rate card when the current one runs out. Don't rack up big bills, but use each card just enough to pay off at end of the month and establish your own credit rating.

Do not make loans to friends and relatives. Like lottery winners, divorcées can find themselves besieged with requests for cash. Greedy family members may suddenly arrive with a sob story about needing money, preying upon older divorcées who have just received a financial settlement.

Invest conservatively; your settlement may well be the only lump sum you will ever see for the rest of your life, unless you are young enough and make enough money to stash away another substantial nest egg, or will be inheriting money from your parents. Don't count on alimony. It may disappear in the future if your ex dies, loses his job, or becomes insolvent, so invest capital in a mix of stocks and bonds that offer some growth, but avoid high risk. Don't invest in any gold mines in Brazil or that surefire thing your brother-in-law recommends. We older women need to preserve capital. Unless you're seriously into following the market, tell the planner to make it easy so you don't have to figure out what to buy or sell each month. My financial planner told me to put my nest egg in the Vanguard Fund, which allocates a large variety of investments, balancing risk with safety. I now wish I had

WHERE TO FIND FINANCIAL ADVICE

Check out Institute for Divorce Financial Planning (www .idfa.com) to find a divorce financial planner.

Read *Help! I Can't Pay My Bills: Surviving a Financial Crisis* by Sally Herigstad, CPA. I love this book. It's simple, easy to understand, with tons of helpful info. If, like me, you hate reading financial advice books, this book is for you.

left stock index funds out of my portfolio, but who knew the stock market would crash in 2008. If you're close to retirement, don't put your money into anything risky. Look into single-premium annuities, which will give you income for life with a large-enough lump sum.

WHO SINKS, WHO SWIMS

Divorcées who sink try desperately to maintain their old life-style because radical change is too frightening. Divorcées who swim plunge into new ways of living. My favorite example is from *Calling It Quits: Late Life Divorce and Starting Over* by Deir-dre Bair. She interviewed a divorcée who wanted to keep her Spanish-hacienda-style house in an exclusive area of Southern California but simply couldn't afford the mortgage. So she rented the house for a year at $15,000 a month to a European execu-tive while she advertised her services as a house and pet sitter. She wound up living the whole year for free, and was planning to do the same thing for another year at an even higher rent, after which she'd be set for life. There were some unexpected benefits: She was delighted with her year of itinerant life, saying it was a "well-earned vacation" that was also physically good for her. She lost weight from walking dogs three to four times a day; she made friends with other dog walkers, and even dated two of them. Now that's thinking outside the box.

Instead of coupling, consider the movement among seniors to live communally, which will help you pool resources. Co-housing communities are becoming more popular—they allow residents to own their own homes but pool a variety of resources, plus alleviate loneliness through communal activities such as nightly shared dinners. These communities aren't necessarily cheap, but if you can afford co-housing it's a great way to transition to life alone. If you find a mate, or want to share your house with family, that's allowed as well. Check out www.cohousing.org.

A recent AARP study found that more than a third of the 1,200-plus women forty-five and older surveyed said they'd be interested in sharing a house with friends or other women, as long as it included private space. "Communal living is catching on among divorced people," says Bair, citing as an example a group of first wives of wealthy men, women who pooled money from their divorce settlements to buy a four-story brownstone in New York City that none of them could have afforded alone. They dine together every night so no one hides in her room and becomes too depressed to get out of bed. This sounds terribly appealing to me. I wish I could move in with them.

Helen, now seventy-five, was in her sixties when she got divorced, and she's been living with the same friend since then. "A friend of mine and I took a cross-country trip to see if we could share such small spaces with each other for a couple weeks," Helen explains. "We survived the trip and joined forces. First we had an apartment together for ten to twelve years, and then before you knew it we bought a house together about six years ago because we enjoyed each other's company so much. It's been wonderful financially. We take care of each other, and it's handy to have someone close by. We do a lot of traveling. We just got back from a national parks trip, and last spring we went to Paris."

Communal living can also mean renting out part of your house, like I do. My renters, a lovely young couple, have become my support system as well as my tenants. They take care of the yard work and any heavy maintenance, and I know I can call on them if I need help. They bring me Latino dishes when they make something special, and I share extra food with them that's too much for me to finish myself. It's very reassuring to me to know they're there, plus I rely on the income. I've rented my garage as a workshop to a couple of carpenters, and if something needs fixing, I know they're around.

Some divorcées stay in their houses and take in boarders, or roommates, others sell their homes and move to condos, and still others move in with their kids. This may sound like a drastic solution, but it can work really well if you get along with your children, *and* you have your own space.

HOW TO FIND A JOB OR CAREER

Most divorcées have to work to make ends meet, either part- or full-time. The benefits of working are more than financial, however. A job will get you out of the house and into a social environment where you can forget about your divorce, at least for a while, and hopefully make friends and other connections. A job is the best antidepressant. I often wish I had one and wasn't stuck with a solitary profession.

Figure Out What Career Path to Take

If you're stymied about what you want to do, first ask yourself what you're good at. If you're still stuck, go a career counselor or take an aptitude and interest test. Also, ask your friends what they think are your talents. Other people can often see gifts that we can't. What do other people compliment you on? What do you get kudos for?

Another possibility is to cross over from a related field. For example, one older girlfriend of mine with a background in accounting wanted to be a writer, so she found work in a tax software company. She was soon writing software "Help" topics; before long she'd transitioned to writing full-time.

Don't necessarily go back to what you were doing before. Terry, a divorced woman in her fifties who had been in real estate development, was out of work a long time. Since it's a fast-moving industry, she was seen as a dinosaur. Terry wound up teaching a course in real estate at the local university. While this didn't pay much, it was a stepping-stone to consulting with universities about their land and buildings. Don't overlook opportunities with low pay that are sources of valuable contacts.

Finally, there's no reason not to go back to school, no matter how old you are. More and more places offer online degrees as well, so you can study at your own pace from your own home. Many offer credits for life experience, which you definitely have.

Attitude Can Trump Experience

As Susan Jepson of Operation ABLE of Boston, which helps people over forty-five find employment, explained to *The Boston Globe*, older women looking for work typically face three major issues: lack of up-to-date computer skills, lack of understanding that the job search process has changed drastically over the past decade, and what she calls " a big, big self-confidence issue."

Confidence is your number one asset when looking for a job. It's something you need to exude in order to succeed in the world of work, but after a hiatus from the workforce plus a divorce your confidence in yourself may be shaken to the core.

There are myriad stories of women talking themselves into all kinds of positions with the right attitude. My girlfriend Teresa, an overweight, unfashionable Italian housewife without a college degree, was offered every job she ever applied for. Teresa's only experience was raising four kids in a small house in Brooklyn, New York, but she radiates the kind of can-do aura that employers seek in their employees. When she walks into an office, I can just see the hiring manager breathing a sigh of relief: *Finally, someone I can trust to take over.* She's the kind of woman who could effortlessly whip up Christmas dinner for thirty in a postage-stamp-size kitchen. She is supremely organized, has enormous energy, knows how to find or make what her family needs, and has confidence that she can do just about anything. That conveys itself to employers.

You can't just snatch confidence out of the ether, however. You need to take some practical steps to project it, whether you feel it or not.

Develop an "elevator pitch." This is a quick synopsis of your experience and what you're interested in pursuing. It should be short enough to impress a potential employer on an elevator ride, recommends Vivian Steir Rabin, co-author with Carol Fishman Cohen of *Back on the Career Track: A Guide for Stay at Home Moms Who Want to Return to Work.* Never say, "Oh I'm willing to do anything"—that projects the opposite of confidence. Instead start the conversation with something that summarizes who you are and grabs the listener's attention. In the second sentence pick three skills relevant to your target field. If you have time, give a couple of results you achieved using the skills you mentioned. Try your pitch out on friends, family, anyone you run into. The more you practice, the better it will sound. When you get to that job interview, you'll be an old pro. For help, check out Seven Steps to Relaunch Success on the book's Web site: www.backonthecareer track.com/steps7.htm.

Do some research to find out what's going on in any field that might interest you. Read relevant trade magazines, take continuing education classes, and attend industry events. The more you learn, the more confident you'll be that you know what you're talking about.

Act "as if." This is one of the oldest confidence-building techniques, but it works. If you act as if you have confidence, it will become a self-fulfilling prophecy. On a job interview try pretending you're someone like Barbara Walters. When you're stumped for a response to a question, or a way to present your experience, ask yourself, *What would Barbara say?* Walters is never at a loss for words, no matter how awkward the situation.

Order yourself a snazzy business card. Include your name and contact information so you don't have to scribble on a piece of scrap paper if you meet someone who wants to keep in touch with you. You can get professional-looking cards for free on www .vistaprint.com.

Pay top dollar for a great résumé. Despite the conventional wisdom that résumés don't get people jobs, unless you have a foot in the door already, a terrific résumé can make you sound like an expert on paper. Talented résumé writers can help in organizing your skills so you look impressive, and underplaying your lack of recent experience. Also, they know how to format a résumé graphically so it's short, attractive, and professional looking. A great résumé will make you feel good about yourself, and make you feel worthy of the jobs you're applying for. Pay a pro for your résumé, don't write one yourself or have the local copy shop do it. Look for a Certified Professional Résumé Writer at www.parw.com.

Network, network, network. Start talking to people, beginning with those you know well. Branch out to those to whom they refer you, and constantly discuss your professional interests and the kinds of opportunities you'd like to explore. These informal conversations essentially function as interview rehearsals as you gradually hone your message. For guidance read the latest edition of *What Color Is Your Parachute?* by Richard Bolles, one of the oldest but still best career guides out there. He outlines how to parlay networking into a job offer.

Make sure you prepare extensively by studying the employer's Web site before an interview. Google that employer and find out what's been going on in that company for the past year for specific talking points in the interview. The more you know, the more you'll stand out from the crowd.

Practice answers to the most common interview questions. Check out the job seeker link on www.quintcareers.com, where you'll find a list of 169 questions that you can practice answering. When asked about your employment gap, answer matter-of-factly that you took some time out to raise your children/take care of an elderly parent/et cetera, but that you're now eager to get back to work. Recognize that having been a mommy can be an asset, not a liability. Sally Herigstad homeschooled her kids for fourteen years and was surprised that employers didn't see that as a negative. In fact some wanted to talk about it. "I could point to my success teaching my kids and nobody could assume I spent those years watching soaps," she said.

Do something meaningful. Being broke is no excuse to take a dreary, dead-end job. Employers are impressed by enthusiasm and love for a particular field. Anything you're passionate about will make you look more desirable to an employer than something you decide on out of desperation.

HOW TO COMBAT AGE DISCRIMINATION

Get credentials, if they apply. Degrees or letters after your name do help!

Never apologize for your age. If you forget something, fix it. Don't talk about your "senior moment." Anybody can forget something—don't remind everyone how old you are.

Try to look "with it." When you shop, look around the store. If everyone shopping there is older than you, try a different store. You don't want to look like a teenager, but nobody wants to look like they went to the outlet mall with the senior bus, either. Ask your hairdresser for something professional but "this year."

Stay reasonably fit. Nothing ages us like forty extra pounds. Ouch!

Don't put dates on your résumé. You don't have to. Nobody needs to know what year you graduated, especially from high school. You don't want to intimidate the interviewer, who may have been in diapers about then.

Recognize that age is not necessarily a disadvantage. One interesting effect of being older is that people often assume you have more experience than you do. You'll be completely honest, of course, but you can't help it if you're fifty-five and people assume you've been in accounting, for instance, for the last thirty years instead of the last six months. "I worked for a woman who had been a bartender for years," Herigstad relates, "and then got her CPA license when she was over fifty. She soon opened her own practice, and I wonder how many of her clients knew how recently she had started."

How to Make Age a Plus

Enter fields popular with women over forty, suggests Sally Herigstad. She notes that even at Microsoft, a company known for its young workforce, the writers' and editors' groups are predominantly female and over the average age for the company.

Think about areas where age *is* actually a plus. I recently read that banks look for older employees because they're more mature and more reliable. If you have no bank experience, don't turn your nose down about starting as a teller. Banks hire tellers for low salaries, but the good ones get promoted quickly. Within a year or so, you could be sitting behind a desk with a vice president sign instead of behind a teller's window.

In fact, don't turn your nose down at entry-level positions in general. Many retail stores look for reliable, older employees whom they can train to be managers. However, before you apply for an entry-level job, ask the hiring manager or other store managers what the promotion opportunities are and how quickly you can move up.

Don't write off areas dominated by young people. In some cases you may have an advantage. For example, most personal trainers are young. But some of us would like a personal trainer our own age—someone who has done more than read about arthritis and plantar fasciitis.

Emphasize Skills, Not Experience

In order to make your years at home sound positive instead of negative, you need to convince employers that you did more than just "stay home." First, avoid phrasing it with those words. "Staying home" sounds passive, and raising children is anything but a passive activity! Point to what you accomplished while raising your kids, such as homeschooling them, or coaching their soccer team, or heading up the PTA. Did you care for an aging parent or a special-needs child? Are you on the board of the homeowners' association, or did you organize programs and fund-raisers at church or your children's school? Did you do any volunteer work? Did you make money in real estate by buying, remodeling, and selling a home?

You don't want to brag about your children and risk sounding like you're living through them, but it doesn't hurt to point out your contributions to their success. Did you get your son started in computer programming? Did you tutor your daughter, and sometimes her friends, in algebra? Did you turn your daughter into a competitive athlete? These are skills you can point out to employers.

If you are working already, don't feel that you're stuck with what you've been doing. You can parlay those skills into another field.

Sheree, a member of my divorce support group, has been working part-time managing the floral department in the local supermarket, a job she hates. She thinks she wants to go to school for real estate appraisal because she used to sell real estate, but is having trouble getting a loan to pay tuition. I asked her what she hated about her job, and she said working in a supermarket. I pointed out that she had retail management experience that she could parlay into a job at another store where she'd enjoy working, such as a Pier One Imports or Ethan Allen, where she could use her home decorating experience as well. She actually hadn't thought of that option and is now applying for other retail jobs.

To figure out what your skills are and where else they would be useful, *Back on the Career Track* has a "Job Building Blocks Worksheet" that's easy to use and helpful. You can also make one for yourself. At the top of the page, describe your old job, whatever it was. Under that, create four sections for job subfunctions; under each of those subfunctions create a list of new opportunities; and under those write down people/companies to contact. For instance, under "old job," Sheree might have written "Manager of Floral Department in Supermarket"; under that her subfunctions might have been "creative flower arranging; supervise workers; interface with top management." Under creative flower arranging, a new opportunity might be "starting a flower shop; working for a florist; or creating and selling arrangements with imitation flowers." Under that, she might put names of businesses to call such as local florists or craft shops, asking if they sell imitation flower arrangements, as well as home design stores that need managers.

LOOK FOR A JOB THAT'S LOOKING FOR YOU

Too many women try to get back into things they used to do before they got married, not realizing how much the world has changed.

For instance, if you apply for a secretarial job because that's what you did before you got married, employers may assume you are technologically challenged, even if you've learned to use a computer and know word processing. Here are some areas to consider where, with a little training or education, you might actually get hired despite your age:

Medical and health care. There is always a need for lab technicians, X-ray technicians, pharmacy technicians, medical billers. Call your local community college and find out what courses they offer to become certified for these positions. Some can be completed in a year, often part-time, and will qualify you for a well-paying job.

Education or child care. Working as a substitute teacher or in a child care center might not pay a lot, but if you love kids it can be rewarding. Nanny work sounds demeaning, but nannies in New York City, for example, can make $50,000 a year or more, especially those with have any background in elementary education.

Taking care of the rich. Be a butler. Like nannying, wealthy people hire "butlers" to organize their lives and homes. If you live in or near an enclave for the rich, and excelled in managing your own home, you can take a course in "butling" and gain certification. Butlers make big bucks. Check out www.butlerschool.com for a description of what butling is all about.

Civil service. You get government jobs by taking a test, which makes age discrimination much less of a factor. There are hundreds of different jobs at the county, state, and federal level, in all kinds of fields for all experience levels. The qualifications for civil service jobs are much more flexible than for corporate jobs—experience often substitutes for education, and best of all it doesn't matter how long ago you left the marketplace. For example, a sixty-two-year-old woman trained by Operation ABLE in Boston, hadn't had a job in twelve years and never had a career. She spent months learning the most up-to-date computer programs, but that did her no good competing against younger women. Employers just assumed she was technologically challenged. She could probably have gotten that secretarial job with a local, county, or state agency, *and* gotten paid more than for a private company *with* job security and health insurance.

After my divorce I applied for a civil service job where my qualifying experience took place twenty years ago. I took the test, got a high grade and a lot of inquiries from various agencies, although none of the jobs were close enough to consider. Another big plus of government jobs: job security and great benefits, including health insurance that you keep after ten years of service. Look for federal jobs at www.usa.gov. For state or local civil service jobs, just plug the name of your state or county and "civil service jobs" into Google; the site will come up.

Consider Working as a Temp

Temporary agencies aren't what they used to be. Kelly Girl is now Kelly Services. Today's temporary agencies employ people at all skill levels for a wide range of jobs. Job contracts often last for three months and can be extended. Many professionals work for temporary agencies on a permanent basis, enjoying the freedom of being able to take assignments as they please.

If you can find temporary work in your field or close to it, you may be able to parlay a temp job into a permanent one. Many businesses now try out potential employees on a temporary basis before hiring, and pay a fee to the agency for employing you. These are the most common temp positions:

- Substitute teacher (these jobs are also available through your local school district and often require only a college degree, not a teaching certificate).
- Computer programmer.
- Administrative assistant.
- Data entry clerk.
- Graphic artist.
- Receptionist.

START YOUR OWN BUSINESS

You don't have to invest a ton of money to start a business. In fact, any business that requires a large investment is probably a bad idea, since at least 50 percent of all businesses fail in the first year. As a recent divorcée you can't afford to lose a lot of money. However, there are many home-based businesses that can be started with little or no money that can be a supplemental source of income, or develop into even more. Before you start one, however, do some research and make sure the field isn't flooded in your area, and that there's a market for your business.

Make an appointment with the local branch of SCORE (www .score.org), which is run by mostly retired volunteers who have owned their own businesses and give free advice to aspiring business owners.

Advertise your business with flyers posted all around town, particularly post offices and libraries. Invest in a classified if they're not too expensive. Don't forget Craigslist.

Good Home-Based Business Ideas

- Babysitting and housecleaning. Don't dismiss them as beneath you. In my area housecleaning pays more than teaching. Babysitting pays at least as much or more than retail.
- Bookkeeping.
- Dog grooming.
- Buying and selling on eBay.
- Making and delivering meals.
- Altering clothes.
- Running errands.
- Driving for the disabled.
- Party/wedding planning.
- Pet sitting and/or running a doggy day care.
- Tutoring.

VOLUNTEER

If you want to break into an area but have no experience—volunteer. For example, if you want to get into public relations, volunteer to do public relations for a nonprofit organization. If you want to be a Web site designer, find a charitable organization that needs a new or improved site.

If you have been volunteering, contact the board of directors of the organization you've been volunteering for and ask them to help you find a job. Boards of directors are usually composed of successful, established, and often wealthy businesspeople in your community. They will be grateful for your help in the organization and anxious to help you in turn.

Volunteer for a political campaign. Again, the movers and shakers in your community are probably supporting and working for their candidate. You can meet influential people while stuffing envelopes. You can also meet the candidate, who may already be an elected official. If your candidate wins, he or she will be hiring people who helped with the campaign.

IF YOU'RE IN YOUR . . .

Forties . . .

If you achieved some success as a professional before you left to raise your kids, haven't been out of the workforce for more than ten years, and are willing to work full-time, the news is very good. In a study of 2,443 college-educated women of all ages, the Center for Work-Life Policy found that 74 percent of women who want to go back to work manage it. In fact, hiring managers are looking for such women, for firms that need women in high-ranking positions.

If you're not in this elite group, consider going back to school. A professional degree will give you all kinds of opportunities you lacked before, no matter what your profession. I still regret not getting a master of fine arts degree in writing. I'd love to teach writing, but no matter how much experience I have, and I have a lot, I'd still need that master's for a teaching position.

Fifties . . .

Consider starting your own business if you have the entrepreneurial spirit. Don't invest every penny you have, however. Start small, recognizing that most businesses fail in the first year. Try to find a partner to share the risk. Consult a volunteer at SCORE. If you can afford it, buy a franchise, which is a much safer way to start a business. The best (and most expensive) franchises have well-known names. Beware of franchises that charge mostly for training and support when the franchise name isn't well known. Check out www.franchises.about.com for some good info.

A consulting or service business is an inexpensive way to start. Work for yourself and market your skills rather than your job experience. Your age will be an advantage as a consultant, since your life experience will be reassuring to clients. You can provide a service or consult in just about any area you're good at, such as organizing, home staging, bookkeeping, personal shopping, or life coaching. For example, Sandra, forty-eight, is a divorce consultant. She has experience as a paralegal in a matrimonial law firm and recognized that women going through a divorce are depressed, confused, and overwhelmed and need to be shepherded through the process.

Avoid multilevel marketing unless it focuses on a great product or service, not on making money by selling to friends. Never invest more than you can afford to lose. Don't choose a business "anyone" can do. Focus on something that uses your particular skills and experience.

Sixties or older . . .

Consider a reverse mortgage. At sixty-two you are eligible to take out a reverse mortgage on your house, which can make it possible for you to keep the house for as long as you live and get an extra chunk of change as well. Reverse mortgages are frightfully difficult to explain, but just think of them as a loan that you pay back out of the equity in your house. You still own the house, but don't have to pay back the bank until you sell the house or die. The bank pays off your remaining mortgage, and gives you a lump sum as well depending on a variety of other factors such as your age, where you live, how much your house is worth, and how much equity you have in it. For reverse mortgage information visit www.aarp.org/revmort, or call (800) 569-4287 for the HUD counseling and referral line. The FHA funds housing counseling agencies throughout the country that can give you advice on reverse mortgages.

At sixty-two you need to decide whether it makes sense to take Social Security or wait until you're sixty-five. You also need to decide whether to take your own or your ex-husband's Social Security, which you're entitled to if you were married for ten or more years. If he worked all his life and you didn't, it probably makes sense to take your benefits based on whatever he's entitled to. If you can wait until sixty-five, do, because you'll get about 25 percent more. However, if you're really strapped for money, or in poor health with a lowered life expectancy, it might make more sense to start collecting at sixty-two. Be aware that if you're working, you can only make $12,000 a year until age sixty-five, or Social Security will take back $1 for every $2 you make. At sixty-five, you can earn as much as you want without affecting your Social Security. Make an appointment with your local Social Security office to find out what you're going to get and what the trade-offs are.

CHAPTER SIX
WAITING TILL THE KIDS ARE GROWN

The Kids Are Never Grown

To Mom, After the Divorce

I really want to know when the whole thing cracked apart,
and more than that I want to know if the myth is true:
that no matter what I do
I will become you.
I swam inside you for almost a year
and you cupped me with one,
then both hands, and you rocked me asleep
and probably you hated me
sometimes for the way I made you so large
and the world a little smaller
and harder to navigate. Sometimes I think about
you when you were this young still,
and your smiles in pictures weren't shot through
with strain and what you see as hopeless wrinkling.
I try to imagine you jumping over fences
and taking long drives in cars, exhaling smoke,
trying like me to act cool
after you'd escaped high school and thought you were free.
You used to have long hair (I saw it in pictures),
and you were thin and probably felt really light sometimes.
(The question I'm trying to ask is

if you ever thought you might not want me there at all.)
When you were nineteen and skipping school
did you imagine one day you'd be sitting in your house
reading books other people recommended,
soaking your hands in paraffin wax?
Did you ever think you'd change the locks
and only give your daughters the key?

But before I can begin this excavation
I should ask if you've been here before:
nineteen, living under the guise of being on your own,
feeling like you can probably do anything
if you want it enough, and trying to dive
back into the empty space left when you broke into the world
screaming, raising hell like always,
trying to figure out what it means that you eventually repeat
all her same mistakes. I want to know if I will end up
fifty like you, scaring off men with my laugh, not caring,
painting my nails bright red and putting my feet up on my desk,
wild after all, alive despite the damage.

—SYDNEY MICHELLE CHAFFEE

Have you heard the one about a couple in their nineties who file for divorce? When the judge asks them, "Why did you wait so long?" they respond, "We wanted to wait until the kids were dead." There's more than a grain of truth in that joke. In fact the only time divorce is not going to hurt your children *is* when they are dead. There's a myth that adult children can handle their parents' divorce and aren't hurt by it. In fact, your adult children may very well be devastated by your divorce. They not only have to deal with the pain of your divorce, but also the assumption that it shouldn't bother them. Grown-ups are supposed to be just that—grown up, not dependent on their families. But, especially today, young people depend on their families throughout their young adulthood, for money, advice, a place they can call home, basically a net they can fall into when life knocks them off the tightrope.

Robert Frost once said, "Home is the place where, when you have to go there, they have to take you in." He expressed perfectly how much we depend on having a home when we go off into the world on our own. Just knowing it's there is profoundly reassuring, even if your children don't come back home. Divorce means that home where they have to take you in is gone. Everything your children have taken for granted was true about their lives isn't true anymore. They have to revise their notions of their childhoods to fit the new reality. This is not an easy task for anyone at any age.

If you think your children know this divorce is coming down the pike, think again. Even though you and their father may have fought for years, or barely spoke, divorce almost always comes as a shock to adult children. My friend Vicki, whose parents divorced when she was twenty-seven, says she actually thought they should divorce because they got along so badly. But when it came the divorce was still a shock. "As long as they were together I could hope they'd work it out. It was hard for me to accept that it was over."

Divorce can seriously destabilize adult children.

Debby, an army brat who grew up on military bases, was twenty when her father left for the general's wife whom he'd been having an affair with and who was pregnant. "I found out my parents were splitting up one day as I walked up my long driveway and passed my dad, who flew by and almost hit me. His things were strewn around the yard, it was raining, and my mom was distraught. I had a hard time after they split. I turned to drink and drugs. All my siblings got into trouble and ended up in jail. I threw myself into a bunch of bad relationships with older men just to get out of the house. It was hard to accept that my father was someone I never thought he was."

I don't have any biological children, but I discovered how painful divorce can be for an adult child when I saw how my divorce affected my foster daughter, Tina, whom my husband and I foster-parented only for two and a half short years, from age thirteen to fifteen. Tina was a street kid from rural upstate New York who spent her life bouncing from her jailbird mom to various relatives and back. She'd been found by the local Department of Social Services in a cold apartment on a freezing winter night, smoking pot with a group of grown men, after her mother had been carted off to jail once again. After Social Services unceremoniously dumped her at our door with no preparation, it took her some time to adjust, since we actually imposed rules on her life, but eventually she came to be grateful that we cared enough to discipline her. Our home was the only stable environment she'd ever known. She loved our peaceful, beautiful house in the woods of Catskill, New York, where she had her own room for the first time in her life plus all the food she could eat, and plenty of love. When, like many foster kids who never give up hope that Mom will finally come through, she left to go back to her mother, her life deteriorated, but we remained in touch with her throughout the years and I tried to help her when she was in trouble and we have remained close. Even though we weren't really her parents, our home was her nest, her cocoon, and she felt she could always come back to if she wanted. She considered us her parents and I thought of her as my daughter. When we sold the house and moved she was bereft, and when we broke up she became bitter.

Even though she was twenty-one and long gone from our lives, she was nonetheless devastated by the news. She said she thought we'd always be together; we were like two peas in a pod.

I was surprised at how outraged she was, feeling that my husband's cheating made it impossible for her to have any respect for him. "He was the only dad I've ever known," she said. "I thought he was different, that here finally was a guy who would never cheat, that he just wasn't that kind of man. He was kind, gentle, and loving. But now he's turned out to be a cheater just like all the other men I've ever known." We were actually the only "happily married" people she knew; we were her icons for happy marriage. What she (and we) didn't realize was that our marriage started going downhill when she left—she was the glue that kept us together.

Children are the glue for lots of couples, and when they leave the bond dissolves, which is why so many boomer marriages break up when the last kid has left for college. It may be coincidence, or due to her early upbringing, but Tina now has no intention of ever marrying. She says, "Why bother, I'd only have to get a divorce." I hate hearing this, but I can hardly disagree. Other adult children of divorce become similarly wary of marriage, thinking it can't last. Brooke Lea Foster, the author of *The Way They Were: Dealing with Your Parents' Divorce After a Lifetime of Marriage,* says she put off marrying her live-in boyfriend for ten years because she was skittish about the prospects of marriage lasting after she saw her parents go through a divorce. "I was in a happy relationship and felt so scared that marriage was going to jinx us and change everything."

If losing the only dad she'd ever known was a bitter pill for Tina and still is, what made it worse for her was how Zeke treated me after we broke up, blaming me for the breakup and for our adopted daughter's emotional problems. I was distraught so many times when we spoke and cried on Tina's shoulder even though I really shouldn't have burdened her with my grief. She no longer speaks with him although she misses him.

This issue plays itself out in the post-divorce lives of many adult children, who go through the shock of not only the breakup itself, but also how the spouses treat each other afterward. Men who feel guilty about leaving will often take it out on the person who made them feel that way—you—and will even try to hurt you post-divorce.

"My dad has tried to turn my younger brother and I against my mother," says Kara, a college student who relishes the time away from her dysfunctional home life. "He tries to get us to go on vacation with him and bribes us with stuff for love in order to make up for what he's done wrong. He wants to look like the cool parent."

Alternatively, if you were the one who left, even if it was for a good reason, you may be in for a shock when your adult child refuses to speak to you and blames you for the divorce.

"It's hard to blame the crazy person so I blame my mother more than my father," says Paul, a resentful twenty-six-year-old whose mother finally left his seventy-three-year-old abusive, alcoholic father. "My mom was clearheaded, and my dad was the crazy one. I'm bitter toward my mother and always will be because she showed cowardice to not divorce my father years before when the situation was not good for all of us."

If you cheated, the reaction will be worse.

When you're in the midst of a divorce, you may lose sight of your children's pain, especially if they've been on their own for years and you think of them as resourceful adults who can be your support system. You may assume that the divorce is only happening to you, that they had a childhood with an intact family so they won't be affected. Nothing could be farther from the truth. Adult children are likely to react with as much shock, anger, grief, and feelings of abandonment and rejection as smaller children. They may be afraid to voice their own fears and hurts and instead try to take care of you and their father.

WHY IT'S SO HARD FOR THE KIDS

"Many parents feel shocked and betrayed when faced with how devastated their grown children are when they divorce," says Noelle Fintushel-Oxenhandler, who with Nancy Hilliard, PhD, co-authored *A Grief Out of Season: When Your Parents Divorce in Your Adult Years.* "Waiting until the children are grown not only provides a sense of timing but of justification." One mother told them she stayed in an unhappy marriage until she was confident her children were grown and had their own lives. She felt she'd earned her divorce and was quite bitter when her children didn't make it easy. The authors explain that many parents are genuinely surprised to see the depth of their children's attachment to the family and its past. After seeing their children leading full and autonomous lives, parents don't expect their divorce to have such an impact.

If you want to spare your children some of the pain of divorce, you need to be aware of what they're going through and how you can make their transition easier.

Adult children suffer a series of intense losses as a result of parental divorce. They lose their family as it has been and will never be again. In *A Grief Out of Season,* the authors explain that while growing up your children have a picture of their futures that you and their father are part of. You and he will come to their weddings, be there for graduations, holidays, and family visits. Divorce shatters all those expectations. Any holiday or celebration becomes fraught with anxiety over which of you will come, will you or he bring the new mate, how will you and your ex get along, should they separate you, seat you together, who should give the toast at the dinner, et cetera. If you think you're anxious about seeing your ex and his new wife at your daughter's wedding, be aware that she's just as anxious about how you'll react.

The bedrock sense of self that your children depend on to know who they are can be shaken by your divorce. They will reevaluate their childhoods in the light of the divorce and come up with different versions of who they were and who they are now. For instance, the daughter who was Daddy's princess and has internalized that sense of specialness will feel betrayed by his infidelity—and her sense of herself as special will be shaken. Debby, the army brat whose father left for the general's wife, says, "It was really hard on my brothers, who were young adults at the time my dad left. They were searching for a role model to look up to. It turned out my father wasn't such a good role model for us kids."

Adult children of divorce often start questioning the point of marriage and become more leery of dating and making a commitment. This can depend, however, on what their relationships are like when the divorce occurs. It can cut both ways. If they're in a good relationship, they may become more committed; if not it may be difficult for them to commit. Stella's oldest son and middle daughter both said that in some ways it made their relationships with their significant others stronger. "The thought of losing that other person made them look at them anew and evaluate what that person meant to them," she says. "My oldest daughter got married a year later. However, it affected my youngest negatively."

The losses go on and on, separating what was once one extended family. As families split apart and take sides, children who take your side in the divorce may stop seeing your in-laws—as could children who take their father's side. The logistics alone can be daunting, especially if everyone lives in different parts of the country. You and their father are no longer one unit, no longer Mom-and-Dad. They have to deal with two of everything: two phone calls to keep in touch, two homes, two stepfamilies, dividing their time, trying not to make anyone jealous. Instead of being a source of comfort, parents become a source of anxiety.

Roles are reversed when there are adult children. You may start telling your troubles to your daughter, relying on her for emotional support, which can be hard on her. Or you may call your son every time something needs fixing in the house, which may make him feel too responsible for you.

"I would come home after school and see my mom in tears at the kitchen table and I felt obligated to sit there and comfort her," says eighteen-year-old, free-spirited Sara. "Her depression started to rub off on me. For a time I felt depressed and wanted to get away from my mother. I am young and just wanted to have fun but I felt like I was supposed to take of her."

Adult children often get caught in the middle of a nasty divorce, with each side vying for their approval. This can be intensely painful for adult children who are used to relying on their parents as the bedrock of their lives. "Divorce means watching the two people we love most turn against each other and sometimes try to destroy each other—and because we are adults we are privy to every excruciating detail," explains Brooke Lea Foster. "They push us to take sides, manipulating us with angry phone calls and emotional e-mails. Instead of sitting down and explaining what's happening, they suck us into the middle."

Adult children may even feel like they've lost their pasts. If they thought they had a happy childhood, they have to think again—to start examining if it was really happy, or if they were deluded. The family history comes into question. If you feel like you've lost your past, they will feel it just as acutely. They may even feel you stuck it out for them, which really can be hard to take—that makes them the cause of your unhappiness all those years. "Adult children lose their sense of belonging," Foster explains. "Divorce shatters their family and their concept of home. Something inside them dies."

The fallout from divorce keeps reverberating over the years, with every new family event, every graduation, wedding, birth, and funeral. Even grandparenting becomes fractured as adult children have to figure out which parent is going to visit their kids when.

HOW TO MAKE YOUR DIVORCE EASIER ON YOUR KIDS

The worst thing you can do is to expect your adult children not to feel strong emotions, not to feel grief and pain just as you do.

Encourage your children to talk about their feelings and try to understand what they're going through. Try to put yourself aside and let them have their own reactions to the divorce. Don't insist they agree with you that their father is a loser, cheater, or whatever else you think of him.

Melissa, who was twenty-four when her parents divorced, says, "It would have been nice if my mother could have recognized my emotions. I wish she had said to me, 'I recognize you're going through a difficult time and I'm sorry I'm not able to support you.' Instead she said, 'It's not your divorce, get over it.'"

The hardest thing to do when you are caught up in your own emotions is to be empathetic, but you will be proud of yourself in the long run if you can do this with your children no matter how old they are.

"Your kids may try to appear stronger than they are," Foster says. "They may appear as if they know what's best. But they're kids and they want to be able to call their mom when they're hurting. You always want to go home again no matter what."

Don't Put Them in the Middle

Putting kids in the middle is the worst fallout from parental divorce, according to all the experts. In these cases, kids had divided loyalties, never could be neutral, and would inevitably become estranged from one of the parents. To try to get your kids on your side, especially if their father left for another woman or is acting like a bastard, is almost irresistible. When I bad-mouthed my ex to Tina, it was supremely easy, because she was outraged at him to begin with. But it made me feel queasy, and I wish now I'd kept my mouth shut. Maybe she would have felt free to contact him and have a relationship with him eventually, which would be a good thing for her.

Foster says the worst stories she came across doing research for her book were the situations in which parents used the kids as messenger or to fight their battles. "There were times in my parents' divorce when I would claim to be neutral but would find myself arguing my mom's side with my dad, which made me profoundly uncomfortable," Foster says.

There is a tendency for parents to go to their adult children for advice. Of course if your husband is trying to screw you out of retirement benefits, you're going to want to tell the one person who can understand; it's natural. But every time you say something negative to your children about their father, you're tearing at their relationship.

It may take a supreme act of will not to try to get your kids to take sides, not to bad-mouth your ex, not to express jealousy when they visit him instead of you. Few of us are that saintly, but remember: You would somehow manage to do this with young children to protect them from being torn apart. You can restrain yourself with your adult children as well. If you lose control, you may regret it, as Stella did. She was sixty-two and her children ranged from midtwenties to thirties when her husband left her for another woman.

"I was very bad with the youngest one who lived here," Stella says ruefully. "She got to witness what I was going through because I didn't have any restraint. She witnessed a lot of the insanity, madness, flailing, and sorrow. I think it freaked her out and it was unfair to her. But that kind of emotionalism just spurts. It's like controlling drinking, drugging, or eating. When you have the compulsion, you can't stop. Seeing my kids triggered me about my marriage and the dissolution of family."

The daughter who saw her go through the worst of the divorce was the one who was negatively affected in the long run. She's with a man whom Stella feels is probably not the ideal candidate for a relationship, but she won't let go because of the fear of losing yet another man. She's even told Stella she's put up with behavior she shouldn't have because of this fear.

Even though you may be going through hell, remember that you're the mom, you'll always be the mom, and they still expect you to be the mom. The role of a mom is to protect their kids no matter how old they are.

Don't Depend on Your Kids for Support

The best scenarios were when moms turned to friends, other family, and therapists for support rather than their kids. This isn't easy, granted, especially for mothers and daughters. Mothers and daughters are close and naturally talk about emotions and feelings. It's just natural to turn to your best friend, your daughter. It's natural to analyze with her why the marriage went wrong, explain why things didn't work out, why he's a rat. Mothers wind up telling children things they shouldn't know. Debby, who had one of the worst post-divorce adjustments, was put in this position. She had to pick sides and sided with her mother, who told her things like, "Don't be fooled by your father because he always lies."

Melissa, who was twenty-four when her parents split and wound up in a happy marriage, is grateful that she wasn't put in the middle, and that her mother didn't rely on her for support. "Fortunately, she looked toward her friends for support," Melissa now says. "At the time I don't know if I could have offered much because I had enough grief and anger of my own. I tried not to side with either of my parents because they both screwed up in many ways. I went back and forth sometimes. It's hard not to." The good news is that adult children do learn positive lessons from their parents' divorce. Melissa is determined never to leave her husband for someone else. She also tries not to argue with him over petty nonsense. "I respect my husband, whereas my mother walked all over my father. It was her way or the high way."

Keep your feelings to yourself as much as possible, especially ones that are likely to really wound your children. Debby, who wound up drinking excessively until she got arrested for a DUI, says, "I feel like my mother hates one side of me because I am half my father. She doesn't like my adventurous side because it reminds her of him."

One of the most painful things a mom can say is, "You're the reason why we stayed together"—which, translated, means, "You're the reason I was miserable for so long." You will make your children feel like they were part of your pain, their childhood was a sham, and all those wonderful childhood moments were fake and phony. Childhood is something we treasure for life, and you don't want to take that away from your children.

Call a Truce with Your Ex

The biggest gift you can give your child is a peaceful and cooperative, if not necessarily friendly, relationship with your ex. It's especially important for you to validate their feelings about the past. Let them reminisce about the past without being negative. Don't try to revise their childhood memories by inserting negative information about what was going on in your marriage at the time.

You will inevitably have to see your ex at family functions and milestone events. Try to be civil at least, and friendly at best. Once enough time has passed, this should become easier—hopefully for both of you.

There are divorced parents who even come together for holidays and birthdays. I recently went to the birthday party of my daughter's friend Katrina, who lives around the corner. I was surprised to see her mother, her ex-husband, and her boyfriend all together at the party. Her boyfriend was doing magic tricks while her ex seemingly was appreciating the scene. When she first got divorced my neighbor was very angry at her ex—in fact, she complained about him to me many times—but she and her boyfriend still invited him for Thanksgiving, birthdays, and other family events. Her ex always came alone since he hadn't found a new partner, and they all had a peaceful time together. Recently, about six years later, I asked her how she felt about him and she actually said, "There's nothing I wouldn't do for him." I was amazed, and awed.

There are even those rare couples who manage to become good friends, even after an initially nasty divorce. I am in awe of

Kay, a fifty-eight-year-old administrator from Albany, New York, who, after going through a lot of rage and bitterness, not only has managed to stay friendly with Joe, her ex, but actually goes on trips with him, his wife Lisa (who, believe it or not, is her brother's ex-wife and her former best friend), and her kids who were eighteen, sixteen, and fourteen when they divorced after twenty-seven years of marriage. (I tell her story in chapter 11.)

"Joe and I maintained a relationship," Kay says. After he left she promised the kids that every Sunday night Dad would come to dinner—and she kept that promise. Even though she had to swallow the urge to retaliate at first, it was more important to her that her children continue to love their father because "he didn't try to hurt them, he was always there for them, and he continued his relationship with them as much as he could." She says her kids will be forever grateful to both of them. "When I see what a friend of mine's ex-wife has done to their kids because he left her for someone else, it makes me sick."

Kay's daughter Sarah agrees. Even though she was extremely "shocked, sad, hurt, and angry" when her parents announced (together) that they were splitting, she now says, "They are both great people, my parents, with three people at the center connecting them. But they never should have been married because they have conflicting personalities. They each went their own way for the better." This doesn't mean there was no fallout in her life, however. She says, "It's hard for me to date now. I want to find the perfect person and I don't want to get hurt. But I don't think divorce is the worst thing ever."

Give Them the News in a Compassionate Way
College students have a name for it: "the freshman call." Parents wait until their child has finished high school and is off to college

before getting a divorce, which they, or at least one of them, may have been planning for a long time. Their son or daughter is already going through the disorientation of being away from home for the first time, adjusting to being on his or her own, and hearing that her family is disintegrating can be profoundly disorienting.

How *Not* to Announce Your Divorce

On the phone. "The hardest thing is when you're away from home and the entire divorce plays out over the phone and e-mail," says Brooke Lea Foster, who went through her parents' divorce over the phone. "It's horrible. You get snippets and constantly feel like you should be there. You feel guilty, embarrassed. You're just getting to know people at college and are too embarrassed to be crying about Mom and Dad when you're being an adult for the first time. When you leave home you rely on home to ground you; when home has an earthquake rumbling under it, you're thrown for a loop."

At Christmas dinner. Your children will feel blindsided if they come home for the holidays only to find out their parents are getting divorced. "My father left right before Christmas and no matter what my mother said, it still would've been bad," Kara says, "though I would have liked her to say *It's going to be okay,* or *Be strong and you can always rely and count on me,* or *I'll always be here for you.* Unfortunately, her emotions got in the way and she was so depressed that she couldn't do or say these things for me."

Without telling your husband first. Adult children bitterly resent it when they feel that the news has been communicated in a sneaky, indirect, dishonest, humiliating, or unnecessarily brutal way. They especially resent it when they are left to break the news to the other parent.

Actually, the best way to tell adult children about your divorce is the same way the experts recommend telling small children. If at all possible, you and your husband should sit down with them together when they have some time to digest the news. If your children are in college, wait until they're home for a long break.

Don't lie. If you were the one who had an affair, own up to it. Don't try to lie to your kids, because someone will tell them and they'll be furious at you for it. If their father had the affair, don't cover up for him, either. They are grown-ups and can deal with it. If they ask about something, be straight with them—without trashing your ex in the process.

This doesn't mean that you should tell your kids every gory, excruciating detail of your divorce. They don't want to know every instance of infidelity or other transgressions. For Kara, "It's frustrating because my mother always wants to bring it up when I come home from college and I don't want to hear it anymore because it's the same story all the time. I get angry because it gets bothersome after a while, and then she gets angry. Sometimes I feel like she is a teenager in puberty because she is still always moody about it."

Don't shove your new boyfriend down your children's throats. When you become seriously involved, tell them casually and let them come to you for more information. Don't introduce him until you sense that they're ready. Ask if they're comfortable meeting him before you do make the introductions. If you're not sure that a new man is going to be a long-term relationship, wait until you are sure. The last thing you want to do is introduce a succession of lovers to your kids.

Give your boyfriend and them time to get to know each other. Don't make the first encounter an extended visit. If you're living with someone, wait until your children have met him a few times and feel comfortable with him before inviting them to stay with the two of you. If your kids are in college and come home for vacations, have him stay in his own place until they're comfortable with him.

Warn your partner *not* to act parental with your adult—or teen—kids. There's nothing more annoying to an adult child than someone trying to be her dad when she's grown up and barely knows him. Also, your partner should stay out of discussions about your ex or their childhood. "The step-parent who tried to revise the family's past or to mediate between parent and child was especially resented," according to the research done by Fintushel-Oxenhandler and Hilliard.

TEENS AND DIVORCE

Teens from divorced and remarried families leave home earlier and get into trouble more often, according to a large study by E. Mavis Hetherington reported on in her book *For Better or for Worse: Divorce Reconsidered.* The Virginia Longitudinal Study (VLS) looked at 1,400 families over three decades, including divorced and intact families. It found that girls in divorced families tend to get their periods and mature earlier, putting them at risk of early sexual activity and pregnancy. The reason for this isn't known, but it is a statistical reality.

Boys get into trouble at school and in the community. Teens are very vulnerable to peer influence, and as that influence grows, a divorced mom who is trying to reestablish her own life has neither the time nor energy to counter it. Hetherington offers some very sound advice for moms of teens:

Don't lose touch with your teen. Keep monitoring who he or she associates with.

Don't be too permissive. Adolescents who receive authoritative parenting are less likely to be involved with a delinquent peer group.

Remember that you are a role model for sexual behavior for your adolescent daughter. Difficult though it may be in the throes of your own sexual discovery period post-divorce, tone it down for your kids. An overtly sexual parent predisposes a child to early sexual initiation.

Try to find a mentor for your adolescent son if his dad isn't involved. Mentors can play a huge role in keeping boys out of trouble, by serving as role models, surrogate dads, confidants, advisers. One important characteristic of all successful children in the VLS was at least one caring and loving adult. In most cases this was a parent, but adult mentors could shepherd a child safely through divorce and remarriage.

Look for a structured, supportive school environment. An authoritative school can help protect against the adverse effects of nonauthoritative parenting.

IF YOU'RE IN YOUR . . .

Forties . . .

You may still have young children at home and have to deal with co-parenting. Unless you and your ex communicate well and there isn't any animosity, this can be an enormous challenge. I learned a lot from my own experience of co-parenting a young child and found the most helpful strategy when conflict arises is getting help from a therapist who has experience with children and divorce. It's almost impossible to avoid all the potential minefields on your own.

The worst mistake parents with young children make is putting the child in the middle. Always keep your child's welfare first when talking about your ex or making decisions.

Another mistake can be joint custody. They sound good on paper, but my lawyer says most joint custody arrangements fall apart eventually. Young children need stability, and traveling back and forth on top of the trauma of divorce can be too much for children. The best arrangement according to many experts is for one parent to have physical custody, with frequent visitation by the other, including weekends. Mom is still the preferred custodial parent in most divorce proceedings, but that trend is changing as more and more dads fight for custody, especially of older sons.

Fifties . . .

You may still have adolescent children at home, probably in their late teens. They may not be past the worst dangers of adolescence, which according to the VLS peak at fifteen in nondivorced homes but tend to continue past sixteen in divorced homes. All the advice above for younger teens applies.

Separation may become more of an issue. Children of divorce can be emotionally immature and more reluctant to leave the nest if their dad is gone. Don't push them out too soon if they still need parenting.

Even children in their twenties can be afraid to leave the nest after divorce. Or they may feel guilty about leaving. Don't hang on to your grown children because you're afraid of being alone. If you haven't found another partner, you may unconsciously be turning your adult child into a spouse substitute. If you have children in their twenties still living with you, take a look at what's keeping them with you. Are you projecting neediness? Have you told them you can take care of yourself? Have you encouraged them to move out?

If college is an issue, be straight with your kids about the family financial situation—what their dad is prepared to pay, what you can chip in, and what they will have to earn themselves. They may have to wake up to the rude reality that all their needs are no longer going to be provided for and they will have to do some providing for themselves.

Sixties or older . . .

You may have children in their thirties and forties with their own families, and assume that your divorce is not going to shake them up that much. It surprised me to find out that no matter how old adult children are, they almost always are going to be extremely upset by their parents' divorce. Your children may be *more* stunned than kids in their twenties, because by the time parents are in their sixties, adult children don't even consider that they might get divorced. The shock can be profound. However, they are likely to be able to deal with the divorce a lot better than college-aged children, because they're mature and settled in their own lives.

Evelyn Kaye, whose blog I quoted in the last chapter, finally left her husband at sixty-nine due to his infidelities, which had been going on during the entire forty-two years of their marriage. Her children were in their forties, and she decided to tell them the truth. They dealt with it very well, which undoubtedly had something to do with their being middle-aged and emotionally mature themselves. "My son and his wife lived near me and they'd seen it happening, but my daughter was in Oregon so she didn't see it," Evelyn relates. "It was very painful to them. My son stood by me, said whatever you want to do is okay, but be sure you know what you're doing. He and wife have been great to me, and kind to their father as well, as were the grandchildren. That's been very nice. My daughter, who'd been through a breakup herself, had a wonderful understanding of what I'd been through. We've got closer as a result. She's worked with her father, and she dealt with him better. Neither of them was angry with him. He was often absent while they were growing up, but his infidelity was a shock to them nonetheless. It's hard for your children to know what's going on in your marriage no matter how old they are."

Discuss who is going to care for their father (or you) if either of you become ill, or if he's already ill. At this age spouses know that one of them is likely to have to care for the other when illness strikes. Since women overwhelmingly live longer, they wind up caring for their husbands. In a late-life divorce, children have to shoulder a burden they thought was not going to be theirs until much later. "My father's a constant worry for me," says Paul. "My mother waited to leave until he was a feeble old man and couldn't take care of himself, which angers me." This prospect can be really difficult for your children, especially if they have young kids of their own.

If you have substantial assets and plan to remarry, get a prenuptial agreement to protect your children's inheritance. It will go a long way toward helping your kids accept your new spouse.

CHAPTER SEVEN
WHAT THE HELL HAPPENED TO YOUR MARRIAGE?

You Do *Need to Figure It Out*

While we'd like to think that time heals all wounds, the fact is that time doesn't heal—time passes. Insight heals. We can't get better until we understand what happened.

—DAPHNE ROSE KINGMA

While doing the work of grieving—and it is work—you will simultaneously be reevaluating and processing just about every assumption you have had in your entire life about love, relationships, and marriage. If you're in therapy, you will be talking about what happened to your marriage with your therapist. If you're not in therapy, I hope you have some wise friends to listen to you and help you gain insight into what happened.

Why bother digging up the past? you might ask. Isn't it better to just move on? Well, no, it isn't. The old saw *Those who don't learn from history are doomed to repeat it* applies. If you don't understand why your marriage failed, you will likely repeat the same mistakes. The divorce rate for second marriages is higher than for first ones. Also, even if you never marry again—and many of us won't—understanding what went wrong is a crucial part of being able to move on. Only with understanding can you get the clarity that will allow you to stop being angry and stop blaming either him or yourself. Understanding what happened is necessary to being able to forgive yourself as well as him.

There are some very interesting findings in the AARP study of divorce over fifty. Most women in their fifties or older said the top killers of their marriages were physical or emotional abuse, infidelity, and drug or alcohol abuse—and they put almost all of the blame on their ex-husbands. And a larger number of men, though not the majority, said it was their own fault. The one thing neither sex would take the blame for, however, was an affair. Among people fifty and older who said infidelity caused their divorce, 93 percent of women and 78 percent of men said their spouse was the one at fault.

These are, of course, the immediate precipitating factors that trigger a divorce, but the mystery is what kept these marriages together for so long. Many divorces occur in the first ten years of marriage. Why do some couples stay married for their whole adult lives and *then* break up? Usually something has changed—the kids leave home, your husband retires or falls in love with someone else (or you do), the drinking gets worse, the emotional abuse starts edging into the physical. In some way the balance of the relationship, which may have been fragile to begin with, tilts too far in one direction or another.

You can attribute the death of your marriage to the ostensible reasons for breakups, such as abuse, alcoholism, infidelity, or even growing apart. But if you're introspective, as I am, you will want to look beneath the surface. The inner search is very rewarding, and though it's often painful, it will go a long way toward helping you heal. You'll find out who you are, and who he is; you'll see what brought you together, and whether it was those very things that in the end drove you apart.

WHAT BROUGHT YOU TOGETHER?

A lot of us fell in love and got married because it was simply what you did at the time. We were expected to get married—and for those of us who were young in the 1950s, '60s, and '70s, those expectations were even stronger—so we married whoever we were seeing when the pressure got great enough, having no idea what we were getting ourselves into. We may have married someone because our parents approved of him, or, if we were rebels, because our parents disapproved of him. Nonetheless, we married someone who reminded us of our family of origin in some way.

I was a different person then. I never would have married him today. We grew apart over the years. Is this your explanation for the failure of your marriage? It's one I've heard over and over from divorced women. In one sense this may be true—but in another the seeds of the end of your marriage were there the day you met. The day I met Zeke, we went out for dinner at a neighborhood restaurant. During dinner he got angry with me about something, I don't even remember what. It never occurred to me that a man wasn't supposed to get angry on the first date, and if he did, there shouldn't be a second date. I thought I'd done something to make him angry, it was my fault and I had to behave better. What I've learned since then is that on some level, his anger was attractive to me. Both of my parents were angry at me a lot, for no good reason, so it felt familiar. I now realize that anger drew me because it was an opportunity to heal those childhood wounds, to finally please the angry dad so that he would love me.

"What attracted you to your spouse," asks Abigail Trafford in *Crazy Time.* "Were you very young? Did you need someone to give you what you didn't get from your parents?" She quotes Suzanne Keller, professor of sociology at Princeton University: "A lot of people have very low self-esteem when they get married. That means you are going to put a lot on the other person to make the world right for you."

Why does beauty marry the beast? No one could figure out what attracted my wealthy, classy friend Ginny to crude, obnoxious Hank. Ginny was slim, cute, and charming; she radiated the kind of class that you can't buy off the rack—it only comes from growing up with money. She had the kind of effortless appeal to men that I've always envied, so I, and the rest of her friends, were stunned when we met Hank, who, though tall and good looking with a charming Australian accent, was also supercilious and shockingly nasty, with a vicious sense of humor. The weird thing was that Ginny wasn't fooling herself about him—she knew just who he was and how obnoxious he was. She thought it was amusing. She got a kick out of his bad-boy behavior. Her family hated him and was dead-set against the marriage. Her friends felt the same. She kept asking me if she should marry him and I kept saying she'd be sorry if she did, but she seemed bonded to him by a glue that was a lot stronger than Elmer's. It was clear to me that he was a social climber who was attracted by her wealthy background and hoped it would rub off on him.

Predictably, her marriage was miserable. He became the kind of hypercritical, bullying, nasty husband we now call verbally and emotionally abusive. He belittled her in front of her friends. In fact, he belittled her friends in front of her as well. I myself was intimidated by him. After they had a son, she went to medical school and wound up supporting the family since Hank was a store manager who made very little. Ginny complained constantly about Hank, but her ostensible reason for staying was her fear that he would never share custody peacefully and would try to turn her son against her. The real reason was that she didn't feel she deserved better. Another reason was that Hank rode shotgun for her—he was the one who stood up to her family. He told off her father and brothers, who were as nasty as Hank, when she didn't have the nerve. Even though she was Daddy's favorite, they put her down constantly.

When her son was a teen, Ginny ran into an old flame, a man who'd wanted to marry her when she was young. Back then she saw him as too adoring, without enough of an edge. But when they met again, she was in her late forties, and she realized what a mistake she'd made. Although he was married with kids, he still carried a torch for her, and she realized that she felt the same way about him—actually always had. They had everything in common; he made her laugh, and he was a decent, caring guy. He was the one she should have married.

No, they didn't run off with each other. But it was a turning point. She finally understood on a visceral level that she didn't have to put up with her husband's vicious, unfeeling abuse. She started seeing herself through the eyes of her old boyfriend, as a desirable, fascinating, sexy woman. She realized in midlife that she didn't want to spend the rest of her days as a punching bag, and left Hank.

To figure out where your marriage went astray, ask yourself what attracted you to your spouse at the start. Were you very young? Did you need someone to give you what you didn't get from your parents? It takes time and racking up some accomplishments before you feel worthy on your own. It took Ginny going to medical school and becoming a successful doctor before she could feel good enough about herself to leave Hank.

Think back to your first date. What was your first impression of him? You can tell everything you need to know about someone during the first fifteen seconds, according to my former therapist

Jim Walters. That might sound a bit flip, but sometimes first impressions, like "That guy doesn't have much to say," are truer than all the rationalizations we quickly pile on top of them, such as "He may not talk much because he's the strong, silent type, or he's just shy."

If I'd paid attention to the first fifteen seconds of our first date, I wouldn't have wound up with my husband. He was much younger than me, jobless, dressed in shabby clothes, and so shy he could barely speak. I rescued him from a marginal existence and gave him a life. Why did I do that? I was forty-one, weighed 235 pounds, and was sure no one else would ever have me. Rescuing him was my first mistake. You might think he'd be grateful, but you would be oh-so-wrong. Men hate being dependent on a woman, and the more she does for them the more punishment they'll eventually mete out. My girlfriends, however, thought I was deliciously avant-garde for hooking up with a much younger man. It was a new trend at the time, and I liked being on the cutting edge. Jim, however, told me the only danger was that Zeke would grow up and leave home someday. That was prophetic. Like so many of my girlfriends at the time, I was into the *Women Who Love Too Much* syndrome. No wonder that book by Robin Norwood was a best seller. So many of us picked a guy with "potential" and tried to mold him into the man of our dreams. Unfortunately, he more often turned out to be the man of our nightmares.

DID YOU MARRY THE WRONG MAN?

Bob, the guy I fell madly in love with after my marriage broke up, who had been through a similarly sterile marriage, had a theory about why so many marriages fail: He said that when you marry the wrong person, the worst thing is that you come to love that person, just through sharing the same bed, the same children, the same tragedies and triumphs. But he's still the wrong person except now you're stuck with him, unable to extricate yourself once the knots of everyday life have bound you together. Still, the marriage is doomed and eventually will fall apart. Bob, a laid-back tennis pro, married an ambitious corporate executive. He spent twenty-five years feeling inferior to her; she never accepted his lack of ambition. They were mismatched from the get-go. Now, if he'd married a flaky artist like me, it might have worked out!

Marion, a fifty-four-year-old librarian, says she married her husband for all the wrong reasons. "My friends disagreed. They said, 'You married him for the right reasons, he just wasn't the right guy.' When I met my husband he swept me off my feet. He was seventeen years older than me, had a Ph.D. from Columbia, worked at a nonprofit helping children, had a home, was solid, steady, smart, foreign, he could cook. Compared to him it seemed like the guys I had dated before were kids. He was solid and mature."

She didn't know it when she married him, but he was an alcoholic. Somehow she stuck it out for twenty-seven years because, as she puts it, "I'm a tough Irish broad. I'm good at making lemonade out of lemons."

When he retired all hell broke loose. "He just shut down, drank more, became solitary, and even moved out of the bedroom. Ultimately he hit me and that was my breaking point. When I left we were fighting and he was punching me in the head." Marion lost everything when she left her marriage, including her husband's extended family to whom she was extremely close. They totally cut her off. She even has to pay alimony, but despite it all, she was relieved to just be away from her abusive drunk of a husband.

Many women marry the wrong guy and then go into denial about it because they don't want to rock the boat. Meantime that boat keeps taking on water over the years. Even though it's slowly sinking, you delude yourself into thinking that it will stay afloat forever. Every once in a while, you do a little bailing, try to fix it, maybe go to counseling, make an effort to communicate, but eventually you give up. Your husband doesn't bother to bail at all. Then a few more waves wash over the bow and before you know it you're underwater.

It's surprising Zeke and I lasted as long as we did. I now see we were more like mother and teenage son than lovers, complete with tantrums on his end and lectures on mine. We shared some values and had a lot in common intellectually, but none of that was anywhere near enough. You also may have realized by now that the glue that you thought held your marriage together was more like the backing on Post-its—hardly sticky at all. Like me, you may have been your own worst enemy when it came to your marriage, the last to know that your marital ship was sinking.

DID HE HAVE INTEGRITY?

Integrity is one of those old-fashioned qualities we are too naive, too lacking in life experience to value when we're young—other qualities seem so much more important, like looks, charm, intelligence, money, successful career, family background, even a sense of humor. What twenty-two-year-old girl in love gives a hoot about integrity? However, it's integrity that can make or break a marriage—make or break a life, in fact. Men with integrity make a commitment and stick to it, through hell and high water. They don't run off with the chickie at the next desk as soon as male midlife crisis hits.

I knew my husband lacked integrity when he refused to bring me to his company picnic because I was overweight and he worried that I might embarrass him. Eventually he changed his tune on that issue, but doing the right thing wasn't high on his agenda, especially if it wasn't easy. He also lied a lot, mostly about little things like whether he'd done something I'd asked him to do. It was so much easier to lie than to face my wrath.

"Our marriage started with an affair and ended with an affair," Stella told me ruefully. She might have known her husband lacked integrity because he had an affair with her while married to someone else. But she was only twenty-three and dazzled by him. "I was the other woman. Initially I wasn't going to marry him because of shame and guilt but then he broke up with his wife. When his wife remarried I changed my mind. From then on I decided I'd make a good marriage to atone for my sins." Stella is one of the many divorced women who told me, "We were the perfect couple." They were married thirty-three years. "I'd say we had an excellent twenty and then it started to go downhill because of his drinking. When he told me about his affair—I was absolutely blindsided. He's always been flirtatious and had 'girlfriends' but had never done this before. I cannot tell you how shocked I was. I trusted him more than anyone on the planet and never thought he'd do that after our history, but he did." Now she wonders why she was so surprised, considering how their marriage started.

So many women find out too late that their husbands lack integrity, and it's always a shock. Integrity is one of those qualities that seems like a given. Only bad guys cheat and steal and lie, right? You would never do such a thing. When our husbands do it, we are stunned—how could this guy who was always so "nice," who loved the children, who took care of his parents, was a great employee, and wouldn't hurt a living soul do such a thing? I have heard of some really shocking things men do, like maintaining two separate families and lying to both wives for a lifetime, like gambling away the house and the family savings, like leaving their wives *and* never speaking to their kids again. It boggles the mind. The reality is that integrity is rare. It's a precious attribute that only the strongest people have. Very few older men leave their wives without finding another woman first. In my mind the ones who do (and I dated one post-divorce) are the guys with integrity.

DID YOUR SEX LIFE STINK?

Sex is the canary in the coal mine. It's the first thing to go when a marriage is in trouble. Zeke and I fought about sex like so many couples who have been married for a long time. He always wanted it, I never did. At the very beginning I enjoyed having sex with him, but sex quickly became a chore. I convinced myself that the sex thing was my fault—after all, I was the one who consistently rejected him. There must be something wrong with me. I had a litany of reasons: I was sure my self-esteem issues had sealed my fate. I couldn't be turned on to a man who truly loved me. I must have some deep fear of intimacy that wouldn't allow me to get close to my husband sexually. I conveniently forgot about his rages and constant criticism. It was a fiction that we both maintained so we could stay married.

If you are the least bit like I was and avoided sex with your husband, you were also avoiding the underlying issues in your marriage. Sex is not just sex, it's an early warning system for all the problems you want to avoid confronting. If your husband avoided sex with you, the alarm bells should have been deafening. Couples make up all kinds of excuses for the lack of sex in their marriages, but there's *always* something else going on.

Shortly after that fateful Christmas when Zeke told me he was leaving, I visited a therapist and told her about the lack of sex in my marriage. She asked if I had any sexual problems. Was I sexually dysfunctional in any way? Could I have orgasms? I told her that I used to love sex before I got married but I always had the hots for unavailable men, adding that I'd always assumed that I wasn't turned on to my husband because he always wanted me. Somehow I thought this would miraculously change because his true love would win me over. Then I thought maybe I was frigid or something, or lacking in some hormones. All I know is I always felt guilty. In one sentence she destroyed the myth that had sustained our marriage. "Sex is *always* a function of the relationship," she said emphatically.

Always!! This wasn't exactly a penetrating insight. I'd just never considered it before, probably because I would have had to do something about it. It was the *always* that got me. Then I thought about it. How could I be turned on to a man who was always furious at me, who punished me with his helplessness, whom I had contempt for? I was his mother, not his mate. That should have been obvious, but I was floating down that proverbial river in Egypt for eighteen whole years.

Does this sound familiar? How was your sex life when your marriage was going downhill? My scenario is extremely common in dysfunctional marriages. The husband wants more sex, the wife wants more affection and communication, wife punishes husband by refusing sex, husband retaliates by throwing his socks on the floor or forgetting her birthday or flying into rages. Or, perhaps even worse, wife wants sex and husband avoids it like the plague, accusing wife of having gotten fat, or not taking care of herself. My girlfriend Valerie was married to a guy who doled out sex like it was a nonrenewable resource. She finally got fed up when he refused to have sex with her on her birthday. At the time, she was going to a Rolfer, and she fell into an extremely passionate affair with him. When she told her husband she wanted a divorce, he couldn't move out of the house fast enough. A few weeks later she decided she wanted to try to save the marriage but it was too late, he wasn't interested.

It was an enormous relief to me to find out that the lack of sex wasn't all my fault after all—we had a screwed-up relationship, and the responsibility belonged to both of us. Whew! I was at least guilt-free in that department, though still cheated on and dumped. The lesson here is that sex is not just sex, it's a stand-in for just about everything else that went wrong with your marriage. Don't fool yourself, girlfriend. If sex isn't working, nothing is working.

WERE YOU SOUL MATES OR CELLMATES?

The idea of soul mates is relatively new. It wasn't much in vogue when I was doing personals dating back in the 1970s. It's become a cliché since then, but in fact the more levels on which two people connect, the deeper their union becomes. The soul level is the most mysterious—maybe it even has to do with knowing each other in past lives (call me flaky, I don't care). And there is a power balance that must be maintained or the whole thing falls apart. That soul connection is based on intimacy, which was missing from my marriage—and was probably missing from your marriage if you're now in divorce court. I thought Zeke and I were intimate but I was mistaking common intellectual interests, values, sense of humor, and the same outlook on life for intimacy.

So what exactly is this elusive quality called intimacy? Why is it so difficult to find? Why is our longing for it so mixed with fear? My guru shrink Jim long ago gave me the best explanation of intimacy I've ever heard. If I'd actually paid attention to what he said, I never would have married Zeke, but I was desperate for a mate, and that trumped common sense. Basically, according to Jim, intimacy in marriage means nothing more than good, direct communication in the context of a sexual relationship. This sounds almost simplistic, but the problems in maintaining such communication can be formidable. "Intimacy is possible only between two people who have a strongly felt and accurate sense of who they are—people who intuitively feel okay about themselves," Jim told me.

Therapists will tell you that most of us are hiding something. Paradoxically, the part that we're hiding may be pretty obvious. I thought I was hiding my fear of being left, but my need for constant reassurance gave it away. When we search for intimacy, we're trying to have verified the part of ourselves that we like the best while ignoring and repudiating the part we secretly hate. According to Jim intimacy demands that, over time, *all* of a person be shared with all of another person. It's a question not of saying everything but of hiding nothing.

This *includes* sharing our weakest, shakiest aspects—ways in which we don't feel as good about ourselves as we'd like the world to think we do. Of course, sharing our insecurities with someone else means sharing them with ourselves. And many people find it enormously difficult to look at themselves squarely and face how scared they feel inside. Instead, most keep trying to find verification of that false version of themselves. This kind of communication is what marriage counselors should teach if they're doing their job.

Sex is often used as a cheap substitute for intimacy. The act itself doesn't take all that much time or effort, and it allows the partners to fantasize a sense of closeness that doesn't really exist. Remember this, girlfriends, when you start dating again. In a love relationship, sex can *deepen* what *is* there—but it can't *create* what *isn't* there. A sexless marriage is a strong sign that intimacy is lacking. However, some couples have great sex but are still not intimate.

Intimacy isn't limited to a sexual relationship, by the way. It's possible between any two people who care about each other. What must be there is the willingness to reveal one's true self, mutual trust and understanding, the sharing of feelings and experiences, and the continuity of a relationship that has lasted over time. We girlfriends can be more intimate with each other than we are with our husbands. In fact, that's often the case. But ideally you are intimate with your girlfriends *and* your husband.

For a nation used to working hard for rewards, it is ironic that we expect intimacy to materialize instantly and effortlessly. It takes both time and effort. Two people need months or even years to achieve a clarity of communication, a sense of belonging, a sharing of events and time. Like any other worthy endeavor, achieving true intimacy takes consistent hard work.

A real commitment based on intimacy involves an emotional bond rather than a legal one. Jim explains it as "a bond you don't wish to dissolve because it's simply too precious. That means being self-aware enough to know when you're in a real relationship. It also means knowing that the next thing shared by people who have already shared a lot is much more precious than the first, even though that first thing seems precious always."

Did you ever have this kind of intimacy with your husband? I know I didn't. A marriage can limp along for a long time without intimacy, but there will always be a sense of emptiness to it, a feeling that something important is missing. You can cover up the lack of intimacy by focusing on other things, like the kids, work, or even mutual interests, but eventually it will catch up with you.

WAS YOUR MARRIAGE OUT OF BALANCE?

Relationships are a delicate balancing act. They may seem to be weighted on the side of one partner or another, but it's always two sides of a coin. Each spouse has to have an equal amount of power in the relationship or the marriage is doomed. It's very revealing to look at your marriage in light of the power balance to get some insight into what went wrong.

Abigail Trafford brilliantly dissects how power imbalances undo marriages in *Crazy Time*. When I read it I had one of those aha moments. Suddenly I understood on an even deeper level what went wrong with my marriage. According to Trafford, the time bomb for crisis is set early, often as soon as two people meet. "You think you're marrying because you're in love; he's so handsome, warm, sensitive, successful, funny. But there's always something else going on unconsciously. We marry to complete ourselves, to get whatever it is we think we don't have. We make a contract early on that we're totally unaware of. One of us is the dominant one, the one who controls the course of married life. The other is the submissive one who is the pleaser or appeaser." In traditional marriages the man is the dominant one and the woman submissive. Ironically, it's often the submissive partner who gets fed up and leaves, to the shock and horror of the dominant one. This may explain why the majority of late-life marriages are ended by wives—who are more likely to be dominated by their husbands.

WERE YOU DEADLOCKED?

Most marriages start out unequal, but if we're lucky they balance themselves as time goes on. Roles can be renegotiated, and power should switch back and forth. Sometimes you are submissive, your husband dominant; other times vice versa. Even in a traditional marriage this can happen, if both partners accept their roles and feel that they both pull their weight equally in the marriage. The key is that they have to treat each other with respect and give each other autonomy. If you're unlucky, like me, your marriage winds up in what Trafford calls deadlock—you both get stuck in your positions and no one moves.

Deadlock can be caused by almost any issue that couples disagree about. For Willa, an old hippie now in her fifties, deadlock struck when her husband put his "principles" first and supporting his family second. She had escaped her uptight, Jewish bourgeois suburban lifestyle to marry a strong-and-silent-type mountain man who worked as a forest ranger. "He was a free spirit, intelligent, self-educated, fit, a spiritual seeker, we had lots in common," she told me. "He was a very independent-minded thinker. I always liked that, someone who figures life out for themselves. He'd done a lot of traveling, been to India. I was looking to get married and have kids. I was in love when I conceived my oldest but I might not have married him if I wasn't pregnant. I moved to Idaho because I thought it was a good place to have kids and then I met him—it seemed like a divine plan."

They lived in a cabin in the mountains where they had to literally haul water from a stream and use a generator for electricity. It was romantic, until they had kids and she discovered he was an "off-the-grid" extremist who wouldn't get a Social Security card, driver's license, or any other trappings of middle-class American life. Eventually the charm wore off. "He didn't pay taxes. One year he had a government job, got audited, and we had to pay an enormous tax debt. I was furious. If he'd filed a return, we would have gotten money back, but he refused. That was the beginning of the end." They were deadlocked for years while she warned him that she'd divorce him if he didn't go on the "grid" and start living like a normal person, but he didn't believe her. When she finally handed him the divorce papers, he begged and pleaded and promised to change. It was too late. She finally walked out on him.

In deadlocked marriages, the power balance between husband and wife mimics the psychological dynamics between parent and child, lord and vassal, lady and servant. "You can spot the signs of couples trapped in Deadlock by noticing who is afraid of whom," says Trafford. "Submissive spouses tend to invest a tremendous amount of power in their mates and sigh a lot. Dominant partners often treat their spouses with contempt and scowl a lot."

She was dead-on about my marriage except for the scowling and sighing, which was the other way around. My husband had a fearsome scowl, and I would tiptoe around trying to avoid one of his tantrums. However, I sure did treat him with a lot of contempt. In my marriage, as in the 1950s TV stereotype of the take-charge wife and bumbling husband, I was the dominant partner and he was the henpecked husband. On TV the henpecked husband just carries on good-naturedly and puts up with being treated like a lamebrain. In real life, though, the henpecked husband is also the passive-aggressive one who punishes his wife by undermining her and, in my case, leaving her for someone else.

"Without equality in a relationship," says psychologist Robert Kirsch, "there can be no wanting of each other, no tenderness or respect. Sex goes to hell. It's only a matter of time before a couple reaches a crisis in a marriage." However, a "matter of time" can be twenty, thirty, or more years. In this context equality doesn't mean you have to reach the feminist ideal of complete sharing of roles. In fact, you can stick to traditional roles and still be equal. In our parents' day—when sex roles were very different and more defined—there were many happy marriages. The key is balance. Each partner has to feel like the other is pulling his or her weight, and each must feel respected and valued. When something changes in the marriage, often the "contract" that keeps you in balance has to be renegotiated. That's where a lot of marriages fall apart—especially when children are born or, in the case of older couples, when they leave—or when one or both spouses retires.

In fact, sometimes a happy couple doesn't seem to be balanced, but if you look more closely they are, even if an unexpected way.

My girlfriend Tara, an accomplished scientist, is married to Ken, who seemingly dominates her completely. She submissively defers to him before they make plans, lets him decide what kind of lifestyle they have, what purchases they make, who their friends are, how they spend their time. She doesn't protest when he clutters up the house with his computer equipment. However, she manages the finances, and he is very dependent on her emotionally. Before they met he was extremely depressed and had been unemployed for years. He is now a successful marketing consultant, and gives Tara all the credit for how his life has improved. He worships her as a person, and is never critical of anything she does. He is also very supportive of her career, and encourages her aspirations. I think she likes being submissive and having a man make decisions for her. I'd hate it, but it makes her feel taken care of and fulfilled. The bedrock of their relationship is mutual respect, something Zeke and I never had. Their relationship might have been thrown out of balance if they'd had a child, which is what happened to us.

Like most couples we limped along with our imbalance until something came along to throw us totally out of whack—Dorothy. All hell broke loose once we adopted a child. Our marital contract needed renegotiating, but we didn't even know what it was, much less how to change it. I was more or less used to and comfortable being in charge and taking care of everything, but I resented the hell out of Zeke for being so helpless and dependent. When Dorothy came along I felt I didn't have the energy or the will to take care of both of them, and I insisted he take over the primary parent role for our daughter. Unlike parenting a teenager, which I did with ease, I found to my horror that that being a mom of a small child was exhausting and no fun at all. Zeke took over primary parenting reluctantly, but hated me for forcing him into it. I had violated our unspoken contract—that I would take care of everything, including him *and* our daughter. He accused me of being selfish and a bad mother, which had a nugget of truth to it. I didn't throw myself into mothering the way I should have. I was too old, it was too exhausting, and I wasn't very good at it. Sex went from minimal to nonexistent. We went from mutual toleration to all-out war.

WHAT CHANGED WHEN YOU HIT MID- OR LATE LIFE?

"You have to admit that 'I'm having a midlife crisis' sounds a lot better than 'I'm a narcissistic jerk having a meltdown,'" said Richard A. Friedman, M.D., in an article he wrote about the male midlife crisis in the *New York Times*. How true. Midlife crisis used to strike in the forties, but these days it seems to extend indefinitely. A man may have achieved all his financial and career goals and wonder if that's all there is. A wife who's been around for twenty or thirty years, who has wrinkles and sags and bags, is a reminder of how he's now on the long slide to the grave. The balance shifts, giving him more power, since older men are often attractive to young women due to their position or wealth. These days they even have Viagra so they can satisfy a younger woman sexually. Since he can't be young again, what he can do is hook up with a younger woman who gives him the illusion of youth. We older women, however, who are judged on our looks, don't have similar options. It's a cruel reversal of the power balance between the sexes that comes with age.

Sometimes the age imbalance is subtle and easily missed until it's too late. For instance, at a divorce retreat in Texas I shared a room with Susan, a Texas matron in her sixties, a plain-looking, large woman who wore a typical southern-matron pink sweatpants outfit. I had never seen anyone in worse emotional shape. She cried nonstop. She literally could not say good morning without bursting into tears.

It seems she had been happily married for thirty years to her childhood sweetheart. They had one grown daughter and were looking forward to retirement. They had everything planned out: where they were going to move when they retired, and what they were going to do. Play a lot of golf I think. She'd had a perfectly happy life in every way, a happy small-town childhood with parents who loved her, and then a peaceful, blissful marriage with a man she adored. Her daughter was successful and happily married herself. Everything seemed perfect until her husband came home one day and announced that he was leaving; it seems he'd met another—younger, of course—woman. Bye-bye Susan. So what else is new? Happens to everyone, right? But it shouldn't have happened to her. I'd never met anyone like her—she was as innocent, naive, and guileless as a child, not a cynical New Yorker like me, who had been dumped before, or a tough southern babe like the other women at the retreat.

Of course she, like me, hadn't paid attention to the power balance. She was the successful one, the one who made all the money; he drifted from job to job. As I've said before, men *hate* being dependent on a woman. No matter how nice she was to him, he was bound to resent her. Facing retirement and lifelong dependency, he was a midlife crisis waiting to happen. All it took was a young chickie to lure him away and it was all over.

Older women, who statistically are in the majority when it comes to initiating divorce, also start feeling their mortality with age. Especially when the kids get older or leave, they allow themselves to feel that they, too, deserve a life. Connie is in her sixties and is planning to end her thirty-year marriage because she is completely emotionally estranged from her husband. They were close, or she thought they were, once upon a time when they were both fiery radicals in the 1960s, but he long ago sank into the slough of despond. It's been a long time since they slept in the same room or even had a decent conversation. She's just waiting until the house is fixed up so they can sell it and split the profits. Men, it seems, have much more tolerance for emotional estrangement than women. Connie says that as long as her husband has enough to eat, a place to sleep, and a TV to watch, he's happy. I've heard this story over and over, as has Deirdre Bair, who interviewed hundreds of older divorcées for *Calling It Quits*, her book about late-life divorce. A typical situation she discovered was a long-term marriage in which the man becomes a depressed lump in the house and the woman feels her only option is divorce. One of Bair's interviewees, a woman in her eighties who had been married for fifty-three years, woke up after transplant surgery and announced to her husband, "I don't know how many years I have left but I don't want to spend them with you."

On the AARP Divorce Forum, "Barb" posted: "Last night, after 25 years of marriage my husband and I decided to split. I stayed for the children and in hopes things would change. I have been controlled by my husband for years. Last year we saw a marriage counselor but he insisted any problems were always me. I have two daughters. One is twenty-five and will be a dentist in two years. The little one just finished her second year of college. My daughters came to me a few years ago and said 'Mom, we would love to do something with you that you like to do, but we do not know what you like.' I cried! I didn't know what I liked either. No one had ever asked me what I liked. So I decided it was time Mom started to find out."

On the same forum "Helen" posted: "After 26 years of marriage and years of wanting to leave I finally found the courage to get divorced. I too waited until my daughters were on their own. The frustrating thing was that many people thought there must be someone else . . . well there was, myself."

FIGURING IT OUT

If you're interested in deconstructing your marriage, make a road map of where you started, the trip you took, and the final destination. This self-analysis has a very practical purpose. Once you see the entire trajectory of your marriage, you can also see the inevitability of its dissolution. This realization will help you move on.

Ask yourself:

How did your relationship start? How did you meet? What attracted you to him? Did he resemble anyone in your family of origin? Were there telltale signs at the very beginning? In my case my husband got angry at me on the first date. In Stella's case he had an affair with her while married to someone else.

How did you feel about yourself at the time? Were you a femme fatale or a wallflower? How did your parents treat you? Were they critical or complimentary when you were a teenager? Even though she was her dad's favorite, Ginny's mom and brothers were extremely critical, so despite her looks and charm she was still convinced that no desirable man would want her. A narcissistic, critical mother can wreak havoc on a girl's self-esteem. My mom was a master of the barbed comment, especially about my weight, and I still don't feel good about the way I look. It's no wonder I married a man who was more interested in my ability to take care of him than in my looks. Did you marry your husband to boost your self-esteem?

Did you or he have unfinished developmental tasks? If you're looking for a positive spin on divorce, try Daphne Rose Kingma's *Coming Apart*. She explains that we not only marry in order to heal the emotional wounds of childhood but also to complete certain developmental tasks. We divorce when those wounds are healed or those tasks completed. Relationships can end gracefully when the developmental process is complete for both partners. Rather than being forever, relationships have life-times—beginnings, middles, and endings. Long-term marriages are more likely to have gone through these stages, completing the developmental process for at least one partner, and so are ready to end. Ginny completed the developmental task of becoming an accomplished woman in her own right who could stand up to her family by herself. In my case, I believe my husband completed the developmental process of growing up while married to me. Unfortunately, I was stuck in the same space of fear and dependency as when we married.

What changed in the balance of your marriage? There is usually some triggering event that upsets the precarious balance of a deadlocked marriage. It may be an affair, a midlife crisis, children leaving home, retirement. Or it may be a triggering event like Ginny running into an old boyfriend, our adopting a baby, Willa's husband's run-in with the IRS. A triggering event doesn't necessarily change the balance, but it does bring the reality of your deadlocked marriage into such sharp relief that it's impossible for you to stay in denial about it anymore.

IF YOU'RE IN YOUR . . .

Forties . . .

This is the dangerous midlife passage. Both men and women get restless and ask themselves if this is all there is. Patterns that seemed fixed forever get called into question. Wives who are going into menopause may become less sexual and more moody, which may provide an excuse for their husbands to stray. Men can be under a lot of stress at work, under pressure to prove themselves to younger colleagues and bosses. The balance in a marriage can shift at this point, especially if you go back to work and your husband starts feeling neglected. If you have teenagers who are becoming sexual, you both may start to wonder what happened to the hot sex you used to have.

Fifties . . .

Kids leave home around this time, so you may be left with a guy you barely know. This is prime midlife-crisis time for men, who are still attractive to younger women and are feeling their mortality. They all of a sudden start spending a lot of time at the gym, get a hair transplant, or a new wardrobe. Before you know it they're hanging out with someone named Jennifer. Affairs are common. With the kids in college, they no longer give your marriage a focus and purpose. If there's an imbalance in your marriage, it will become glaringly obvious in the fifties. The stories of men who dump their wives during this time are legion. You, on the other hand, may be really sick of putting up with an emotionally empty relationship and have no interest in taking care of the lump on the living room couch anymore.

Sixties or older . . .

Men retire in their sixties. All of a sudden you're faced with a guy who's there all the time and who is mourning the loss of his identity—his job. He's depressed and taking it out on you. Your retirement plans may get derailed by his behavior. You may have a career of your own that you're not willing to give up to retire with him. Retirement can really do in a marriage that was limping along somehow until then. You may be sick of being the caretaker; you may see time slipping away and want a life of your own before it's too late. Your children may be grown, with children of their own, and not need you anymore. You may feel that it's finally time for you, and your children can deal with it if you leave. Women in their sixties are likely to be the leavers when a late-life marriage ends.

CHAPTER EIGHT
REINVENTING YOURSELF

How to Become Who You Really Are

There's an enormous advantage to getting divorced when you're older. You've completed your adult tasks of raising children and pleasing a husband. You're more resilient, you've survived some crises already such as possibly the illness and death of your parents, you've coped, you can put things into perspective. Now you get to carve your own life instead of waiting for another sculptor to carve it for you.

—ABIGAIL TRAFFORD

Who were you when you got married? Did you have any idea? If you got married in your early twenties, as so many older divorcées did, you were probably clueless.

Either you hadn't found out yet who you were, or you gave up part of yourself to be who you thought your husband wanted you to be. The best marriages allow the partners to discover themselves, to change and grow. If you're reading this book, you probably weren't in one of these marriages—and in fact, not too many people are. Marriage is not an institution that encourages self-discovery.

Maybe you married a man who told you who he wanted you to be. You may have organized your life around his, done what he wanted, and supported his goals. You may not have known what your own needs and wants were. Even if you had some idea, marriage itself can turn women into clones of their own moms. All of a sudden the spunky girl who hitchhiked through Europe at twenty, or studied microbiology, or sang in nightclubs becomes a "wife-and-mother." This role can be pretty constricting—even more so twenty years ago when you started raising your kids.

People are getting divorced at older ages because life doesn't end at forty anymore. Women see they can fall in love, marry, travel, make new friends, and start a new career or business at fifty, sixty, and even older. We see a future for ourselves where before there was none. At this point in your life you have the luxury of going back to square one, of finding out who that quirky, independent, outspoken woman is who has been hiding under that wife-and-mother identity all these years. This task can be immensely scary as well as exhilarating.

THE "WIFE" SYNDROME

To free us from the expectations of others, to give us back to our-selves—there lies the great, singular power of self-respect.

—JOAN DIDION

No matter how much we try to be true to ourselves, marriage changes us, makes us into "wives," who by definition defer to their husbands. I never thought this would happen to me because though I was the daring older woman who turned the tables on the traditional male–female roles by marrying a younger man. Boy, was I wrong. I had to tone myself down to not piss off my self-conscious, fearful husband who would do anything to avoid embarrassment. I couldn't talk too loud, say anything too outrageous, change tables in restaurants or seats in the theater, or call attention to myself—or worse, to him—in any way. I can't say I managed to turn into a well-behaved wife, but I sure tried. My divorce allowed me to become again who I once was, a ballsy broad who doesn't give a damn what people think. What a relief that was.

Men can kill your self-esteem and turn your lioness into a meek lamb. Meredith, an accomplished economist and teacher, who left her lawyer husband when she was fifty-five because he had destroyed her self-esteem with his domineering, controlling personality and constant put-downs, says, "I had a bad self-esteem problem prior to the divorce because I'd been listening to him tell me for years that I was stupid, dumb, a bad teacher and a bad mother. That's why our kids had problems, according to him. Anything that happened was my fault. He was so mean that I was going to write a book called *At Least He Never Hit Me.* I'm still in the process of figuring out who I am." Meredith adds thoughtfully, "It's a fun adventure, but very painful. You have to reach down into your core and find out you're to blame, too. I had to admit I allowed him to do these things, I shouldn't have."

For just one example, Meredith's dream vacation was to go to Chichen Itza. For her entire marriage she told her husband that's where she wanted to go. But despite taking vacations in Mexico seven times, they never went to Chichen Itza, because he always wanted to go to Acapulco or Mexico City. "I should have said I want to go to Chichen Itza or gone by myself," she says now. "I let him talk me out of it. After we'd been divorced for five to six months, I called my old high school boyfriend and we started dating. It took a lot of courage to call, but it was great fun. When I told him I wanted to go to Chichen Itza, he made reservations."

LIFE TRANSITIONS

Divorce is one of life's major transitions, and it can be one of the most freeing ones. Life is about change and evolution.

Sometimes change is intentional, planned, and purposeful, and sometimes it's unforeseen, unexpected, unplanned. It's those unforeseen transitions that are the killer. If you were the one who planned to leave and then left, you have it somewhat easier because at least you were past the first stage of transition—awareness.

New Paltz, New York, psychotherapist Denis Jelley, M.S.W., outlines the stages.

The Five Stages of Transition

Awareness. There's a point where you know the change is coming. The awareness could be an epiphany, like "Why didn't I see this coming. I should have asked for a divorce a long time ago." Or it could happen over time, a slow realization that it's time to leave or that your marriage isn't working.

Acceptance. During this phase you are still feeling the emotions around divorce, such as anger, sadness, anxiety, but you have accepted that it is a reality.

Rediscovery. Finally you get to find out who you really are and what you want in your life. This is the fun part of divorce. You get to re-create your life, dream big dreams, try new things. Jelley recommends that you research your passions, to see if you can realize them in some way.

Commitment. You figure out where you want your life to go. You focus your intention on your goals and objectives, you commit to moving forward rather than staying where you are. It's easy to remain stuck. Believe, visualize, stay positive. Think *The Secret.*

Action. You put your plan into action. If it's too scary to do all at once, take baby steps. Take a smaller risk to build your confidence so that you can take a big one.

DIVORCE DYNAMITE

You've probably also heard the saying *What doesn't kill us makes us stronger.* I got a kick out of what Internet blogger Michelle Mills wrote in response to that old chestnut after going through a few deaths in the family, a hurricane, and a variety of other tragedies in a short time: "Well, I think I'm strong enough now, thank you very much." She went on to reassure her readers that she'd be back as soon as she weaned herself off Xanax. Amen to that.

I'm always tempted to ask people who say things like, "Cancer was the best thing that ever happened to me"—if they had it to do over again, would they *choose* to have cancer? Divorce is kind of like cancer. Maybe you wouldn't choose it, but since you're stuck with it, you might as well start making lemonade out of that lemon, girlfriend.

Like the mythical phoenix that rose from the ashes, you can and will rise from the ashes of divorce if you just let it happen and don't get stuck in bitterness and regrets. We've all run into the divorcées we don't want to be, the ones who ten, even twenty years later are still raging against their ex, blaming him for every downward turn their life has taken since the divorce.

Right before my husband left, I had dinner at a friend's house. Her other guest was a blowsy blond divorcée in her fifties who could not stop talking about her custody battle with her ex. My immediate impulse was to be sympathetic because her son had been taken away from her by this evil ex-husband, who had dumped her for a younger woman. Now, granted, her ex was a wealthy man who had the advantage when it came to court battles. As she went on and on, describing all the intricate details of each legal maneuver, I realized I knew the evil ex and his new young wife. We all live in the same small town. I'd seen her son at their house during a meeting of an organization we both belonged to. She talked about her child as if he were little. But I knew he was now sixteen. Years after the divorce this woman was still obsessed with fighting a custody battle for a sixteen-year-old boy who wanted to live with his father—a custody battle she couldn't possibly win even if she'd had all the money in the world. By sixteen—or even earlier—most judges will award custody to the parent the child wants to live with. Clearly, fighting with her ex was this woman's reason for living; the custody battle was the way she kept connected to him, and how she kept her rage alive. What a sad way to live, I thought at the time. It was an object lesson I thought back to many times during my divorce.

YOU AND I ARE THE PHOENIX

Elizabeth Lesser, cofounder of the Omega Institute, explains in *Broken Open* (Villard) what it's like to come alive again after divorce:

> *We too can reproduce ourselves from the shattered pieces of a difficult time. Our lives ask us to die and to be reborn every time we confront change—change within ourselves and change in our world. When we descend all the way down to the bottom of a loss, and dwell patiently, with an open heart, in the darkness and pain, we can bring back up with us the sweetness of life and the exhilaration of inner growth. When there is nothing left to lose, we find*

the true self, the self that is whole, the self that is enough,
the self that no longer looks to others for definition, or
completion, or anything other but companionship on the
journey.

I think there are two paths you can take after a major trauma like divorce—bitterness or emotional growth. I chose emotional growth, or rather it chose me. The phoenix that rose from the ashes of my divorce was a kinder, gentler me. I'd always been arrogant, thought I knew all the answers, thought I knew what made relationships work. I held on to grudges for years. I wrote people off when they didn't meet my expectations. I was judgmental, lacked compassion for people whom I saw as weak or lacking. I judged myself harshly as well. On the flip side I was extremely oversensitive to slights or what I perceived as rejection from others.

The crucible of divorce really tested me to the full extent of my sanity. I was traumatized not only by being dumped but by being unable to care for Dorothy, who needed constant supervision and support. I'd easily been able to deal with teenage Tina when she lived with us—even though she was very rebellious—and thought I could deal with anything, but seven-year-old Dorothy's acting-out behavior—extreme enough to be dangerous at times—pushed me to the breaking point and beyond. I was desperate. Eventually I had to admit that I didn't have what it took to give Dorothy the structure she needed. I had to humble myself to ask Zeke and Almira to take her more and more of the time. And I had to absorb their blame and contempt because they saw me as a failure as her mother, and their attempts to turn her against me. I hit bottom— even fantasized moving back to New York City and starting a new life. In the end I didn't leave, and I didn't break. In the way of the phoenix, the universe took care of both me and Dorothy. We are now blessed with a remarkable school program and a therapist who is helping us heal our relationship and has enabled me to forgive myself for my failings as a mother.

I also made new friends and reunited with old ones. Having to admit failure with Dorothy taught me what I most needed to learn—humility. I learned that I had limitations, and that I had no corner on the truth. I tried to stop judging others and accept people with all their failings and flaws. I no longer take everything personally. I don't write people off anymore. Divorce showed me how flawed, how vulnerable I am, and by extension how vulnerable all of us are. It gave me the gifts of compassion and empathy, valuable gifts indeed. If that's not the Phoenix Process, I don't know what is.

There are all kinds of issues we women grapple with, issues that need to burn in the fire before we can rise from the ashes or become who we really are. Those issues include fear, anger, cynicism, shame, and just about any other human emotion that cripples us. I encourage you to look at your life in the light of what you want to leave behind in those ashes. For many of us the desire to please others has crippled us throughout their lives. In order to really change, to find our true selves, we have to respect our own needs and learn to follow our own inner desires.

For us older women this can be a huge challenge. We were raised at a time when taking care of others was the only role women were supposed to have. Then we went through the turbulent changes of the 1960s and '70s when those expectations changed, but we were still stuck with the programming we grew up with. Divorce is an opportunity to finally break free of that caretaker role and try out a new way of life. But it isn't easy.

I was moved by one woman's post on the AARP forum, which pretty much said it all. This fifty-four-year-old schoolteacher who'd been married for thirty years finally decided to leave her husband. She related one incident that was really striking for its emotional sadism.

She had always loved to travel, but he'd refused to travel with her. He called her at school one day and asked her how she'd like four days and nights at the beach for a birthday present. "I cried. I was so happy," she wrote. "Then he said 'April Fools.' Last night as we were dividing up our lives he said that there was nothing wrong with that—I should not have gotten upset. That just confirms I am doing the right thing. I love life. After everything that's happened, I see love and happiness waiting for me. I compare my life to the movie *Awakening*. I am awake now. I have been struggling not to go back to sleep. I took my students to the Frist Center for Visual Arts to see the masterworks. I sat and admired the beauty in the Van Gogh with the field of green grass waving. I heard the song by Sting, *Fields of Gold*. And in my mind I was free—and laying there enjoying the beauty of feeling. I have written too much. I hope to inspire whoever is reading this. Have faith in yourself. Nothing can be better than freedom." To that I say, *Amen.*

DON'T DIE WITH THE MUSIC STILL IN YOU

Dr. Wayne Dyer says, "You are here to fulfill a destiny. You can sense the inner pull toward playing the music that is within you. That inner yearning is your cue." We ignore that inner yearning while we're married because we're too busy taking care of others. The inner voice to *be what you came here to be* intensifies when you move away from your destiny. To find out what your music is, he says, you have to take the time to notice the moments of your life that make you smile, laugh, feel happy, meaningful, and valuable, the times you look forward to, the times that you are so lost in a project that time vanishes. These are the daily moments that nudge you to follow that path of bliss.

For me that moment occurred thirty-five years ago when I was an unhappy caseworker in a state agency for delinquent youth. I got laid off and was surprised at how liberated I felt. I was broke at the time, but instead of being upset about my uncertain financial future, I felt like I'd been released from prison. I'd always wanted to write, and I spent the next six months collecting unemployment insurance and writing a novel. Then I was lucky enough to get a steady gig as a freelance writer. I knew I'd finally found my calling.

At the time I was in therapy with my wise shrink Jim Walters, whom I've spoken of before. He was the only one to support my aspiration to be a writer. My parents had grown up during the Depression and were obsessed with security. Jim believed in me and kept on pounding into my head over and over, "There is no security, there is no security," when I obsessed about winding up on the street. He finally convinced me that even if you have a civil service job, security is illusory. Anything can happen to you at any moment, and spending your life slaving away doing something you hate just for security is the path to a wasted life. This is equally true of a wasted marriage.

I'd been a magazine freelancer for many years, but after my divorce I realized I didn't want to spend whatever was left of my life trying to sell boring articles that I didn't want to write in the first place. I decided to put all my energy into trying to sell a book, which was my dream. That's how this book was born.

Many divorcées describe their divorce as being let out of prison—or at least they do a few years later when the grieving period is over. There aren't too many times in our lives that we can start over, but divorce is one of them.

The most inspiring story I've come across is that of Lydia, age fifty-nine. This poor woman suffered physical, mental, and emotional abuse for twenty-five years before finally escaping to a women's shelter. She'd been so beaten, belittled, and blamed that she feared for both her life and sanity. Her husband, a powerful, successful, charismatic man, had convinced everyone, including her children, that she was the crazy one and he was the sane one. He screwed her out of every penny as well during the divorce.

So there she was with absolutely nothing—no job, no children, no money, no family—her parents were gone and her extended family lived long-distance. In order to survive, she worked as a nanny, because she was good with kids. She had a few English as a second language credits so she taught some ESL courses as an adjunct. She had taken up yoga for exercise while married and became adept at it.

She had to reconstruct her life piece by piece. "There was no major turning point. I built a beach one grain of sand at a time. I thought I'd have it all together in a year, so I figured out how to be the happiest I could be with what I did have. Now I teach yoga, which I love, and English as a second language, which is very rewarding because I'm helping immigrants. I'm also a part-time bridal consultant. I enjoy helping brides coordinate their outfits and find a flattering dress, but the pay sucks. However, the work I do is meaningful. I tried being a receptionist and that almost killed me. That's one of the ways I survive, meaningful work."

Lydia has an intensely spiritual outlook and says, "My religious ties gave me emotional strength. I felt God would help me get through it. I have a close personal relationship with God." She also has a circle of close friends who support her.

Reinventing your life as a divorcée doesn't have to be as extreme as Lydia's journey, or even that of Elizabeth Gilbert—the author of the delightful *Eat, Pray, Love,* who left her husband and went on a journey to Italy to experience pleasure, India to explore spirituality, and Indonesia to find something she calls balance; or Frances Mayes, author of *Under the Tuscan Sun,* who renovated a villa in Tuscany after her divorce. It can be as easy and simple as fulfilling a dream of giving great dinner parties.

Marion, a fifty-four-year-old librarian who had always loved giving dinner parties, finally left her husband with just the clothes on her back after twenty-five years of putting up with his alcoholism and verbal abuse. "I moved in with a good friend for six weeks. I remember sitting there crying, 'I'm fifty-three years old and I don't have a can opener.' My friend kept telling me that money is only good for the freedom it buys you. My home is very important to me. I always fantasized that if I left I'd live in a chic apartment with a river view and give elegant dinner parties. As it turned out I had just enough money to rent an apartment in a beautiful high rise with a view. I bought furniture and ultimately I got back into the house and got my precious things.

"My husband and I had given dinner parties together, which I enjoyed, but I never learned to cook because he did all the cooking. So I learned to cook and started giving elegant dinner parties for my friends. I got a wine bottle opener that I don't need a man to use. Now anyone can come over at any time without my worrying that he'll insult someone. I used to hide his drinking and our fighting because I felt alcoholism was shameful. I never wanted anyone to feel sorry for me. Now I have friends over once a week. I feel that if I don't work really hard to entertain my friends it doesn't count," she says laughing, "but sometimes I actually let them call out for food."

HOW TO GET YOUR GROOVE BACK

Divorce is hell on a girl's self-esteem. Whether you were dumped or did the dumping, being a failure at marriage can make you feel like a failure at life. Divorce can assault your feelings about your attractiveness as a woman, ability to accomplish your goals, likability, even whether or not you're smart or talented. If you were married to a controlling or competitive man, you may have exited from your marriage feeling like a total loser who can't do anything right, whom no man would ever look at again. No matter how many well-meaning friends and family members tell you this isn't true, the only way you can restore your self-esteem is to prove your worthiness to yourself. I have always hated those general "how to love yourself" tips, which to me have no relationship to reality. Here, then, are some real-life techniques that have worked for me and for the divorcées I talked to.

Face your fear and do it anyway. If there was something you were afraid to do before or during your marriage, screw up your courage and do it anyway.

Judith, a ladylike Texas divorcée who spent her life closeted in an affluent suburb of Houston, was accustomed to dressing in color-coordinated pantsuits and lunching with the ladies. After her divorce she started riding a motorcycle, although she had always been terrified of them. "Biking is a metaphor for life," she says "Motorcycles for me were a metaphor for fear. I was afraid of everything; the zip had been zipped out of me. On my own I could become myself. Doing the things you've been afraid of shows you can do them. It's the only way to gain confidence."

Escape from your everyday reality. After leaving her husband, Lola, fifty-eight, a craftsperson who lives in upstate New York, dyed her hair purple and went to the Burning Man Festival in Nevada. Burning Man is a two-week event during which you live in the middle of the desert in a tent, bring in all your own food and whatever else you need, and basically check out of ordinary civilization for the time you're there. There are thousands of people at Burning Man—mostly artists—who create their own little community for the duration. She made the decision to leave her marriage during the first festival, but went back the year after her separation to experience it again. She says, "Being there is a total fantasy. You can be whoever you want to be."

Not being as adventurous as Lola, I went to a divorce retreat at a luxurious Texas spa, which gave me the chance to compare notes with other divorcées and get pampered as well. If you can afford it, take a trip to a spiritual retreat or spa where you will be away from your everyday worries and can spend some time looking within.

Do whatever it is your husband prevented you from doing when you were married. If Evelyn can do it at sixty-nine, it should be easy for the rest of us. "I have moved on in terms of getting my life to be what I want it to be," Evelyn says. "He was into the nice house, his work, formal dinner parties. I like travel and teaching. He never let me get a dog so now I have one. Everything had to be perfect for him. I'm much more casual. I'm finding out who I am. Sometimes I feel lost and question why I did it. I ask myself if it was a good thing to stay so long. That's what I can't deal with. But until I get decrepit I'm going to move forward."

Remember who you once were. If you can't figure out who you are now, or even what you like to do, think back. What did you love before you got married, what kind of young woman were you? Did you love to dance, to travel, to go to the theater or concerts? Did you stop doing any of these things when you got married? I had a pretty wild life when I lived in New York City. I partied in clubs, drank in bars, picked up guys, and danced all night. The bar scene isn't exactly available to sixtyish women, but dancing is. I didn't dance during my marriage because my husband was too self-conscious to get out on the floor. Since the divorce I've gotten into swing dancing. It makes me feel like I'm back in high school, when we called it the Lindy. I don't go out dancing alone that often, however, because I have a problem asking men to dance. You can't just sit there and wait to be asked when you're my age. I know my struggle with shyness keeps me from getting out there and doing more things. I've found it helps to join a group, where eventually you know the people and feel comfortable.

Learn something new. Sara Davidson, author of *LEAP! What Will We Do with the Rest of Our Lives?* says learning is one of the best approaches to change because it requires you to take the initiative and get out in front of the wave instead of letting it break on you. "Becoming a beginner again is like traveling to an exotic country. All your senses start firing." She interviewed a woman who went back to college at the same time as her son, and a high school teacher who went to the Fletcher School of Law and Diplomacy at fifty-four. She figured that years of herding teenagers would serve her in dealing with heads of state. Davidson herself took up ski racing in her fifties and interviewed other aging boomers who took up everything from improvisational dance to writing poetry to producing musicals. All of her interviewees were vital and enthusiastic about the rest of their lives.

GROW OLD GRATEFULLY—AFTER ALL, WHAT'S THE ALTERNATIVE?

One of the hardest struggles we older divorcées have is aging. When you're married, you feel you can relax about getting old— your life is settled, you have a mate to walk into the sunset with. You may be upset about your wrinkles and sags, but at least your husband still thinks you're beautiful (hopefully). Divorce turns that sense of security on its head. When my husband announced he was leaving, after wailing "But how will I survive?" I was hit with the reality of having to date again. "I'm fifty-eight, who will want me?" I moaned. Aging is rough even when you're married. It's hard to lose that male gaze when you walk down the street, to feel you've become invisible. Ironically it was easier for me because I'd always been the fat girl whom guys didn't look at anyway. I think it's harder for you girlfriends who used to be real lookers.

Women deal with aging in different ways. Lola has dyed her hair purple; she wears big purple glasses and, when I met her, a fitted black T-shirt, baggy black pants with large green polka dots, and clogs. She's not going gentle into that the good night, and since she's still quite a beauty with a great figure, she gets away it. She met a guy at Burning Man and is having a steamy long-distance romance. One of the advantages of living in my town, the old hippie mecca of Woodstock, is the large number of old ladies in 1960s garb. I am currently wrestling with the jeans-or-no-jeans dilemma. I look at women my age who haven't given up their jeans, and unless those jeans are dark, tailored, and worn with high heels, they look schlumpy. If you're already short and plump, faded jeans are not a good look, but they're hard to give up. I've made some progress: I've transitioned to black jeans and jeans skirts–they're a bit more flattering.

The upside of aging these days is that there are no rules anymore. We're not our mothers. We don't have to look respectable, or tailored, or grandmotherly, or tone ourselves down or gussy ourselves up. You get to look however you want, to express who you really are. Of course if you're working in a law firm you have to dress appropriately, but after hours all bets are off. I do have a fashion icon, however: my girlfriend Dinath, who at fifty-six always looks stunning. She has a straight red pageboy bob and puts together youthful, fashionable layered outfits with jackets and heels that make her look twenty years younger and at least that many pounds thinner, but effortlessly—not like she's trying to look younger. Of course Dinath was a fashion designer, so that helps a lot. As Nora Ephron says in *I Feel Bad About My Neck,* "If only one-third of your clothes are mistakes, you're ahead of the game."

There is one big upside to divorce—almost everyone loses a ton of weight. Even I lost weight, and that's not my usual coping mechanism. Take that weight loss and run with it. Literally. Get out and exercise. Shed those sweats, get your hair done, get a manicure and pedicure, put on makeup, buy some new clothes, and you will start feeling like a woman again. If you're in a dying marriage, chances are you've let yourself go, out of either despair or rebellion: "I'm not going to try to look good for that asshole." Well, now you've got to look good for yourself. No matter how old you are, you're still a woman. I schlepped to my therapy appointments each week in the same jeans and T-shirts for a year. Kali gently prodded me to try a new look. Once I got interested in dating, I gussied myself up and even put on makeup, which I hadn't done for years—my husband hated it.

If your fashion sense, like mine, is left over from the March to the Pentagon in 1967, ask your Dinath, your fashion-forward girlfriend (I'm sure you have one), to go shopping with you and help you go through your closet. Be ruthless. Just wear what she tells you and you'll be fine. Don't insist on keeping that Grateful Dead T-shirt. There's sure to be a teenager you know who would love to have it. When you have that makeup consultation, stick to the advice you get. (I really have to do that—I still find it a terrible hassle to put on makeup every time I leave the house.) Let your hair go gray if you want to make a statement, but get it styled fashionably. I've tried to let mine grow out three times but always crawl back to my hairdresser for coloring before I get to see how horrible I really look. I'm currently in another go-gray phase and I hope I make it to my whole head.

For inspiration watch *What Not to Wear* on the Discovery Channel. At the least you'll feel better about your own wardrobe after seeing what's in the closets of some of the participants.

IF YOU'RE IN YOUR . . .

Forties . . .
Lucky you, you're still young enough to reinvent yourself a couple of times before you wind up in a nursing home. You may be hampered right now by survival concerns—say, taking care of your kids—but you can still follow your dream. Just keep it there in front of you as you move forward in your life.

Willa was in her late forties when her marriage broke up. Her ex-husband had no money, while she had three kids and lived in a small town in Idaho. She had to take a string of jobs to get by, including teacher's aide, rural mail carrier, special-ed tutor, women's shelter support person, and counselor for the developmentally disabled. She was an accomplished musician but could not make any money playing classical piano or flute. Her husband had discouraged her from playing, to the extent that when her mother gave her a piano he put it under a leaky roof and refused to fix the roof. She'd pretty much given up on music when a friend asked her to teach her son the flute. At first Willa refused; she wasn't interested in teaching. Finally she agreed, and rediscovered her passion. She's been teaching music to young people ever since, eventually becoming music director at a private school. Also, she's back to performing in cafes and churches.

Fifties . . .

Fifty is the new forty, so you're far from over the hill. Actually, you're in the prime of your baby boomer years, and you have a lot of company in reinventing yourself. Boomer women are doing everything from starting new businesses, to fighting AIDS in Africa, to even having babies again via assisted reproduction. Anything you wanted to do in your thirties, you can pretty much do in your fifties these days, including marry again if you want to. (You better be careful to marry the right guy this time, girlfriend!)

Many women in their fifties are starting new careers, and lives. In *For My Next Act: Women Scripting Life After Fifty,* author Karen Baar found that women increasingly are starting new careers in our forties and fifties. Representative Nancy Pelosi, House majority leader, did not even run for political office until she was forty-seven and the last of her five children had left home. How's that for a model? In addition, during research with women who achieved eminence in their fields between the ages of fifty-five and ninety, Sally Reiss, Ph.D.—a professor of educational psychology at the University of Connecticut—has found that the later years are very productive for the development of women's creativity.

Baar quotes Heidi Hartmann, Ph.D., president and CEO of the Institute for Women's Policy Research, "If you're fifty-five and you think it's too late to go to college, think again. The older you are, the longer your life expectancy, so start thinking in terms of living to age ninety. If there's a degree you want to get, go ahead and do it."

Sixties or older . . .

Get on the road and travel. This is the time to see all those places you've always wanted to see, visit the far corners of the world. Women in their sixties are even joining the Peace Corps, which may be a bit rigorous but can be extremely rewarding. By the time you start collecting Social Security, get that reverse mortgage on your house, and watch your kids graduate from college, you may have enough money to go on the road. If you always dreamed of traveling with your husband after retirement, take that trip yourself. You may even have more fun, meeting new people and going to places he'd never consider visiting. Check out www .travelchums.com to find a traveling companion. About 25 percent of members are over fifty. You might even find a single man to travel with.

Consider moving to a different country. Your retirement income will stretch much farther in Mexico or Costa Rica, for instance, and you'll be joining a community of interesting expats. San Miguel de Allende in Mexico, for example, is populated by American retirees, many single women among them, who are interested in the arts.

CHAPTER NINE

DATING AGAIN

On That Little Screen and Off It

i'm not a control freak i don't care what you do as long as you're a faithful person and don't cheat, one thing you should know is i'm in trouble with the law for dwi's but that dosen't make me a bad person. i'm trying to change. [sic]

—HARLEY GUY, FIFTY-FIVE, MATCH.COM

During the throes of a difficult divorce, it's easy to assume that you'll never find love again. But that's simply not true. If you really want to find it, you will. At the very least you can find a companionable relationship. The good news is that, despite the male demographic advantage, more than 75 percent of women in their fifties have a serious exclusive relationship after their divorce—often within two years. The key is simply wanting it badly enough to take some risks, to put yourself out there and start dating again.

However, dating after twenty or more years of marriage can feel a little like Alice falling through the rabbit hole. You're lost in an unfamiliar world where everything seems reversed; where you wind up doing the pursuing; where you may want sex more than he does; where men are more interested in women your daughter's age than in you; a world that seems to have rules except you've forgotten what they are. Unfortunately, the rules for dating haven't really changed since high school. You're still supposed to wait for him to call, not have sex on the first date, and flatter his ego. The difference is that after fifty, there are so many more women than men that men think they can call the shots. Your job is to let them know that they can't—you are so special that they still have to court you and win you no matter how much competition there is.

Soon after my husband left, when I was still too shell-shocked to even think about dating, I ran into a friend at a journalists' convention who was sporting a very handsome gray-haired fellow on her arm. I knew she was single, around my age—late fifties— plain looking but very charming. I wondered who the guy was. She said she'd been dating him for a while. He was intelligent, educated, a professor in fact. She'd met him on YahooPersonals.com. I assumed this was an aberration, that she'd just gotten lucky. I was wrong. I eventually found out that the Internet has revolutionized dating for women over fifty.

Luckily, Internet dating came along at the right time. It has almost leveled the playing field for women like us. The Internet gives you the opportunity to find older men you never would have met otherwise and to cast a big net outside your immediate area. There is a cornucopia of older men—and even younger men—out there ripe for the plucking. You just have to be ready to make a few compromises. The guy my journalist friend was dating had a slight disability. She said it amazed her how many women had passed him up because of it.

Most of you know how to meet men in your community—the key is get out there and do what you enjoy. Chances are you'll meet some like-minded men. Internet dating is a long shot for long-term romance—so many men are either emotionally unavailable, married, or both—but it *does* happen. We all know women who've found love on the Internet. It is certainly worth trying, just to get back into the dating game and flex your dating muscles Just don't expect too much.

LITERARY LADY SEEKS LUSTY LADDIE
(MY MATCH.COM PROFILE)

I'm a Woodstock, NY professional freelance writer, with many different interests, ranging from extremely lowbrow (*American Idol, The Bachelor*—oy vey) to reasonably highbrow (jeez, what was the name of that foreign movie I saw lately?). I'm a bit outdoorsy—I do actually go outdoors on my way to my car—and love nature if it's not running after me with bared teeth. I'm not into any sport that involves hitting a ball in the hot sun. I can't see why sweating and sunburn appeal to people. When it's hot I want to be in a lake (I'm a long-distance lake swimmer). When it's cold I want to be in the ski lodge drinking a hot toddy or in a hot tub, preferably with a hot guy. I hate laundry lists of interests because I find they're meaningless until you actually talk to and meet someone. If I read another profile that lists walks on the beach I'll scream. I love to sit on the beach—preferably under a large umbrella. I'm kinda cute looking, plumpish but not fat, love to schmooze, gossip, read, eat gourmet food, go to movies.

I just want a smart, funny guy. Should like good food, books, movies, trashy TV shows, and be willing to listen and get to know me. Non-negotiable demands: Smart and able to laugh at himself. Must be kind and have integrity. Fabulously wealthy couldn't hurt.

STILL SEXY AFTER ALL THESE YEARS

I don't know if your marriage was a libido killer, but mine sure was. I literally hadn't had any sexual desire for eighteen years, since I started living with my husband. I had spent all my sexual energy avoiding sex with him. Except for a brief crush on our carpenter, which I wouldn't have done anything about, I had never looked at a man sexually. Now I was long past menopause and supposedly long past my sexual prime. My body didn't know this, however. It started twitching every time an attractive man came into the room. All of a sudden I was evaluating every man I saw as a sexual partner. I was on fire, all the time. Pent-up demand, I guess.

Most of us, no matter how old we are, aren't ready to be put out to pasture after divorce. Sexual desire doesn't disappear with age, but may actually increase after you recover from the stress of your divorce. Even if the younger generation, specifically our kids, think it's gross that we still want sex, we are the baby boomers, we set the trends, and an active sex life at all ages is now one of them.

I had met my husband and three previous boyfriends through personal ads, so Internet dating was a natural for me. Nine months after my husband left, I became obsessed with Internet dating. I would stay up nights trolling dating sites for men—it sure beat feeling the pain of the end of my marriage. If I was lucky, I could find a date for the weekend on Wednesday. Unfortunately, like any addiction, it was a temporary fix.

The ups and downs of Internet dating can be dizzying. Be careful not to get caught up in the roller-coaster ride. One day I was high on having lined up three potential dates, the next day they'd all disappear—they'd fail to return calls, or e-mails, or both. I hate this aspect of Internet dating. You can instant-message or e-mail someone for weeks, even talk on the phone regularly, start fantasizing that this is the man of your dreams, and then he disappears, never to be heard from again. It's almost impossible not to build up expectations about a guy you haven't met and then feel really let down when he drops you. The reality of the Internet is that there is no reality. You don't become a real person to the potential date until you actually meet him—and even then he may never call you again. That's why it's a good idea to try to meet as soon as possible, before too many fantasies build up on either side.

When it came to sex, I found the tables had turned since my youth. Once upon a time I thought all men wanted was sex. Now that's what I wanted—desperately. Young women still complain about being hit on, but I was praying to be hit on when I went on a date, especially if the man was attractive. Ironically, I found older men were the ones who wanted to get to know me first. Or maybe they had performance anxiety and were afraid they couldn't get it up. I didn't have a hard time finding dates, but I did have trouble finding men who wanted sex as much as I did.

Sexual experimentation is not unusual for older women who've been married for a long time. Those of you who married young may have missed the sexual revolution completely.

"I married my college sweetheart at twenty-one and stayed married for twenty-eight miserable years until I discovered he was gay," says Taylor, fifty-six, a college administrator who became a hot ticket post-divorce. "I never had good sex or a loving relationship in my life. When I first separated I started dating someone at work who proposed to me, but he wasn't in my league, he wasn't bright or educated. Then I met a thirty-year-old triathlete who had a body you couldn't believe. He was dumb as a rock but the first time I had sex with this kid you had to scrape me off the ceiling. I had no idea this was what sex was supposed to do for a woman. He'll always have a place in my heart because the sex was so fantastic. Then, while I was seeing him, I started an affair with my doctor who was forty-two. Then I ran into a twenty-three-year-old who wanted to come over to have sex. Then there was the thirty-six-year-old aspiring writer. But it was all physical. I've been in a relationship for three years now with a seventy-two-year-old man who is the love of my life. He's also great in bed."

I wouldn't recommend promiscuity to anyone, however. It probably won't find you a mate, and it may cause you a lot of anguish. I don't regret it, but I gave it up because eventually it became really depressing. Actually, studies have shown that women who have a lot of casual sex after divorce are more depressed than those who don't. Sex, like a drug, provides a short-lived high. And then there's the risk of sexually transmitted diseases. I used sex to distract myself from all the pain I was in, to indulge a rescue fantasy: Another man would come along and heal the hurts of being dumped. Many of you may have this fantasy—if you could only find someone else to love you, everything would be okay. I'm here to tell you, girlfriend, that it doesn't work that way. The only way to heal that hurt is time and work on yourself. Finding another relationship too soon can backfire big-time. Eventually I recovered from the need to escape the pain, accepted my unmarried status, and learned to live alone and be okay with it—at least most of the time.

Ironically, it doesn't seem to work this way for men, especially older men. Men simply can't survive without a woman, and very few let much time go by after their divorce to find someone else. They get remarried after divorce a lot more quickly than we do, and not only because they have more opportunity. They've been taken care of their entire lives by a woman, and they really don't know how to take care of themselves. We, on the other hand, were their caretakers, and we're happy to be relieved that burden. We're not so anxious to remarry or even live with a guy. I can't imagine giving up half my closet space, much less half my life at this point.

You may hear people advise you to avoid men who are recently separated. Ignore that. Any guy who's been on the market for more than a few years may be a commitment-phobe. Both of the guys I had relationships with after my separation were recently separated. The first one married the next woman he dated after me; the other one dated around for a short time and then moved in with a woman. Years later they are both still with those women. Take my advice here: If you want to find a guy, get him on the second go-round. Few men will wind up with the transitional woman, the first one they date after the divorce. Many settle down with the *next* one. Unfortunately, I was the transitional woman for both my guys.

The Wacky Iraqi

I was very lucky that my first Match.com date was with Harry, who billed himself as the Wacky Iraqi. I can't resist telling you the story. You'll learn a few Internet dating lessons along the way. In his photo Harry looked like an elderly, dissolute elf, but his profile was offbeat and funny enough to overcome the ugly photo. An Iraqi Jew who grew up in India, he was fascinatingly exotic. As he described himself modestly:

> *Most body parts work—some are brand new and work better than others—and I am in reasonable health. Up to two pills a day! Average height, weight, intelligence, hearing, etc. I am insensitive sometimes when the joy of saying something witty overcomes my better judgment—the Q'uranic sura about evil intent being essential to being evil does not impress the infidels. I have few hobbies—reading, investments, politics, traveling, dancing (under duress). Basically a modest man, with much to be modest about.*

Unfortunately, Harry lived in New Haven, more than a hundred miles from me. I was ignorant enough about Internet dating at the beginning to think that distance didn't matter. Take it from me girlfriend, it does, especially with older men. They are much in demand, particularly if they're as cute and financially well off as Harry, and don't have to travel very far to meet eligible women. Despite the fact that Harry cast a wide net, fish close to home were much more attractive. Distance was no impediment to e-mails and phone calls, however, which is what we did for a while.

Harry wanted to know what I meant by "a few extra pounds"— the category I had checked on Match. "I should tell you that your face is promising and if few extra equals under 50 in your part of the world I may be able to avoid too much libidinal anguish," he wrote.

I had agonized over the weight categories on Match. Was I "large," "a few extra pounds," "average," "athletic and toned"? Forget the last category—I settled for "a few extra pounds" since forty was a "few" in my opinion. My picture was misleading. Since my face was thin, no one envisioned the size of my rear end. I finessed the question by telling him that I considered myself "pleasantly plump." I took five years off my age as well, figuring I could pass for a bit younger. I recommend not fudging much on age or weight on dating sites—it will backfire when you meet the guy. Men hate it when women claim to be slim when they're not. However, if you can deal with juggling the dates in your life story, feel free to pare a few years off your age. You can admit it eventually—but not until the third date or so.

I spoke with Harry a couple of times on the phone and liked him better each time. We dickered about where to meet. He wanted to come to Woodstock, but I wanted to meet in between because it put less pressure on me. Long-distance first dates can be a disaster. If the guy travels 200 miles to meet you, you can hardly send him back after a cup of coffee. Unless you meet somewhere in between, you'll be stuck with him for the entire day or evening. With Harry I gave in. I didn't regret it. The minute I saw him, I was smitten. He looked younger than his pic, and though not conventionally handsome, he was strong and fit, with a mischievous twinkle in his eyes and a sly smile. His confidence, his male energy turned me on.

He handed me an enormous cake with HAPPY BIRTHDAY ERICA written on it and three cannolis. New Haven is famous for its Italian bakeries. I asked him why he'd had "happy birthday" written on the cake since it wasn't my birthday. He said he couldn't think of anything else. I was charmed.

We spent the evening together, talked and joked, went out to a lecture, and found we had lots in common, except for politics. Harry was very polite and didn't make a pass. I was too shy after so many years away from the dating scene to make one myself. I was still operating by the *no sex on the first date* rule. I didn't know if this was still de rigueur on the dating scene, or what was expected these days. How many dates would I have to wait? I had no idea. I'm sure you have no idea, either. The rule of thumb I've heard from other girlfriends is the third date, but feel free to put sex off until you're really ready no matter how long it takes. The upside of dating older guys is that they're not controlled by their hormones. They can wait and will like you better if you make them wait. They're nervous about performing anyway. At the end of our first date, Harry sat on my couch, patted the spot next to it, and told me to sit there. He cuddled me sweetly and I sank into his chest. When he left he stuck his tongue into my mouth and kissed me passionately. I just about swooned. It had been a long time since I'd been kissed like that.

We e-mailed back and forth for a while but he didn't mention visiting again. I felt like this was almost coitus interruptus. Here I'd had him in my grasp and let him go. How was I going to get him back? I kept making my sexual intentions clear in my e-mails, despite his unexpected protestations that he wanted to be my "friend." Ever the wag, Harry wrote:

Sex with a woman at my age? I am considering the priesthood and celibacy. I hear there are some nice Italian nuns there nowadays. Perhaps even some Indians? I have a lot of physical problems. My knees are weak. My eyes are dim. I have colic. Among other things too sad to think about. I don't know if I can satisfy you. All that pent up demand. Let me think on it. I don't know if I can be passionate about anything anymore, but I can still make love once a year whether I need it or not.

Finally Harry showed up very late on Wednesday night. By the time he arrived I was exhausted from housecleaning, food shopping, trying on sexy nighties, leg shaving, hair blowing, making up my face, and all the other tasks I'd forgotten about when it came to having a man visit. I don't think I'd shaved my legs during my entire marriage. When he arrived we basically fell into bed, awkwardly. Even though I felt self-conscious and was far from having an orgasm, feeling him inside me was unutterably exciting. Harry was a pretty unimaginative lover by the standards I'd had before marriage—but as my first experience post-marriage he was wonderful. He made me laugh, he wanted me, and he was very, very male. Unfortunately, after staying an extra night, he left and never came back. He e-mailed coldly. "I will stay in touch and may even come up sometime. Just don't expect it and don't demand a date right now. I know any date becomes an expectation."

I was crushed. I felt as if the sexual floodgates had opened for me, and I wanted more, more, more. I discovered after more Internet dating that sometimes a man will travel to meet you if sex is in the offing. Men like novelty, and a new woman is always enticing. What they won't do is have a long-distance relationship unless they fall madly in love.

Hurt, I wrote Harry off, then a few weeks later I decided I was being silly—that I'd rather keep in touch with Harry than lose him completely. I started e-mailing him and sharing my love life with him and asking him about his, which was pretty entertaining. At one point, after I'd been complaining about a lack of lovers, he gave me some wise, if brutally honest, advice:

> *At our age sex is an iffy thing —it does not always work. But you should not take it personally. You do have a bigger butt than someone would expect judging by your face, but there may be those who like a bigger butt. And these things are superficial and should embarrass one to think in those terms so no one wants to say anything. If someone likes you the sex part follows. And yes, you are right, the Internet makes guys fantasize about women. Besides their ideals were formed when they last courted 20–30 years ago so these ideals of beauty are what sticks in their brain. So any woman over 50 seems older than the 20–30 year olds they dated before they last got married. And it is probably true that men lose the libido and drive at some point so need a younger form to stir it up. I seem to do OK for a while but will occasionally skip a firing!!!*

Keep well. And stay composed and don't panic. There are
tons of men after your ass. Harry

Men over fifty really are different from younger guys. They're
more scared—of not being able to get it up, of being exploited,
of being hurt. They're bitter veterans of long, often sexless marriages. Some are totally defeated, no life left in them. The upside
is that they're not as fussy about looks as younger men—they want
someone they can talk to. Sexually, men over fifty have problems
with impotence, mostly due to health problems like heart disease,
high cholesterol, and diabetes. Luckily, Viagra had come along
just in time for my divorce—and yours. I initially ruled out guys
who used Viagra, then decided that if I wanted a man over fifty I'd
better get used to the idea of drug-induced erections.

The Shaman Lover

I got all fired up when I read this passage in Elizabeth Lesser's
Broken Open. I knew a Shaman Lover was exactly what I wanted.

And there is another kind of Shaman, the kind I call the
Shaman Lover. The Shaman Lover is a man or a woman
whose destiny is to heal the heart-sick with the sweetness
of love, and to give the gift of fire to those whose passion
is frozen. Some call the Shaman Lover a temptress
or a knave, a siren or a snake. Sometimes this is true;
sometimes the Shaman Lover has bad medicine to offer.
Sometimes the smartest response to the allure is to run
away. But sometimes the Shaman Lover has been sent by
fate to blast us open, to awaken the dead parts of our
body, to deliver the kiss of life. If we succumb, we are
changed forever . . . There is something primal—even
dangerous—about this kind of experience. Passion, sex,

and the dark side of a love affair can ignite a parched heart, and burn a life to ashes. At the same time, the stirring of Eros in the body and heart revives the soul's water, and nourishes rebirth. This is the classic descent and resurrection process—where life arises out of death.

While searching for my shaman lover, I had dates with many duds who were not only not shamans, but schlemiels, including an Indian massage therapist with whom I'd madly flirted in sexually graphic terms on the Internet. I was crushed when he made it obvious that he wasn't attracted to me when we met. I learned from that experience to meet first, have cybersex later.

Finally I met "him" through, what else, Match.com. Bob was fifty-five, five years younger than me, a short, handsome, boyish-looking tennis pro—a funny, dynamic guy who totally charmed me. To my surprise he found me irresistible as well. Our relationship was explosive for the next three months, including some of the best sex I'd ever had. I even had multiple orgasms for the first time in my life. At age sixty!! It happened just as Abigail Trafford writes:

You fall in love—a coup de foudre—*and the block of lead in your chest miraculously melts; you can't believe it, you laugh, you dance . . . It's like being a teenager again. Just touching each other, looking at each other, you feel you've known each other forever. You make love as you've never known it could be . . . You've been dead so long in marriage, it's time to be alive again, to be born again. Falling in love is your emotional midwife. You know it's too soon, too much like jumping into a lifeboat that you know leaks and has no oars. But you smile, feeling so*

good after feeling so bad for so long. Therapists call this
the search for the romantic solution. But it's usually not
a solution. You crash. Puff, the magic dragon of love is
gone.

I never had this kind of love as an adolescent, and it's a very adolescent kind of love. Unfortunately, the essential characteristic of a *coup de foudre* is that it is temporary, it's a fantasy that can't go on. Bob wanted to see others. I couldn't accept that and broke up with him. Puff, he was gone. If you are lucky enough to find this kind of intense, passionate affair post-divorce—and many divorcées I spoke with did—you should be prepared for the pain when it ends, which can be worse than the pain of divorce. I went through hell when Bob and I broke up, but I don't regret a minute of that relationship. I wrote this in the heat of my affair with Bob. It's embarrassing now, but it was true then, and it still is.

I don't think I have ever been in love or understood what
love is until now, at age sixty, I've finally fallen in love
with a man who loves me equally. I am shaken, moved,
turned into jelly by this love more than I ever was as a
teenager with my first crush. I am experiencing something
that is supposed to be the province of young people, but
the intensity of it for me now, tinged with the specter of
death, is almost unbearable. He is truly my first love,
and he will likely be my last love, which adds poignancy
unknown to young lovers. I never understood how this
passionate connection is essential for a marriage to last,
to thrive, to weather the disappointment, tragedy and
boredom that are the stuff of everyday life. Without it my
husband and I were squabbling roommates, not lovers.

I was lucky enough to get left. At sixty I was able to begin my life again. How very sweet that was. This time around I was able to reinvent myself as a desirable woman, long past the age when women are considered desirable. I never believed that old saw about beauty coming from within, but my lover says he sees into my soul and I am beautiful. That is more than I ever expected from a man, and I am blessed to have experienced it.

I was right about Bob being my last love, in the sense of being totally consumed by love, swept away by it, drowning in it. I don't know about you, but I don't want to love like that again. Love should not be that euphoric; it shouldn't be like a high from a drug. There's some other kind of love—the kind that grows rather than explodes. I'd like to experience that kind of love before I die. All-consuming passion isn't just the province of the young, and neither is the foolishness that goes with it.

INTERNET DATING ISN'T SCARY

"I registered with twelve online services when I was fifty-eight," relates writer Kathryn, now sixty-five. "I figured that even if I didn't meet anyone I might get a story out of it. I met a number of quality men (and several not-such-good-quality), both online and in person. I dated a college professor for a while, but there were no sparks. I had a torrid phone relationship with a shrink in another city, but when we met in person (he flew here) it turned out we couldn't stand to be in the same room together.

"My now-husband just happened to live about three miles from where I was living at the time. He came from one of the minor dating services. I'd never paid for that one till I got a letter from a guy whose profile seemed perfect for me (a history professor in the Midwest). I paid to read his letter, which was wonderful, we spoke on the phone and arranged to meet in two weeks when he got back from a trip.

"The very next day I got another letter on the same minor dating service. The guy hadn't even put up a profile, so I would never have paid to read the letter. But since I already belonged, I read it. It was even more wonderful than the one from the history professor. The next night we talked on the phone for two hours. The next day, a Sunday, I met him for brunch. As soon as we met, I *knew*. He came home with me to watch a baseball game and we have been together ever since. Even though we had a few acquaintances in common, it's very unlikely we would ever have met if it weren't for the Internet."

If you're afraid of Internet dating, you're not alone. Most older women I've spoken to are. Either they don't know how to post a profile, they don't know how to screen potential dates, or they're afraid of the dangers of meeting strangers. All of those obstacles can be overcome if you make up your mind to learn the ropes.

You do need some *chutzpah* or an old-fashioned sense of adventure to undertake Internet dating. But there is no reason to be fearful. Personally I think the danger factor is way overemphasized when it comes to Internet dating, especially for older people. I dated through the personals when I was young, and the Internet when I was sixty. Older men were a lot more courteous, truthful, and reliable. Unlike my experiences when I was in my thirties, I never got stood up, and I never met anyone even remotely dangerous. What I did find you have to watch out for is the married men. There are lots of them out there pretending to be single. One of my tips below tells you how to weed them out.

EVERYTHING YOU WANT TO KNOW ABOUT INTERNET DATING BUT DIDN'T KNOW WHO TO ASK

When I talked to older women about Internet dating, I found their biggest hesitation was ignorance of the basics—how to write a profile, how to post it on a dating site with photos. Many of you may need a basic introduction to the Internet. Don't be embarrassed about your ignorance. If you're over fifty and computer-phobic, you're not alone. Go take a class or call a computer consultant. You'll need an introduction to the basics of the Internet to use it for dating.

Here are some basic tips to get you started:

If you want to dip your toe in without investing money, try www.plentyoffish.com or www.okcupid.com. They're free. Or pay to join Match.com or YahooPersonals.com. They have the biggest databases, and the more prospects, the better.

Post a good head shot and one good full-body shot. Photos are extremely important. They should be recent and be just of you, no kids or grandkids. One pic of your pet is okay. If you've got a great figure, show it off, girl. A little cleavage goes a long way. If you don't have any good photos on your computer, ask a friend with a digital camera—almost everyone has one these days—to take some pictures of you and e-mail them to you. Then you can post them on the dating sites.

Don't write the same boring profile as everyone else. Leave out walks on the beach and dining by candlelight. You don't have to list all your accomplishments, interests, children, or anything else. Just write something short and intriguing about yourself—anything—and leave the details for the first e-mail or phone call. If you can't think of a thing, write about what you're doing at the moment. I like the ones that use the word *you,* such as "I'd love to travel to the Greek Islands with you." Be breezy, be funny, be yourself. If you're totally stymied ask a friend to help you write your profile.

Feel free to lie a little, but not much. It's okay to take off a few years and a few pounds, but guys are infuriated by women whose photos were taken twenty years and 200 pounds ago.

HOW TO SORT
THE WINNERS FROM THE LOSERS

Married men give themselves away by not posting photos and not giving out home numbers. Don't ever date a man who won't give you his landline home—not office, not cell—number. Call that number and make sure the machine has his voice on it. If he only gives you his cell or office number, trust me, he's married. Do not go for the excuse, "Oh, I just moved and the phone's not turned on yet." Tell him to get back to you when he has one. This technique is a surefire way to screen out the married men.

Avoid guys who are not only recent separatees, but nonseparatees. I can't tell you how many times I heard, "I'm separated but I'm still living at home and looking for a place." One guy was living in the basement because he wanted to be near his kids. He did have a separate phone line, but any man who can't even wait to date until he has his own place is not separated.

Insist on a photo, unless you don't mind dating Quasimodo. I'm pretty flexible about looks, but there has to be some chemistry.

I have my limits. The few times I agreed to meet someone without seeing a photo (they always have good excuses), I was not pleasantly surprised.

Make the first meeting short, preferably just for coffee or a drink, and have an appointment to get to after half an hour or an hour. Leave him wanting more. I prefer the drink to coffee. I found that meeting at night for a drink gives you the opportunity to look your best. Let's face it, girlfriend, if you, like me, look your age, you're going to look younger in dim light in full makeup. Also, this coffee thing is overrated. It's so much more sophisticated to meet at a bar, and I feel so much sexier after that first cosmopolitan.

Don't agree to meet until you've spoken to him on the phone for at least an hour. Then follow my surefire phone-call formula. If you don't, you will regret it, guaranteed: If you fall in love with him during the first phone call, there's a fifty–fifty chance there may be some chemistry in person. If the phone call is iffy or blah— or worse, really boring—there is zero chance you'll like him on a date. Do not make the mistake of thinking he will improve in person. It absolutely never happens. When you talk to someone on the phone, there is a fantasy factor—you want to imagine he'll have some redeeming qualities in person even if he's boring or obnoxious or talks incessantly. Here's what I say to get off the hook when they ask for a date: "I'm really sorry, but I don't feel we're compatible." It's short, inoffensive, and impossible to argue with.

Don't put up with nonstop talkers. This is my least favorite male behavior, and almost every guy is guilty of it. Some of them relax after a while and start listening, but they may need a reminder. Kali suggested a great tactic to derail the guys with verbal diarrhea. After letting him talk for fifteen or twenty minutes, interrupt and ask, "Is there anything you'd like to know about me?" If that doesn't initiate a little give-and-take, either end the phone call or start looking for the exit.

Don't ever, and I mean never, do any suggestive flirting through instant messages or e-mail until after you've actually met the guy. You'll find that lots of men just want cybersex, which is infuriating and insulting. They don't admit it; they just start asking suggestive questions. It's incredibly embarrassing to build up fantasies on either side and find absolutely no chemistry in person. Have all the cybersex you want after you get to know each other.

HOW TO PROTECT YOURSELF EMOTIONALLY

Be aware that many, if not most, guys on the Internet are emotionally unavailable, especially if they've been dating for a long time. Guys get hooked on the kid-in-a-candy-store aspect of Internet dating. It's just too damned easy to keep surfing for someone else if you don't meet their every fantasy. Men over fifty have a demographic advantage that they never had before they got married, and it goes to their heads. Don't get emotionally invested until you've gotten to know a man really well.

Pay attention to whether or not he's hidden his profile after a couple of dates. If it's still up there, he's probably a player. Take it as a warning sign to proceed with extreme caution.

Avoid casual sex. I've said this already, but it bears repeating. It's irresistible to many women to sleep around at first. It sure was to me. After all, you've just been let out of jail. If you must, go ahead and have some one-night stands. Just don't do it for too long, and be aware that your self-esteem is fragile and can't tolerate too many *he never called* episodes. Remember that we women are programmed to get attached, and the rejection that comes with casual sex gets harder the older you are. When you're twenty-five and he doesn't call, you know someone else is around the corner. When you're fifty-five, it can be a long way to that corner. Also, remember that sexually transmitted diseases don't care about your age—use a condom.

Drop the search for Mr. Perfect. Take the advice of Alice Solomon, author of *Find the Love of Your Life After 50!* The perfect man is just not likely to turn up at this stage of your life, if he ever was. She recommends taking the mega-list of all your criteria and dumping it. Anywhere from three to five must-haves is plenty. And stop with the height, weight, and amount of hair a guy should have unless you want to be alone for the rest of your life.

Follow the stupid "rules." You probably know what they are if you grew up in the 1950s or '60s, but if you need a refresher read *All the Rules: Time-Tested Secrets for Capturing the Heart of Mr. Right* by Ellen Fein and Sherrie Schneider. Also take a look at *He's Just Not That Into You* by Greg Behrendt and Liz Tuccillo. I tend to go into full rationalization mode when a guy doesn't call, so my girlfriend Roz gave me this for my birthday and it helped. I absolutely abhor the rules, but I can't deny that they work. Solomon agrees. Always let the guy make the first move. Don't be too eager. Remember, older men were brought up in the same era you were, when men were supposed to do the pursuing. If he doesn't suggest a meeting after a few e-mails and one or two phone calls, forget it. If he doesn't call soon after the first date, write him off.

Keep your expectations low and you won't be disappointed. Unless you're lucky (which happens), you will probably get rejected and do the rejecting more than a few times. If you can deal with this, keep dating. If you find it unutterably depressing (as I did eventually), give up Internet dating. Yes, you do have to kiss a lot of frogs to meet that balding, second-time-around prince.

AGE AND THE "IT" FACTOR

You're never too old to be attractive to men. I'm sure you've noticed that there are women who attract men no matter how old they are. They have what I call the "it" factor. They're not necessarily beautiful, but they radiate self-confidence. A case in point is Edna, my friend Wendy's mother, who had men pursuing her into her eighties. Edna was a former glamour girl who retained her charm and youthful personality until she died. She pretty much looked her age, though, and dressed in ridiculously young clothes, but I guess men liked that. She acted as if she was gorgeous even when she was very old and always just assumed she'd be the center of attention wherever she was. She had a quality of focusing her attention on you that was very flattering; it drew women as well as men to her.

Many divorcées I talked to had once been man magnets, but lost their confidence after divorce, especially if they had been left. Others have a rock-solid sense of their appeal that wasn't shaken by divorce.

Maria, for instance, who's sixty-one, was left by her husband of twenty-five years—whom she absolutely adored—for another woman. Nonetheless she has had no trouble finding men. Slim, short, with shoulder-length curly graying hair, it doesn't hurt that she's adorable and looks at least ten years younger than her age. But I've run into many gorgeous women in their sixties who bemoan their lack of dates. What's different about Maria is her attitude.

"I did have a rebound affair after my husband left," Maria told me. "It was great because I found out I might be able to have a relationship one day. After that I didn't date for about two years and it was good to be with myself. Then I thought I'd like to share myself with someone, so I went online at the insistence of my therapist, and met someone. He's fifty-eight, lives about forty miles away but is thinking of moving here. It's nice, I'm not in love but I'm in 'like.' He's in 'like' big-time. He has a totally different energy than my ex-husband, he's more low-key, not so dynamic. We've been seeing each other for five months, and I just agreed to have sex with him—I wanted to know if I really liked him first." When I asked her if she was worried about not finding love again, she responded: "My worry was not if someone would love me but the other way around."

With that attitude she has what it takes to find love at any age. If she could bottle it, she'd make a fortune. I'd be the first on line to buy it:

- Confidence that she's attractive.
- Feels okay about being alone.
- Sees a relationship as "sharing herself" rather than getting a man to love her.
- Puts off sex until she's sure how she feels.

Another friend has *always* been very attractive to men even though she's short and dumpy with a bad complexion. We were all friends when we were single in our thirties and my girlfriends and I would constantly discuss what the hell she had that we didn't. She's now in her sixties and just told me that she still has no trouble attracting men. I think I finally figured it out. She's very charming (charm is key), has a sense of personal style, and radiates friendliness combined with a rather haughty attitude. Somehow she conveys that she is the arbiter of what matters in life, an aura that gets both sexes working for her approval. She's supremely confident and draws people to her. Such women are very seductive—and the key is that they don't try to attract men, they just assume that men will be attracted to them. That's the "it" factor.

HOW TO DEVELOP YOUR "IT" FACTOR

There are ways of attracting men even if you're not a babe and never had that kind of sexual self-confidence.

Be friendly. Most men (and women) are basically insecure and want to be around women who make them feel accepted. Women with the "it" factor actually like men, and enjoy their company. Many women prefer the company of other women when it comes to friendship. So many of us divorcées are bitter and angry at the male sex. I heard over and over from Internet dates about women who hated men, who had been abused by their husbands and took it out on every man they met. You are not going to find another mate with that kind of attitude.

Be yourself. This is another one of those pieces of advice I hate, because how do you know who the hell you are anyway? However, I've been around long enough to know that I tend to either freeze up in the company of an attractive man, or I talk too fast and try too hard to be ingratiating, which has to make him uncomfortable. I rarely can just relax and convey the essential, irreverent me.

I notice that sometimes when I'm involved in doing something else, a man will start flirting with me. For a while after my divorce I ran speed-dating events. I was packing up after one event in an upscale restaurant and was surprised to notice that a rather handsome, nattily dressed man in his fifties stayed late to help me. He started chatting with me, asked where I lived, and said he'd date me if I lived closer. I realized that men like him almost never came on to me. I'm sure if I'd sat across from him during the event he wouldn't have written me down on his card, but here I was just doing my thing and he was interested.

Try acting "as if." If you're insecure like me when in the company of an attractive man, pretend you're Sophia Loren or Marilyn Monroe. Ask yourself what she would do. Would Sophia stand there feeling awkward and insecure? Not on your life. She'd be wondering whether it was even worth her time to talk to him.

Lose weight and get in shape. I hate to recommend this since I've always struggled with my weight and wish being slim weren't such an asset in the dating world, but there's no way around it—it is. Luckily, you may not have to try too hard—women traumatized by marital breakups usually find that the pounds melt off during the first year. Every divorcée I talked to who found a long-term relationship post-divorce mentioned losing weight as the first step to restoring her self-esteem. Most also started exercising. Women with the "it" factor may not have the best figures, but none are fat.

Take care of yourself. Get manicures and pedicures, get your hair done regularly, update your makeup and wardrobe, wear heels if you can tolerate them. Buy expensive face and eye creams and use them regularly. No matter how many wrinkles you've got, gussying yourself up will do wonders for your self-esteem. If you look like an attractive woman on the outside, you'll start feeling like one on the inside. If you want to get the occasional Botox or Restylane shot, go ahead, girlfriend. Anything that makes you feel better about yourself. I'd avoid a full face-lift, though. General anesthesia is just too dangerous, and the results are often not that appealing.

"My biggest fear when I got divorced was my age," says Taylor, who discovered how to get the "it" factor at age fifty-six. "I'd never dated in my life and was clueless how to go about it at forty-eight. I have a nice shape, so I had that much going for me. Things were starting to sag so I really worried about that, and I eventually joined a gym. I do weight training six days a week to help with cholesterol. I started taking care of my skin. My idea of a moisturizer used to be Vaseline; now I use good products. The first time I had a manicure and pedicure I was fifty. I've learned to really love being a woman and to nurture that part of me. No matter where I am, I wear clothes that fit, designer jeans, heels, jackets. I turn heads. I make no bones about being fifty-six, I don't lie about my age, I brag about it sometimes when I see people ten years younger who look dreadful. I have a firm and shapely derriere. I told everyone at my daughter's wedding that I had a great butt and even invited them to touch it."

The law of attraction really works. If you really want to find love again, and believe it can happen to you, it will. A negative attitude is the biggest deterrent to finding love later in life. However, you also need to be able to handle it. When a possibility for love comes over my horizon, I go into a panic and forget about the "rules." Looking back on the two men I fell in love with after my divorce—both of whom were terrific guys—I realize I screwed up both relationships by being too clingy and desperate. Let that be a lesson to you. No matter how old you are, if you believe that you are a "catch," you will have a chance of getting caught.

MEETING MEN
OFF THAT LITTLE SCREEN

Most women, no matter what their age, still meet men the old-fashioned way—in the course of their lives, not on the Internet. They do, however, put themselves out there to do it. No one yet has met anyone sitting at home watching TV, although I wish it were possible. Perhaps if your cable goes out and a single, older cable guy comes to the house to fix it. (Why are they all so young???) Here are tips based on real-world success stories:

Go dancing. Despite the predominance of women, dancing is a good way to meet men because single older men know dancing is where the girls are. My girlfriend Joan Price, sixty-five, author of *Better Than I Ever Expected: Straight Talk About Sex After Sixty,* met her husband-to-be at a contra-dancing class. She came on to him but he didn't want to date her at first. She decided to become his friend anyway, and after about a year they started dating. He told her he wouldn't date her at the beginning because he wanted to make sure she was interested in a serious relationship, not just casual sex. Ya gotta love that guy. She wound up marrying him.

Tell everyone you're looking. You never know who is going to come up with a single man you might be interested in. The best dates are fix-ups by a friend who knows the two of you.

"After my divorce I started putting out energy that I wanted to meet someone," fifty-six-year-old ebullient, charming, though not-quite-slim Mae told me. "I looked good, dressed good. No matter where I went, I started talking to people and let it be known I was available. I'd talk to people on ticket lines, while bicycling in the park, to people doing things I was interested in. I changed my mind-set and told friends I was looking. I happened to be at a friend's house when Walter came over. He'd gone to high school with us and was also going through a divorce. The minute he came in, we started talking about what it's like to get a divorce. By the time the evening was over, he asked to drive me home. At first I said I'd walk, and then he drove me the five blocks. He called me two days later and the rest is history. I lived in New York and he was in DC that year, but we saw each other every other weekend at least. For one year it was a long-distance relationship and then he retired and moved in with me. We're really happy together."

Be open to the unexpected. After fifty you may not find Prince Charming, the guy your mother always wanted you to marry. You may have to be more flexible. Susan Richards, best-selling author of *Chosen by a Horse* and *Chosen Forever*, was fifty-five, long divorced, and had no interest in remarrying when she met Dennis Stock, a well-known photographer, on her book tour. He was unlike anyone she'd ever known: attentive, adoring, brilliant, fascinating. He wrote her irresistible e-mails. She writes about his first e-mail: "I had never received such a communication from a man. It was breathtaking in its straightforwardness, its eloquence and its undisguised declaration of interest." She didn't realize at first that he was seventy-eight, and was ready to drop him when she found out. When she expressed to her friend Allie her fear that he could die, Allie responded, "He will die. The question is, do you want to spend some time with a remarkable man or not?" They almost broke up because he wanted sex and she didn't. It wasn't because she didn't find him attractive, she did, but she'd decided she was no longer interested in a full-time partner. "I was too old, too independent, too, well—I felt too unsexy," she writes. However, their romance seemed fated. Twenty-five years earlier, not knowing who he was, she had bought his house. And then on her book tour, they'd met at an animal sanctuary—both were passionate animal lovers. Dennis kept pursuing her, she got over her fears, and eventually she fell in love and married him, finding the kind of happiness she had never known with a man.

Do what you love, the men will follow. This is a truism, but that doesn't make it less true. Women who meet men get out there, doing stuff, going to classes, hiking, dancing, traveling, skeet shooting, skiing, bird-watching, working for a political party. The more places you go and the more you do, the more chances you'll have to meet someone. It's just playing the odds.

Don't forget the supermarket. The produce department has spawned some interesting romances.

IF YOU'RE IN YOUR . . .

Forties . . .

You are a lucky girl. You're at the bottom end of the baby boom, and lots of men in their fifties are looking for you. It's not true that men want women twenty years younger. They want a woman a few years younger whom they can talk to *and* who still looks good, and you, girl, still look good. At least I did at your age. My Internet dating guru girlfriend Kathy was in her forties when she divorced, and she's never lacked for dates. She's now with a fifty-year-old man who worships her. Internet dating should work for you since there are lots of men in their late forties and up on Internet dating sites.

The downside of dating in your forties is that you probably still have kids at home, which complicates things enormously. Be careful not to mix dates and kids until you know the relationship is really serious—and I mean remarriage-material serious. If possible, date when your ex takes the kids, but if you're a single mom it's going to be a lot harder. You can date, but no sleepovers unless you set one up for the kids, too. Join Parents Without Partners for support (www.parentswithoutpartners.org).

Fifties . . .

You are still a hot ticket, especially if you're fifty-five or under. The baby boomers are hitting their sixties, and you are still young enough for baby boomer men who actually are looking for a woman near their own age. This is not the least bit unusual, especially in areas where men aren't spoiled by seeing hordes of supermodels every day, like New York City. In upstate New York where I live, men are much more open to women their own age. Younger men will find you fascinating as well, so consider dating down, about five or ten years.

At around fifty-five the male dating pool diminishes, so it may be time to ramp up your efforts if you really want to find a man. Most divorcées in their fifties *do* find love if they make the effort. That means getting and staying active. The best way to find a healthy, active man is to become active yourself. Older men tend to go out for sports to keep in shape, and women in their fifties who hike, bike, ski, play tennis, and do other strenuous sports are in short supply. I've heard many complaints from athletic older men that they can't find women their age to keep up with them. One handsome serious hiker in his late fifties told me women even lied about their hiking ability to get him to go out with them, but when he took them hiking they faded after a mile. He lost interest as well.

Sixties or older . . .

Do not give up hope. I talked to many divorcées in their sixties who found love.

The odds are a lot better than you think. According to the 2003 census, there were 1,704,000 divorced and unmarried woman older than sixty-five, compared with 1,082,000 men. That means a ratio of less than two to one, so if you follow the advice above for women in their fifties about getting active and simply getting out there, your chances to find love will increase as well.

If you're athletic the odds will improve immensely. Check out the golf course. It's not exactly a strenuous sport, and it's predominantly male. Older men on dating sites often look for a woman who plays golf. Hiking clubs are a treasure trove of older men.

The political angle is a good one if you're in your sixties. Many retired men volunteer to work for their political party. Get out there and stuff envelopes or make phone calls for the Dems (a plug for my party) and you may be surprised at how many men you'll find doing the same.

Dress up whenever you go out. Drop the jeans and T-shirts, even for the supermarket. You never know when you might meet someone, and the act of dressing up and putting on makeup is psychological preparation for a romantic encounter. When it comes to meeting a man late in life, the intention to make it happen, and belief that it's possible, is everything.

Don't overlook younger men. The two men I got involved with after my separation were both five years younger than me and they didn't care about my age.

CHAPTER TEN

BUT I LOVE HER

Coping with Betrayal

When he's late for dinner, I know he's either having an affair or is lying dead in the street. I always hope it's the street.

—JESSICA TANDY

Do you ever get over it?" I asked my cousin Ellen during the depths of my despair. She'd been dumped for another woman in her late fifties and a few years later seemed to be doing just fine. "No, you never get over it," she told me. "But you do get past it." She's right. Just like any trauma, you put it behind you eventually. It took years, but I've put it behind me and I am here to tell you that you will too.

Our society's casual attitude towards infidelity doesn't make it easy, however. In order to heal you need to acknowledge the depth of the wound—that what you're going through is serious, that infidelity is up there on the scale of the worst things that can ever happen to you. It's not easy to see the tabloids regularly trivializing infidelity by featuring titillating scandals about men dumping their wives for another woman. In 1950 Ingrid Bergman's affair with Roberto Rossellini ruined her career. Today's Hollywood stars play musical beds with impunity. Even Woody Allen's career wasn't affected after what amounted to a combination of adultery, incest, and pedophilia.

The taboos against adultery, and especially against leaving your spouse for someone else, seem to have almost totally disappeared. The values we grew up with in the 1950s and '60s such as commitment, honor, fidelity, responsibility, and integrity—even that old warhorse, duty—seem to no longer carry much weight. Romantic love, no matter how ephemeral, trumps them all.

The issue of morality when it comes to infidelity may not get much press, but it's a frequent and intense subject of discourse among us older divorced girlfriends. We understand that infidelity is a fact of life, especially considering that we're living longer and being faithful to one person for 30 or 40 years can be a tall order, but we don't approve of society's casual attitude towards it. We certainly don't approve of older men dumping their aging wives for a younger version.

It hasn't helped that the divorce laws have relaxed the rules on adultery as well. What used to be grounds for divorce now don't matter to the courts one way or the other. If no one cares who cheats, then the mate who has been betrayed has to live not only with betrayal but with being a tired cliché. It's humiliating to be the discarded first wife—and it doesn't even get you much sympathy anymore. We may be a joke to the media and our friends may tell us to get over it already but the blow—to our children, our families, our egos, our futures—is profound.

The damage of divorce, especially when infidelity is involved, is like a wave rolling outward to cover more and more territory, affecting not only the wife and the children (even if they're adults) but the entire extended family, which often winds up splitting into warring factions. Grandparents lose the right to see their grandchildren, parents of adult children may be estranged from them for a lifetime, aunts and uncles may never see their nieces and nephews again. Even Woody Allen lost custody of his children—and they lost a father—but *the heart wants what it wants* was his rationale.

WHAT GOES AROUND

Have you ever been the other woman? I have. No matter what they say, being the other woman is a hell of a lot easier than being the betrayed wife. When I was in my twenties, I went out with various married men and fell in love with two of them—one while I was in college and another whom I worked with after I graduated. Despite the fact that both had small children, I saw their wives as mere obstacles to our love. It never occurred to me that there was anything wrong with breaking up a marriage. The women's movement was in the future, and in the meantime I was a child of the 1960s who assumed marriage was a bourgeois invention that should be trashed along with the establishment. My second married boyfriend left his wife, but I didn't feel guilty even when I later found out she committed suicide because of our affair. My ethical development was sorely lacking, I'm afraid. To my eternal shame, I only felt sorry for myself. Maybe what goes around did come around—back to me. I didn't escape my karma.

If you're wondering who's to blame for the relaxation of social inhibitions against adultery and divorce, the answer is, we are. "We have met the enemy and he is us," as Pogo once said. We baby boomers were the ones who tore down traditional family values and started the sexual revolution when we decided that personal fulfillment was more important than duty, responsibility, and obligation. We were the ones who declared that "till death do us part" was conditional on being happy in your marriage.

It's not surprising that in midlife, one or both of us look around and say "Is this all there is?" or "I'm living with a stranger." Since

there are no longer social inhibitions against divorce to keep people together, the marriage is put to the test—and it often fails.
Men in midlife are surrounded with temptation. Before my husband started cheating on me with a colleague he'd been "friends"
with for years, he'd come home regularly with tales of other office
affairs. As the realities of aging begin to dawn on men in their forties to sixties, they become depressed about what they've missed,
what they haven't accomplished and never will. When one turns
around and looks for the likely cause of his misery, there you
are—the aging, critical, nagging wife who doesn't "understand"
him, who isn't sexually interested in him or vice versa. And there
she is, the woman at the next desk who sees him as an interesting,
accomplished older man. Voilà! Affair.

We women aren't immune to the siren call of an affair either.
We're out there in the workplace too, and when your marriage
sucks the temptation to do more than just flirt with the guy at
the next desk can be irresistible. Even though I was the victim
of betrayal, I understand that we're all human, affairs happen,
even decent people leave their marriages because they fall in love
with someone else. In the end what's important is those old values: accepting personal responsibility, trying to make amends if
at all possible, and avoiding the temptation to trivialize infidelity
or blame your spouse for your behavior. It is possible to leave a
marriage honorably, with your self-respect intact, even if an affair
is the reason. (An example is the story of Kay and Joe in Chapter
Eleven.)

WHATEVER HAPPENED TO INTEGRITY?

Edith Wharton, in her story "The Reckoning," wrote about a modern (for the early 1900s) couple who marry with the understanding

that personal freedom is paramount and that marriage is only a formality, to last only as long as they're happy together. If and when they cease to love each other, they are free to separate. Ten years later her husband falls in love with a younger woman, invokes their agreement, and leaves, which totally devastates her. In fact she had done the same thing to her first husband: left him when she fell in love with her second husband. At the end of the story, she visits the first husband and apologizes. He reminds her that the law protects her; she doesn't have to let her husband go. She responds,

> *The law represents material rights—it can't go beyond.*
> *If we don't recognize an inner law . . . the obligation that*
> *love creates . . . being loved as well as loving . . . there is*
> *nothing to prevent our spreading ruin unhindered . . . is*
> *there?*

The passage about there being an inner law, an obligation that love creates, is what the 1960s generation overlooked. Although her prediction wasn't true in Wharton's day, it is now: We don't recognize that inner law anymore, or that love creates an obligation, so we *are* spreading ruin unhindered.

When I need a moral compass, I turn to Rabbi Jonathan Kligler, the rabbi of my synagogue. I'm lucky that Rabbi Jonathan, as we all call him, belongs to the long Jewish tradition of *tzaddiks* or wise men. You may have visited your priest or minister for guidance at some point in the divorce process, especially if infidelity was involved. Most religions are pretty clear that adultery is a sin, but religion doesn't play much of a part in our lives these days. However, religion still has a lot to offer when it comes to sorting out moral questions.

Even if you're not Jewish, I invite you to learn from my rabbi's words, which certainly resonate with anyone who considers herself an ethical, moral human being. I'd like to note that Rabbi Jonathan is a Reconstructionist rabbi, which means he's very liberal. Judaism is one of the few religions that see divorce as a necessary evil, maintaining that it's preferable to a life of married misery. His sentiments may sound conservative, but his worldview is not.

"All the values the boomers threw out are coming back to haunt us," Rabbi Jonathan told me. "Self-gratification has become a lifestyle. Even though monogamy and the nuclear family haven't been around since time immemorial, nonetheless their breakdown represents something negative for our society. The feminist analysis of patriarchal marriage has something to do with the breakdown, but the dissolution of social agreements we've made doesn't serve anybody."

Ouch! As a feminist I can attest to the incongruity of someone like myself upholding the sanctity of marriage, but I'm not a young radical anymore, I'm a betrayed wife, and that puts a whole 'nother perspective on the feminist analysis of marriage as a patriarchal institution.

There's no way to minimize betrayal, Rabbi Jonathan reassured me, which made me feel immeasurably better about what I was going through. "You've given your word. You're only as good as your word—integrity depends on that," Rabbi Jonathan continued. "The quality of our life and relationships is only as good as our integrity. If we want to live compromised ethical lives, on a deep level we'll pay for it. Of course many people aren't interested in being emotionally or intellectually aware. They're content to go through the motions and may not discern the effect of betrayal. If your game in life is winning, then other people are objects to be manipulated so you can win. But there's another game out there with rewards that aren't easily tallied; you can't add them up on a ledger. That's the game of seeing how aware, loving, and kind you can be."

BLAMING THE VICTIM

From my current vantage point, six years later, the actual hurt and anger of being cheated on and left has passed. I recognize that my ex may be weak but he's only human, and we're all at the mercy of our emotions to one extent or another. Our marriage sucked, he had a midlife crisis, fell in love with someone else and left, what else is new? It's a very old story. Infidelity is forgivable, but what held me back was his vindictiveness and anger. Have you been wondering why the man who cheated on you is also so furious at you? Where does he get off blaming you when he was the one who cheated? When Zeke told me he was leaving, I kept asking him why he was so angry at me; what did I do that was so terrible? "Why do you always think everything is about you," he'd snap at me. I guess he meant it was about her—he fell in love with someone else. Then why was he so angry at me? Why did he blame me for the demise of the relationship, why did he seem to feel entitled to leave me for someone else, why the constant rage? In my interviews with divorcees, I heard repeatedly about the vindictiveness of unfaithful exes. I recently posted this on my blog on www.divorce360.com:

Why do unfaithful spouses try to destroy you AFTER they leave?

I'm thinking about this because a friend of mine, who's in her seventies, has just forgiven her ex, or at least is able to talk about him with understanding and equanimity, THIRTY years after their divorce. He cheated, left her AND went to court to get custody of their children even though he didn't want them. He just wanted to destroy her, for reasons that she still doesn't understand. She won, but her life was a living hell and her kids suffered tremendously. Thirty years is a long time, but when a husband (or wife) not only cheats and dumps you but then tries to do you in, and screw up your kids, that makes it really difficult to move on.

I've been struggling with this because my ex not only left me and moved in with the affair partner, but then he undermined my ability to mother my child effectively by convincing her I was a bad mother. How do you get beyond that?

I find that so many cheating spouses not only cheat, but then go on to try to destroy the person they cheated on. Why is this? Guilt? All I know is bitterness tends to linger when that happens and when people tell you to "get over it" you want to strangle them.

My post hit a nerve. There were many comments, including:

It's easier for them to walk away and not look back if they can destroy what little self-esteem you have left. The guilt of what they did to their families, it does eat away at them, even if they choose not to see it. They turn it into hate for us, for making them feel the way they do.

I never understood why he felt the need to try to assassinate my character when he was the one in the wrong. I was already being destroyed by what he was doing, but apparently that just wasn't enough for him . . .

I was the one that was cheated on, I was the one that was hurt as well as I was the one that tried to forgive and forget. . . . But he turned what happened all on me, it was my fault that he cheated, it was all me.

I suppose the guilt from infidelity leads to this kind of vindictiveness but that's hardly an excuse. The incongruence between you makes it all worse. He's already found a new partner and doesn't feel the loss of the marriage. You, on the other hand, are shattered, terrified of the future, and collapsing on friends and relatives. His happiness is the unkindest cut of all. He's already detached from you, or is in the process of detaching, which makes him excruciatingly insensitive. For us older women this scenario is even more painful, since the departing husband has found love, usually with a younger woman, and we know that we're unlikely to do the same—our years of prime sexual attractiveness are over, and available men will be few and far between at our age. I was furious that my husband waited so long to leave when he insisted he'd been unhappy since day one. Then why hadn't he left on day two when I was young enough to find another partner? He admitted he never could have left unless he'd found another woman, which was honest at least.

Another devastating aspect of betrayal and being dumped for another woman is the feeling of total powerlessness. There is really nothing you can do about it. He made the decision, he made up his mind to leave you for her. You can't convince him to come back, you can't change his mind; the only person you can change is yourself. Trying to punish him for his betrayal never works; in the end you will only look foolish and be sorry you gave him the satisfaction.

If you're still struggling with bitterness, if you haven't gotten over the betrayal or its aftermath yet, give yourself a break, and give yourself a lot of time. The seventy-five-year-old friend I mentioned in my post lived long enough to see her ex marry three more times, lose the respect of his children, and destroy his own life. When I asked Rabbi Jonathan about recovering from infidelity, he said "I want to support your readers by fully acknowledging the depth of this hurt. This kind of betrayal is morally bankrupt, the person bankrupts himself by doing it, then it takes work to build up credit again in your account."

TWO GIRLFRIENDS, TWO DIFFERENT LOVE AFFAIRS

When it comes to marriage, divorce, and infidelity—there are no black and whites, only shades of gray. Consider the cases of my two girlfriends, Sarah and Kim, who were having affairs while my marriage was on the rocks.

Sarah had been in a clandestine relationship with a married man for twelve years. She was a bohemian writer in her fifties who led a very independent life and actually was happy with the arrangement. She didn't want a live-in lover to cramp her style, but she did want sex and love, which he provided. He was a very conventional man who couldn't bear to leave his family, even after the kids were grown. For all those years he carried on the fiction that he was a devoted husband, father, and grandfather, and Sarah got sex and love without the annoyance of having to share her bathroom.

Kim, on the other hand, was a pretty, conventional, middle-class forty-five-year-old housewife, married to a perfectly nice businessman, with whom she'd raised two lovely daughters, one a senior in high school and one in college. Bored to tears with her husband, she started searching on the Internet for an old flame, Frank. They rekindled the fire. There were some minor obstacles, however. Frank was married and lived in Florida. He had a wife and three kids—all under eighteen.

There was no deterring true love, however. Despite two spouses and five kids, they started an Internet affair that became progressively more torrid, eventually turning into an actual affair. They declared eternal love, felt that they had always loved each other, still loved each other, should have and would have married when they were young if her parents hadn't broken up their romance. It was, fated. They were sure they were meant to be together.

Frank moved to New York, and they both left their mates to be together. The mates both went into severe shock, retaliating in the way betrayed spouses usually do, by attaching bank accounts and hiring killer attorneys. Kim's daughters seemed to adjust, but her mother and sister stopped speaking to her. Frank's son stopped speaking to him. His wife became obsessed with revenge, tried to turn his kids against him, and took him to the cleaners big-time.

I was caught in the middle since I was friends with both Kim and Frank, and, despite my own situation, I understood their dilemma. Kim would ask me plaintively, "What am I supposed to do? I'm only forty-five. Harold [her husband] is a nice man and has never treated me badly, but do I have to spend the rest of my life with someone I don't love?" Frank, on the other hand, was married to a woman who had total contempt for him. When they'd gone to marriage counseling and the counselor asked her to talk about his positive qualities, all she could come up with was, "He doesn't drink." I know what she meant. He wasn't exactly Mr.

Adorable. A gruff, control-freak criminal lawyer given to explosive rages, he intimidated just about everyone except Kim, who turned him into a puppy dog. He felt totally alone, sure that no one would ever love him until she came back into his life. He could not pass up what seemed his only chance for happiness. They were soul mates, et cetera, et cetera. Even though I was in the reverse situation, I sympathized with them because I knew their dilemmas, and I didn't know their betrayed spouses.

In the end Sarah's lover's wife died. He stuck by her till the end, taking her to all her chemo appointments and staying at her bedside during her terminal illness. "I admire him for that," Sarah told me. "I wouldn't respect him if he'd deserted her when she really needed him." They now live together and she's part of his family, which Sarah actually found that she likes. However, they both are very careful to maintain the fiction that they met *after* his wife died, not before.

Frank and Kim got married, and after five years are still happily married. According to her, the biggest downside is that he took a big financial hit, which means they won't be able to retire as early as they'd hoped. Their families have adjusted more or less, but the wounds run deep. When I asked her if it was worth it, she told me, "Of course. He's my sweetie. It's been hard but life is complicated anyway. We've had a great time together." But Frank is still estranged from his son and daughter; Kim hasn't spoken to her sister in years, and her relationship with her mother remains problematic. "What I've learned?" she says. "That other people taking sides is never good for children." When I asked her if she had any regrets, she told me she wished that she'd left before she had the affair.

I don't know about you, but I wouldn't have cared a whit if my husband had just had sex with someone else. I would have actually given my blessing to an occasional fling if it meant we could have preserved our marriage and our child's happiness. During our many heated discussions where I'd plead with him not to leave, Zeke would bring up Sarah's situation, declaring fiercely that he refused to live a lie like Sarah's longtime lover. He compared himself to the character Meryl Streep played in *The Bridges of Madison County*. He neglected to mention that Meryl stuck with her marriage for the sake of her kids. To me, the French have it right when it comes to infidelity. You can't stamp it out, people will stray, we're all human, but while having an affair is acceptable in France, you're supposed to keep a secret and limit your emotional involvement. Leaving your family for your lover is strongly frowned upon. This solution is far from ideal, but at least it limits the damage.

If it seems like I'm advocating staying in a bad marriage because you made a vow, or for the sake of the kids—I do realize that sometimes that's *not* the right thing to do. Some marriages *should* end, not only for the sake of the parents, but also for the sake of the kids. It's just hard to know which marriages. My own parents separated for six months when I was ten, and in retrospect I think I would have been better off if they'd divorced. They were so unhappy together and my mother took much of her misery out on me, which made my adolescence hellish. But an affair is the wrong way out. I have a lot of respect for Carl, a fifty-five-year-old guy I dated who left his wife of twenty-five years, *without* having an affair first. He did fall in love with a young woman he worked with, which was his wakeup call. He didn't pursue a relationship with her, but the feelings she stirred in him made him realize he wasn't willing to settle for a loveless marriage for the rest of his life. His kids were grown and gone—he told me he never would have left if they were still at home—but his wife didn't want him to leave. Yes, initially his wife was devastated by his departure, but the respectful way he did it made the transition easier for her. They've now managed to become friends.

No matter how much I want love, and I've been a love junkie myself big-time, I'd happily live a lie if it spared my daughter one moment of grief. But then I wasn't tested by finding my "soul mate" while married. I'd like to think I'd do the right thing, but I'll never know for sure.

CHILDREN AND INFIDELITY

Most children weather divorce without serious emotional damage, although they may suffer subtle psychological problems later in life such as self-esteem or relationship problems. Some children do just fine and others fall apart—depending on the temperament of the child and the circumstances of the divorce. The more amicable the divorce, the better the communication between the parents, the better the children fare. There may be a lot of disagreement about the effect of divorce on children, but nearly all the studies agree that a high-conflict divorce is the most likely to harm children, and infidelity usually results in a high-conflict divorce, especially if your husband stays with the affair partner.

You probably know this already but it bears repeating, despite all the pain his cheating has caused you, don't badmouth your ex's girlfriend to your children. Take the high road and don't put your child in the middle, especially if your child is going to be spending visitation time with the girlfriend. Even though it feels like it's going to kill you, zipper that mouth. You'll be proud of yourself down the road.

Many of you older women don't have to deal with this particular ring of co-parenting hell, but you may have to deal with teenagers or young adults who are at a stage where they're sorting out their own moral positions—and seeing a parent hurt can derail their development in many ways. Teens have trouble with sexuality under the best of circumstances, but when they see a parent who is unfaithful it gives them permission to go wild sexually themselves. Considering the epidemic of teen pregnancy and STDs, your kids can wind up in big trouble. Sons are particularly at risk, says Frank Pittman, author of *Infidelity and the Betrayal of Intimacy*, because "fathers often take sons into their confidence, forming a secret alliance with their son to hide things from the wife and mother . . . Sons of philanderers who grow up to be philanderers themselves often recall their fathers' revelations as the beginning of their underground sex life." On the other hand, sons may take the side of their mother and refuse to have anything to do with their fathers.

Teenagers and older children also take sides, usually the side of the betrayed spouse, and you may be in the paradoxical position of trying to get your kids to forgive their dad who cheated on you. If you're a compassionate mom, which I'm sure you are, you don't want them to lose their dad. When my twenty-eight-year-old computer consultant saw the title of this chapter, he said, "My dad left for another woman when I was thirteen. I didn't speak to him for years." I can only imagine how devastating this was for him and his mother.

In my divorce Zeke foisted Almira on me way before I was ready to deal with her. At the beginning, when Dorothy lived with both of us, he'd bring her to school events and poor Dorothy would have to run interference between us. I was humiliated, begged him not to do this, not to put Dorothy in the middle, but there was no reasoning with him. He felt since Almira was parenting Dorothy part-time, she had the right to show up.

This scenario is all too frequent. Everywhere I go I find the victims of a parent's infidelity. When I described my book to the manager of a local copy shop, a woman in her forties whom I barely know, chimed in with the story of how her father left for another woman, whom her mother would refer to as "the whore" whenever she called. She felt forced to choose between her mother and her stepmother, and couldn't form a relationship with her stepmother as a child, which she would have liked to do. Dorothy's first therapist warned me not to force Dorothy to choose between me and Almira because it would make the situation even harder for her, so I have made huge efforts never to bad-mouth Almira in front of Dorothy. That day I yelled at her in the parking lot on Dorothy's first day of school was, I'm proud to say, the exception. Well, okay, I admit it, I've lost it a few more times.

Stepmothers and ex-wives can become a toxic combination for children when Dad marries or stays with the affair partner. And if she is a bad stepmother and mistreats your child to boot, the situation becomes immeasurably worse. I suppose I should consider myself lucky. Now that I am finally past the hurt and anger of Zeke's betrayal, I've let Almira know that I'm grateful she's doing such a good job helping to raise my daughter. But although she is genuinely devoted to Dorothy, Almira needs more time to accept me.

WHY IT HURTS SO MUCH

In *Breakup: The End of a Love Story*, Catherine Texier expresses how it feels to be left for another woman:

> *It's one thing to be with a guy and see that he's losing interest and maybe you are too, and quite another to have*

built a family and two literary careers and a house and eighteen years of shared companionship, the passion still going full swing in spite of the mounting tensions, and to feel the plug being pulled out overnight without warning. Like being shot in the back by a cop.

The women I talked to who had been left for another woman all described the experience in extreme terms:

"I cried every day for two months, I still cry two years later," Stella, sixty-two, admitted. Her reaction after being left for another woman after thirty-three years of marriage was frighteningly typical. "I railed and screamed in the car and burned his suit in effigy in the backyard, every witchy, crazy, demented thing you can think of. I drove by their house and hid in the bushes. I could be at work, get overwhelmed and go into the mini gym and cry and walk on the treadmill as fast as I could until it passed. I lost thirty pounds but gained ten back. Jangled nerves, twitching eyes, hyper alert. So sad like you wouldn't believe. This is the guy I'd been with since age twenty-three, the only guy for more than half my life and all my adult life. It was depressing that he was pulling away into alcoholism anyway but this was the *coup de grâce.*"

Romantic rejection actually triggers changes in our brains, according to anthropologist Helen Fisher, who has studied the chemistry of romantic love. Her research was an eye-opener for me. It answered a lot of questions about my own reactions to being cheated on and rejected and will probably shine some light on yours. She describes how brain scans of rejected people suggest that they secrete excess dopamine and cortisol during the initial phase of rejection. That's why rejected lovers get frantic and tend to relentlessly pursue the beloved. They may also take humiliating measures to reconnect—anything from writing letters to storming into the other woman's home to begging for him to change his mind. Paradoxically, along with the stress and the impulse to protest, abandoned lovers also feel renewed passion, which has a biological basis. Dopamine is the chemical in the brain that is associated with romantic love. But when love is thwarted, dopamine-producing neurons in the brain's reward system *prolong* their activities. As the beloved slips away, the very chemical that contributes to feelings of romantic love becomes even more potent, creating protest and romantic passion—which impels the abandoned wife to go to extremes to get him back. I certainly sprang into action as soon as Zeke told me he was leaving and tried desperately to hang on to him. All of a sudden I felt intense love and attraction for him when previously I'd felt mostly indifference.

If you ever wondered, like I did, where the intense rage that we jilted wives experience comes from, brain chemistry goes a long way to explain it. It seems that love and hate/rage are connected in the brain. The primary rage system is closely linked to centers in the prefrontal cortex that anticipate rewards. The common response to unfulfilled expectations is known as frustration-aggression. In short, when people and other animals begin to realize that an expected reward is in jeopardy, even unattainable, these centers in the prefrontal cortex trigger fury. "Why does passionate love turn to hate and rage?" Fisher asks. "Because love and hate/rage are connected in the brain." Both love and hate produce excessive energy, drive you to focus obsessively on the beloved, and cause intense yearning. They can exist simultaneously, which is why we vacillate wildly between love and hate when in the throes of being rejected. You can be terribly angry at a rejecting husband but still very much in love. This reaction explains why jilted lovers stalk and sometimes kill their exes, or even resort to suicide. Men commit the majority of homicides while women may attempt suicide. Luckily, many suicidal women fail to kill themselves, often because they're attempting to manipulate the rejecting husband into returning. However, many do succeed. Even though our strongest drive is survival, the drive to love can triumph even over the will to live.

Eventually these feelings wane and you must deal with another form of torture, hopelessness and despair. In one study of more than one hundred men and women who had been rejected recently, some 40 percent experienced clinical depression. The expression *dying of a broken heart* is not just hyperbole. Heart attacks and strokes can be caused by severe depression. These statistics probably come from a study of rejection in college students where most psychologists do their studies. If clinical depression is that common after rejection when you're just dating, imagine how severe it is after twenty years of marriage.

It's amazing so many of us survive, and actually bounce back to find a better life. As severe as our response is to grief, for almost all of us the will to survive is stronger. We're programmed to forget and go on. I often think of what it must have been like in earlier days when women lost so many children before age five. They managed to get over their grief and bore more children or the human race wouldn't have survived. We have inherited this ability to grieve and go on. The expression "time heals" comes from our genetic inheritance.

Of course not all of us suffer equally. How we react depends on many things, including our upbringing. "Some people make secure attachments as children and have the self-esteem and resilience to overcome a romantic setback relatively quickly," Fisher explains. "Others grew up in loveless homes fraught with

tension, chaos, or rejection, leaving them clingy and defenseless."
Biology plays a part as well. We all know women with sunny dis-
positions, who always see the glass as half full. They take everything, including divorce, with more equanimity and bounce back
more quickly.

In order to move on, it helps to be clear about exactly what
you're missing and grieve for those specific losses. As Wendy, my
therapist girlfriend, advises, "The grief you suffer from infidelity is a different type of grieving. You lose the status of beloved.
You're no longer the one he calls every day, someone else is.
You're no longer the center of his life, someone else is. That is the
unkindest cut of all." For us older women, the grief is not only for
the marriage but for who we used to be. You're not the same young
girl you were when he met you, so you may need to grieve the loss
of your sexual attractiveness, since you're facing aging as well as
betrayal. If you're missing a real connection, as I was, you have to
grieve that. Or you may have to grieve no longer being the retired
comfortable lady with the nice lifestyle, being the object of your
husband's sexual desire, or simply being the beloved.

LIVING WELL IS THE BEST REVENGE

Shirley Glass, whose practice focused on infidelity, knew from
clinical experience that living well is the best revenge. "There
is no revenge as sweet as living a joyful life," she reported in her
book *Not "Just Friends."* Glass would even suggest to betrayed
wives that someday they write a thank-you note to the affair partner for taking a cheating man off their hands. At the time they
were going through the pain and anguish of betrayal, they couldn't
imagine doing such a thing, but "several ex-wives have smiled at
me years later and said, 'You were right. She did me a favor. I hear

she's as unhappy now as I once was.'" Some of them even wound up feeling sorry for the affair partner, who wound up stuck with their loser ex-husbands.

For inspiration read *Revenge of the Middle-Aged Woman* by Elizabeth Buchan. It's a witty, ironic story of Rose, a magazine editor in her late forties who is blindsided by her fiftyish husband's affair with her young assistant, Minty. They all work at the same magazine, and in quick succession Rose loses her husband, her job, and her house to the heartless Minty. She sinks into a terrible funk, but is determined to start a new life, which she does with grace and dignity. In the meantime her ex-husband and Minty's life go down the tubes as Minty turns into a shrew and makes his life miserable. Eventually her ex asks to come back, but he's already had a baby with Minty and is stuck with her for life. In the meantime Rose has made another, happier life for herself and has moved on. Read it and weep—and then have a good laugh. Rose is a great role model for us all.

I have heard many of these stories from divorcées, who often went on to have a happy marriage with a much more suitable mate after being ditched by a cheating spouse. Even if they don't find true love, they often find fulfillment in other ways, including a successful career, good friends, travel, and a happier life. They discover that it's good riddance to their oppressive, controlling, critical, cheating husbands. Susan Becker—who was dumped for a younger woman, and whose "Letter to Harry" I quoted in the first chapter—now says, "What I do know is that my husband's final gesture of cutting me loose was the kindest thing he has ever done."

CHAPTER ELEVEN

FORGIVING THE BASTARD AND MOVING ON

Forgive Yourself First

Forgiveness means giving up all hope for a better past.

—LILY TOMLIN

There are as many books out there about forgiveness as there are about how to make your marriage work. Almost every counselor, clergyman, and self-help guru seems to have an opinion about forgiveness, and most of those opinions have the same core message: *You need to forgive for yourself, not the other person. Forgiveness is the only way to let go of the negative feelings that are eating you up inside, that he may not even be aware of. If you don't forgive, you are doomed to be bitter and blaming forever. You need to forgive in order to move on.*

For some divorcées that works. They're able to forgive because of their personal beliefs, their religious faith, their ex's expressions of remorse, the circumstances of the breakup, or just a sense that it's the right thing for them. Others get stuck in bitterness and don't forgive *or* move on. Still others move on successfully without ever forgiving what their husband has done.

Both forgiveness and the desire for revenge are natural human responses to being hurt. We want to forgive—to let go of hurts, to move on—especially if we don't want to hurt others, such as our children or ourselves, by having to be tortured with ongoing anger and bitterness. Or we may want to repair our relationship with him for the sake of the children and feel that we need to forgive to do that. The desire for revenge is also a natural human response to being hurt. We want justice when we're wronged; it feels unnatural to just accept and forgive without some kind of restitution. These two desires are often at war after divorce. The real goal, however, is to make peace with yourself so you can heal, which certainly doesn't involve revenge, although justice may help. Getting sidetracked by the search for revenge, usually through the courts, or trying to forgive whether or not you feel like it or are ready to do it, are both futile paths only leading to more pain.

The problem is that we're taught we *must* forgive in order to heal, to stop carrying around all that anger and hatred. But how is that possible? The very definition of forgiveness means you're supposed to stop being angry about something you have every right to be angry about. In order to do that you have to twist yourself and your emotions into a pretzel, or admit you've failed at yet another aspect of your marriage—your divorce. That's just more guilt being pushed on you, as if you didn't have enough.

I contend that you *don't* have to forgive unless you feel like it, or unless your ex has made amends. You will not necessarily suffer if you don't forgive. Forgiveness is not the only way to heal from hurt, betrayal, or emotional or physical abuse. You will move on anyway because unless you consciously hang on to your hurts, nursing them with more and more attention, they will naturally fade with time. We are human, our wounds heal, hurts of the past recede into the past and the pain lessens over the years. Forgiveness often happens organically, after enough time has passed.

You need to understand the basis of forgiveness as a spiritual concept before you can decide for yourself whether or not you want to, or need to, forgive him. To me the most important aspect of forgiveness is not to forgive him but to forgive yourself.

WHAT WOULD JESUS DO?

Part of the forgiveness dilemma is the meaning of the word itself: According to Wikipedia, which seems to have supplanted the dictionary when it comes to definitions these days,

> *Forgiveness is the mental, emotional and/or spiritual process of ceasing to feel resentment, indignation or anger, against another person for a perceived offense, difference or mistake, or ceasing to demand punishment or restitution.*

In other words, in order to forgive you have to stop hating—or at least stop being so angry at—the offender. You can't even be indignant. You can't even be a little bit pissed. This is a very tall order for many of us—especially if betrayal was a factor in our breakups. However, it's what Jesus did, and since we are basically a Christian society, that has become the gold standard for forgiveness. Again from Wikipedia:

> *According to traditional Christian teachings, the forgiveness of others is amongst the spiritual duties of the Christian believer. God is generally considered to be the original source of all forgiveness, which is made possible through the suffering and sacrifice of Jesus and is freely available to the repentant believer. As a response to God's forgiveness, the Christian believer is in turn expected to learn how to forgive others. The Lord's Prayer teaches:*

*Forgive us our trespasses as we forgive those who tres-
pass against us.*

Both Judaism and Islam see forgiveness very differently.
Unlike the Christian approach, which is based on doing what
Jesus would do, Jews base their beliefs on doing the right thing.
In the Jewish tradition you're not obligated to forgive someone
unless they've sincerely expressed remorse and convinced you
of their sincerity. In fact the offender is mandated by God to ask
for forgiveness three times; only then is the victim religiously
required to forgive. However, if the wrongdoer does not apologize,
there is no religious obligation to grant forgiveness. Additionally,
in Judaism, a wrongdoer must apologize *to those he has harmed* in
order to be entitled to forgiveness. A person can obtain forgiveness from God only for wrongs done to God, not for wrongs done
to other people.

Most of us, myself included, are so steeped in the Christian tradition that we're unfamiliar with this approach to forgiveness. I certainly had no idea what my own religion taught until
I researched it for this book. This knowledge took a weight off
my shoulders. You don't have to forgive the bastard unless he
apologizes, repeatedly. I was amazed to discover that I wasn't
obligated to forgive Zeke—ever—unless he expressed remorse
and asked for forgiveness. I have prayed so many times to be
able to forgive, while waiting and wishing for an apology, any
apology. I so much want to feel better and drop the bitterness I
am still burdened with. I want the ice around my heart to melt,
for Dorothy's sake if for no other. It's a terrible burden for a child
to have her parents despise each other. I would forgive him with
great relief if he even once asked me to. But he never has, and,
in fact has made it clear that he doesn't feel one jot of remorse.

Guilt, yes, for hurting Dorothy. Remorse for betraying me—not even a whisper.

Gary Egeberg, the author of *The Forgiveness Myth: How to Heal Your Hurts, Move On and Be Happy Again When You Can't or Won't Forgive,* likens mandatory forgiveness to being kicked in the shin. "If someone deliberately kicks you in the shin, it would be ridiculous to be concerned about the condition of this person's foot rather than attend to your own bruised shin, but that's what forgiving feels like for many. Rather than caring for yourself after he's hurt you, you're supposed to focus on him by extending goodwill or forgiveness. This is true even if he fails to apologize, refuses to get you an ice pack, or worse, lines up to kick you again." Sorry, I don't think so.

I'm not alone in this struggle. Many of you want to forgive your husband and can't find it in your heart do to so. Then you wind up feeling bad about your inability to forgive, which just adds insult to injury. Why do you have to forgive to move on? I wondered. Why forgive a husband who betrayed you, abused you, was cruel, dishonest, and never expressed remorse or apologized, in fact blamed you for his bad behavior? As women, haven't we done enough time on the cross? Isn't it more appropriate, not to speak of self-respecting, to say, *To hell with him, he has to live with his sins. I'm focusing on myself.*

This is not to say that forgiveness doesn't help heal the hurt of divorce—it definitely does. Someday I'd like to look back on our marriage with a sense of equanimity, an ability to remember the good times as well as the bad. Kali says, "You have to see your ex as a flawed human being like yourself. He's made mistakes and so have you, but eventually you need to forgive him for being only human." Yes, I'd like to let go of the anger, but I'd also like to regain my past. If you've seen *Eternal Sunshine of the Spotless*

Mind, you'll know what I mean. In that film, Jim Carrey and Kate Winslet are lovers who break up. Kate Winslet's character elects to have a futuristic procedure to erase all memory of their relationship. When she doesn't recognize him, Jim Carrey decides to have the same procedure. As his mind is being erased, however, he realizes that he is losing all the wonderful memories of their time together, so he fights the process. It's a funny, surrealistic, emotionally resonant treatment of how it feels to be so desperate to get rid of that pain you're stuck with when you break up that you're willing to erase your entire past. It brought home the message that I'd lost eighteen years of my life due to the way my marriage ended—there were good times during those years as well as bad but the good ones had disappeared. I cried for about twenty-four hours after seeing that film. Someday I'd like those years back—they belong to me. But forgiveness is appropriate only if and when you feel like it, when it happens naturally, not because it's something you're supposed to do, something mandated by God. So give yourself a break, girlfriend. Work on yourself and let him go. Let God forgive him, it's not your department.

FORGIVE YOURSELF FIRST

The person you *really* need to forgive after a divorce is not him, but yourself. We women tend to take responsibility for the destruction of our marriages no matter who does the betraying or leaving. Somehow it's our fault—we weren't good enough wives or mothers or sex partners or listeners or caregivers. We didn't understand him, we judged him, we didn't put up with his faults. *We* were the ones who failed. If he found someone else, it was because we took him for granted, weren't nice enough to him, didn't want to have sex, wanted to have too much sex, didn't take care of ourselves, got old, got fat . . . the self-blame goes on. In order to move on for real, *you* are the one who needs forgiveness, not him. Releasing those feelings so you can heal has nothing to do with forgiving him. You even need to forgive yourself for failing to forgive, to move that anger to a smaller and smaller compartment in your mind and heart where it simply doesn't take up space or bother you anymore.

Patricia Wall, my expert on the tribal origins of our relationships, agrees. She says that when your partner is gone you need to release the wound to be whole again. "As women we automatically blame ourselves when the tribe is fractured, even if he's the one who did the fracturing. Releasing actually has nothing to do with him, it's a completely internal process of healing. We associate it with forgiveness because the process of healing yourself includes dismissing the power of the person who wounded you— forgiveness takes back your power from him so he can't hurt you anymore. Fundamentally, for a woman who has been betrayed, forgiveness is about taking back the power to decide you are whole, valuable, and own your own fire. It's a way of chucking him out of your cave so he has no more power over you."

The word *forgiveness* is the problem. It's too loaded with the assumption that somehow what he did was okay. That's not the case. You're not excusing him. You're releasing yourself from the conflict he created in your tribe. You're reclaiming your domain over that tribe.

I think this is what many of us wind up doing, without officially forgiving our exes, or even dealing with the issue. It's what I've done. The more time passes, the less emotional energy I spend on anger or feeling hurt. We move on organically. The marriage was in our past, we have changed and become different women, we have new lives, new interests, new mates. Initially anger is appropriate, and women who don't get angry are often in deep denial. Anger is a necessary part of healing, especially if there's been a betrayal, but moving on doesn't necessarily have to involve forgiving. It can just mean acceptance of reality. As long as we've forgiven ourselves.

For a long time I blamed myself for the problems in my marriage. I have forgiven myself for those failings by becoming more and more aware of what actually went on in my marriage, realizing that he was equally responsible for its failure. In the end, all I feel is enormous regret, and that's a burden we all struggle with when it comes to the mistakes we've made in life.

HOW TO FORGIVE YOURSELF

Bonnie Russell, who operates www.FamilyLawCourts.com, says women in particular have trouble forgiving themselves. We're afflicted by the "shoulda, woulda, coulda" syndrome. "I should have seen it, known it, realized it," followed by "I wasted twenty years of my life." She recommends setting aside five minutes, setting a timer, and really wallowing in it. "Beat yourself up. Most people can only do that for less than three minutes. By three and a half minutes, they're glancing at the timer. The trick is to stay with it because it's so unpleasant. When the timer finally dings, you'll be so happy! These thoughts will creep back later, but the good news is, when they do women happily say, 'Honey, I already beat myself up over that, I'm moving on.' And more importantly, they act on that, and do."

Rabbi Jonathan acknowledged that my forgiving Zeke wasn't appropriate right now since he hasn't expressed any remorse, still blames me, and I'm still entangled because of our co-parenting situation. However, he recommended that I should

FIVE MINUTES TO SELF-FORGIVENESS

Rabbi Jonathan gave me some great advice about how to forgive myself that's applicable to most of us:

- Focus on the ongoing situation so you can look in the mirror in the morning and know you're not adding fuel to the fire.
- Forgive yourself for being so pissed off.
- Accept the nature of the current situation, instead of indulging in self-recrimination.
- Don't do things you'll feel sorry for. This includes sending inflammatory e-mails (my major weakness).
- Don't get off on the high of battle. This doesn't mean giving up, just not behaving in a vindictive way.
- Forgive yourself for marrying him in the first place. (I beat myself up for this but have to remind myself that I couldn't have been anyone else than who I was at the time.)
- Forgive yourself for not being able to forgive.

turn it around and consider apologizing to him instead, letting him know I'm aware of my weaknesses and that I have many regrets. "You don't need to forgive him," Rabbi Jonathan told me, "you could seek his forgiveness as a way of letting go of the past and telling him that you're in a different space now. Forgiveness is about what happened in the past. The dramatic part of forgiveness is that it's disarming. Seeking his forgiveness might clear space in the kind of nonlinear way that relationships work. It might also relieve you of having to defend yourself against your own failings." This advice applies to all of us who are struggling to forgive.

He explained that forgiveness requires humility. The whole business of seeking it or giving it means you're not trying to control the situation. That doesn't mean you won't stand up for what is right, but you're not trying to control him. "The mystery of forgiveness is that it allows the next thing to happen. It's unknown what the next thing is. That's not in your control. Forgiveness is about giving up control, releasing the past into the past, letting your life go on."

I balked at this, not being able to imagine actually asking Zeke to forgive me, although I know I have much to be forgiven for. "If it's too much of a stretch to reach out to him," Rabbi Jonathan reassured me, "be as generous as possible to yourself and behave in the right way in the future." When you still have to deal regularly with someone as I do with Zeke, forgiveness just makes it easier. If two people are dug into positions. nothing will happen , but if one person is willing to move something might change. So far that person isn't me. It might be you, however. If you can find it in your heart to ask forgiveness as a way to heal, give it a try.

TWO WRONGED GIRLFRIENDS, TWO AMAZING FORGIVENESS AND MOVING-ON STORIES

Both Kay and Lydia have been divorced for a number of years— eight years for Kay and ten for Lydia. They have both long ago forgiven and moved on despite circumstances that would seem to make it impossible. Their stories are inspirational and will give you an idea what is possible down the line, after the initial pain has healed.

Kay

Kay met Joe when she was very young—she was a freshman and he was a senior in college. Now fifty-eight, she is an administrator from Albany, New York, and has been divorced for eight years. Although they both were the same religion, they were very different in every other way. Their marriage was tumultuous. He came from a divorced family, she came from a close, loving family; he was socially inept, she was a social butterfly; she liked to spend money, he was a tightwad; he was controlling and put her down all the time, she took it. After nine years of marriage, they had three kids in rapid succession, the first when she was thirty. Before she had kids she thought about leaving, but then she became pregnant and stopped thinking about it.

"I was never very independent," she explains. "I was worried at first about what kind of father he'd be, but he turned out to be a great father. But we never learned to communicate. Talking was a waste of time to him, he didn't like thinking aloud. I remember hoping my first pregnancy would be a boy—I didn't know if a girl could handle it. But something changed after we had kids. He stayed up at night, he took care of the babies without complaining. His personality didn't change, however. He was very mercurial and criticized everything about me, from my spending habits to the way I put the dishes in the dishwasher. Then he started taking vacations on his own. At some point it became clear that things were going on that I didn't know about."

After the kids were born, the couple became very close to her brother and sister-in-law, Lisa, who had kids of similar ages. The two families lived near each other, vacationed together, went to the track together since both owned harness horses. They even went to Disney World together every year for fourteen years. Her husband and her brother worked in the same office.

Even though no one thought Kay and Joe's marriage would last, they made it to their twenty-fifth anniversary and threw themselves a party. Not long after that, she began to notice that Joe and Lisa were spending too much time together. One day her brother took her to lunch and played a tape of Joe and Lisa talking that made it clear that they'd been having an affair for quite a while.

"I must have known on some level, because I was upset and sad but not really astounded," Kay says. "We tried marriage counseling, but it was pretend therapy because he wasn't being honest. Finally I brought in the tape to prove that he was lying. Joe admitted to the affair, promised to stop it, said he loved me and didn't want to lose his family. For the first time he cried, and when we got home he told me that the family was the most important thing to him. I told him he had to give up Lisa and tell our children what he'd done, that he'd done something foolish but he'd decided to keep our marriage together."

They spent another fruitless year in counseling with yet another therapist. Even though Joe denied that he was seeing Lisa, it was clear that he'd started again. This counselor felt there was nothing more she could do because he was being dishonest. As hurt as Kay was, she knew Joe had had affairs before that didn't mean much. He'd grown up with a father who had affairs. But this one was different. He couldn't give Lisa up. She read his e-mails to her, and it was clear he was really in love with her.

"What upset me the most was that I'd been very close to Lisa and couldn't believe she would do this to me. I'd done so much for her—we were friends. That summer he told me he wanted to keep both of us in his life. He promised to give me everything I wanted if I let him do that. It was a ridiculous proposition, so I dismissed it and told him to leave."

After he left, somehow they maintained a relationship, cool at first, but they always talked about the kids. "He always asked me how I was doing and it was clear then and still is that he'll always love me. If he could have had it his way, he would have had both of us. I promised my kids that every Sunday night their dad would come to dinner, which he did."

Kay says that most of the hurt was to the family, not between her and Joe. Despite her pain over the breakup, she stayed on good terms with Joe because of her kids. She wanted them to love their father. He didn't try to hurt them, she insists;, he was always there for them, and he continued his relationship with them as much as he could.

"People thought I was crazy. I could have done so many things to hurt him but I didn't. I just couldn't. I have a sign on my desk with an Asian saying: If you devote your life to seeking revenge, first dig two graves. That struck something in me."

This doesn't mean that Kay is some kind of saint. At the beginning she did vengeful, childish things like ordering dogshit and having it sent to Lisa's house. She called her names in front of other people in church. "When this happened I was in terrible pain and let some out, just not in front of my kids. I wrote poetry about the pain I felt and what he'd done and sent it to Joe. He read it and was very hurt. All this happened during the first years, but slowly I climbed out of the pain and was able to forgive."

Even though Joe never really said, *I'm sorry, I shouldn't have done it,* what he did show was caring and fairness. "He never apologized, it's not his nature, but he showed his remorse in his behaviors. He put down enough money so I could get a Lexus. My kids call it the 'guiltmobile.' I got a fair settlement including alimony for life." When she had surgery both Joe and her new boyfriend were there. Joe sat with her when she had chemo for lung cancer. "My brother would berate me for being friends with him but my ex-husband was there for me. I know if I need something he's a person I can call. He never blamed me and he never will."

Kay says she couldn't have done anything that would make her children more sad and unhappy than they already were because of the divorce. "I don't understand people who do that. I think that by not hurting them I ended up helping myself in the long run. By maintaining a friendship with Joe, I felt stronger and more prepared to go on by myself. I wasn't alone, he was there for me no matter what. My kids will be forever thankful to both of us."

As for Lisa, Kay was her dear friend and loved her before this happened. Kay knew her marriage to Joe was problematic. Paradoxically she felt that if Joe had broken up their marriage and then left Lisa, she would have been even angrier. She could accept that he broke up their marriage because he was truly in love, not for no reason. Today she accepts that Joe and Lisa were meant to be together, and respects that. Eventually she was even happy for them. "I looked at Lisa and said, *I can make this work.*" Now that Kay has remarried, happily this time, she and her new husband and Lisa and Joe even go away together on vacations. "When we start making plans my kids call it the cuckoo convention. I told myself there are much worse things in life than this. I have even gone to Lisa at church one Sunday and said, 'Lisa, I wasn't very nice to you, please forgive me, I'm sorry.' She apologized as well."

Eventually even Kay's brother admitted she'd done the right thing. "To this day people are amazed when I say I was lucky," Kay told me. "But I am. I didn't have a husband who left me and my kids. I had someone who was always there for me and always will be. We weren't friends in our marriage but we are now. For me to be able to focus on the good things is easier than wallowing in hurt and pain."

Many divorced couples manage to maintain a cordial—even friendly—relationship for the sake of the kids. Maybe they don't go on vacation together, but they do care about each other. My neighbor invites her ex-husband to Thanksgiving dinner and other events every year with their kids and her boyfriend. My friend Russell Wild and his ex-wife Susan Ellis Wild wrote *The Unofficial Guide to Getting a Divorce* together, despite the fact that it took time for them to negotiate a friendly relationship. Kay is just remarkable because of the circumstances. There aren't too many ex-wives who could forgive a husband who cheated with a sister-in-law, much less go on vacation with the two of them.

Lydia

Lydia, now fifty-nine, was married for twenty-five years to a man who abused her physically, verbally, and emotionally. They met in college, where he was a professor fifteen years her senior. She was a New York Jewish girl stuck in the Midwest in the mid-1960s, where her parents had moved. Even though she was cute, she'd only dated cultured, bright, New York Jewish guys, and all of a sudden she couldn't find a date.

She was dazzled by David, who was also Jewish and from Long Island, in addition to being a nationally famous painter. As an art student she now realizes she confused being in love with his work with being in love with him as a person. She probably married him out of desperation because she couldn't adjust to life in the Midwest.

Like a lot of abusive men, he was extremely manipulative, and didn't start actually beating her until she was nine months' pregnant and he knew she wouldn't leave. She then proceeded to have three more children and stayed in the marriage because she thought it was best for the children and felt that if she'd made a mistake she had to suffer with it.

It helped that she loved being pregnant and nursing, lectured for La Leche League, and was very close to her kids. "When you have so many kids, you don't have time to focus on your marriage," she told me. Today she says her kids remember a happy childhood and have somehow screened out the abuse. "They remember all the projects, the secret walks. Their father was involved with them somewhat, but he didn't play ball or kid games—he was too old, too tired, too busy with his painting." Lydia now realizes that she had kids to escape the marriage. "It was a kind of solution."

She says she was lucky she never got seriously injured. "The worst incident was when he tried to throw me through a plate glass window," she told me dispassionately. "He didn't succeed in throwing me through the window, but I had bruises." Like many abused women she didn't report him, because she was afraid she couldn't support the kids alone. She interceded when he tried to hurt the children, but in reality she couldn't always be there to stop him.

When the children were teenagers, she wanted to go to graduate school to get a teaching certificate. He refused to allow her to have any independence, accused her of stealing the family's money, and closed her bank account. During the last few years of her marriage, she grew truly despondent, lost hope, and hatched a suicide plan, even doing a trial run to make sure it would succeed. Luckily, she came to her senses and realized that it was the marriage that had to go, not her. When her husband refused to allow her to go for therapy, she told him about her suicide plan and threatened that he'd have to take care of the kids if she killed herself. By then he'd convinced both her and the children that she was the crazy one and he was the sane one. Eventually he relented, and she got help that led her to escape the marriage, fleeing to a battered women's shelter. "Through the counseling they led me to Safe Home. To leave an abusive situation you need a trained expert."

Financially, she wound up with nothing and is still barely scraping by. But she says, "I got screwed financially but felt like a success because I didn't get murdered. He did everything he could do to stretch out the divorce, wouldn't give me a Get [a Jewish divorce], told the children I left in a menopausal fit." Although they'd begged her to leave for years, at first the children refused to talk to her. "They had to believe I was crazy in order to continue to love their father, who had always told them I was a nut case." Eventually however, they came around. She is now close to them.

Why did she stay with him? "I liken it to putting a frog in a pot of water on the stove and then keeping on raising the heat. Eventually it's too weak to get out." Has she forgiven him now that ten years have passed? Surprisingly, the answer is yes. "I can forgive him because not forgiving him gives him power or control over me. It's easy for me to say, 'I forgive you, you had a loused-up childhood and you didn't have what it took not to become an abuser.' I hope he's gloriously happy with his new wife because I'd like my kids to see one of their parents happy. He still doesn't admit that he ever abused anybody."

About the anger she obviously still has, Lydia explains:

"I think it's important to get angry. My problem was that I didn't get angry then, I just accepted and accepted. But you have to learn to let go of that anger. When I talk about what happened with him, I remember the anger I had but I'm not attached to it, it's water under the bridge—anger is like having poison left inside.

"Instead of saying *I was an idiot,* I choose to reframe everything into strength rather than weakness. I was strong enough to figure out how to survive all those years and keep my kids alive. I was strong enough to raise kids who aren't abusers, I was strong enough to leave although I had no way to support myself.

"Yoga helped me get through. I had a fear of inversions, of standing on my head. When I had to learn to overcome that, it helped me—I put my world on its head by leaving my husband. My religious ties gave me emotional strength. I felt God would help me get through it. I see my ex has a holy soul just as I do; he's just not as attached to a higher level. There are five levels of soul; the highest levels are the god within you. People like him are on lower levels. At the end of every yoga class you say *namaste,* which means 'the holiness in me salutes the holiness in you.'

"Yoga helps with forgiveness. When you can't do a yoga pose, we say forgive yourself for not being able to do it. If you can't forgive yourself, you can't forgive anyone else. During *Tashlich* [a ceremony during the Jewish high holy days in which you take bread crumbs and throw them into moving water, symbolically casting your sins away] I took the rose petals from my rosebush put them in the creek and said, *That's my anger, it's going down the stream and he's losing complete control.* I work hard every *Tashlich* to get rid of any anger that creeps up."

There is much to learn from Lydia. If she can forgive, anyone can. The key for her was realizing that her ex's childhood made him who he was, that he didn't have the strength to overcome that childhood, and that we all have a holy soul, but that he is simply on a lower level of development as a human being than she is. I particularly appreciated this insight from yoga and the Eastern traditions, since it gives you a way to forgive without actually making the offender's behavior somehow okay, or inconsequential. I liken it to forgiving a child for attacking you. That child doesn't know any better, and neither does your ex. He's simply lacking in integrity or limited in understanding and consciousness, and you have no choice but to accept that and move on.

MOVING ON

There are three stages in the divorce recovery process. During the first phase, you flit from one thing to another. You may date different men, get rid of old friends and make new ones, travel to new places, try out new jobs. Abigail Trafford calls this the Hummingbird phase. "Hummingbird people aren't able to reestablish themselves as new entities because they never allow themselves to confront the pain and anxiety of divorce or a new life. Their wings flutter too fast," she says. My Hummingbird phase included a long detour from grieving with Internet dating, which became an obsession.

The next level is foundering. You fall apart emotionally, you lose your job, your new romance breaks up, you can't seem to make enough money to get by, you despair that things will ever get better. Some people never stop foundering. We all know women who are still hanging on by their fingernails ten years after their divorce, bouncing from job to job, man to man, shrink to shrink. This is the stage where you can get stuck in cynicism and bitterness. When Bob and I broke up I floundered, searching desperately for a replacement, finally having to accept "the reality of my situation," as my girlfriend Roz put it.

Moving on for real is the phoenix phase, where a new you rises up from the ashes of divorce. You've gone through all the pain and misery, moved past your anger, forgiven or not, whatever feels right to you. You've gone through the final stages of grief and let go of your marriage. You've become a separate, self-motivating individual who doesn't depend on a man to make a good life for yourself. Most importantly, you accept yourself as a flawed human being; you forgive yourself for screwing up your marriage. You finally become who you really are, even if that's a very different woman from who you were when you were married, or who you ever expected to be.

Moving on doesn't happen in neatly defined stages. It's an imperceptible process that happens while you're doing other things. It's halting—two steps forward, one step back. One day you think you've moved on and then you regress—over and over again. The most important thing to remember is to keep forgiving yourself at each stage. If you regress and do dumb things, like sleeping with your ex (it happens), bad-mouthing him to the kids, or making a scene at a family event, pick yourself up, brush yourself off, and start all over again. Remember to tell yourself it's okay, you've been through hell and you deserve to screw up—once, twice, or a zillion times—until you're ready to stop screwing up.

One day you look up and realize you haven't thought about your ex or your marriage for a whole hour, then a whole day, a whole week, and so on. You get involved with other things; you catch yourself thinking about the project you're working on, or the guy you're involved with, what to invest your money in, how to help a friend, how your kids or grandkids are doing, redecorating your living room, buying a new house, a trip you've always wanted to take. Life, in all its complexity, just takes over. Your marriage recedes into the past, seeming almost as though it happened to someone else. You realize that you're doing things you never would have done when you were married and you congratulate yourself. The pain gets smaller and smaller, taking up less room in your consciousness.

This doesn't mean you will never again feel the pain and rage you initially felt. Triggers will come up and you'll be right back there. In a divorce support group I went to immediately after my husband left, when I was totally consumed with my own anguish and desperate for some relief, I was horrified while listening to a woman who had been divorced twenty years ago. She talked about all the old, bad post-divorce feelings coming up recently because her ex-husband had died. However, when I expressed my dismay that she still had those feelings, she reassured me that she had long ago moved on; it was just that her husband's death had brought up a lot of unfinished business and bad memories that she needed to process. I was greatly relieved but still uneasy. I couldn't imagine then how you could actually move on and be back at square one twenty years later at the same time. Now I understand since I'm in both places regularly. It's like grief for a loved one. You mourn, you move on, but when something reminds you of that person a fresh pang still grips your heart.

Some experts assert that it takes a year for every five years of marriage to recover. That sounds about right in my case. However, co-parenting can complicate the moving-on process. If you still have to interact regularly with your ex and that interaction is hostile, you can get stuck repeating the past. I expect that when my daughter gets older, it will get easier for me to totally disconnect. Still, most of the time my mind is on other things—my writing, my friends, my house, my health, my finances or lack thereof (don't get me started on that subject)—not him. Every once in a while, though, when he does something to really piss me off, I'm right back in that place where I feel helpless, hopeless, and homicidal. Thank goodness we have finally reached a truce of sorts, where we avoid e-mail flame wars and communicate mainly through my daughter's therapist.

You may also sink into feelings from the past when you run into him at those unavoidable family functions such as weddings, graduations, and so on—especially if he's with a woman twenty years his junior—but those feelings will pass quickly. When I listen to the excruciating pain of recent divorcées, I realize how far I've come. I totally empathize, but am so grateful not to be there anymore.

Please trust me on this, girlfriend. The divorce journey is long and arduous but it does end, it really does. When you're finally there, write him that thank-you note. Never forget . . . he's history, you're not.

RESOURCES

Here is a compilation of my favorite books, Web sites, and other resources.

BASIC SURVIVAL—THE TOP TWO

If you don't read anything else, read these two books:

Lesser, Elizabeth. *Broken Open: How Difficult Times Can Make Us Grow.* New York: Villard, 2004. This book will give you hope that you can emerge from the trauma of divorce wiser, stronger, happier, more in touch with your purpose and passion. Lesser shares stories of people, including herself, who have accomplished this transformation.

Trafford, Abigail. *Crazy Time: Surviving Divorce and Building a New Life.* New York: Harper Perennial, 1992. My bible of divorce. Original, insightful analysis of what happens when marriages fall apart. It explained to me what went wrong with my marriage. Unlike most books by experts, this one is written by a journalist whose long, lively anecdotes make the book easy and fun reading.

INSIGHT AND EMOTIONAL SUPPORT

Bair, Deirdre. *Calling It Quits: Late-Life Divorce and Starting Over.* Bair interviewed nearly 400 older ex-wives, ex-husbands, and their adult children and came up with a fascinating book about how the boomer generation is coping with divorce.

Colgrove, Melba, Ph.D., Harold H. Bloomfield, M.D., and Peter McWilliams. *How to Survive the Loss of a Love*. Los Angeles: Prelude Press, 1991. Comforting affirmations, poems, snippets of advice. Pick it up when you need a lift.

Egeberg, Gary, and Wayne Raiter, M.A., L.I.C.S.W. *The Forgiveness Myth: How to Heal Your Hurts, Move On and Be Happy Again When You Can't or Won't Forgive*. Richfield, MN: Original Pathways Press, 2008. A contrarian view of forgiveness that promotes and fully explores the view that you don't have to forgive to move on.

Falk, Florence. *On My Own: The Art of Being a Woman Alone*. Harmony Books, 2007. Falk illuminates the essential role that being alone plays in women's lives. Inspiring stories and great advice.

Fisher, Dr. Bruce, and Dr. Robert Alberti. *Rebuilding When Your Relationship Ends*. Third edition. Atascadero, CA: Impact Publishers, Inc., 2002. A divorce classic, this book outlines the stages you go through after divorce very clearly and compassionately. The model that the authors use of rebuilding block by block, moving up the mountain to freedom, is very helpful and reassuring.

Fisher, Helen. *Anatomy of Love: A Natural History of Mating, Marriage, and Why We Stray*. New York: Ballantine, 1994. Fisher offers new explanations for why men and women fall in love, marry, and divorce, and discusses the future of sex in a way that will surprise you.

————. *Why We Love: The Nature and Chemistry of Romantic Love.* New York: Holt, 2004. Fisher argues that much of our romantic behavior is hardwired into our brains due to the brain chemicals norepinephrine and dopamine.

Kingma, Daphne Rose. *Coming Apart: Why Relationships End and How to Live Through the Ending of Yours.* Boston: Conari Press, 2000. Kingma points out that we shouldn't view divorce as a failure. We marry to complete developmental tasks and often divorce when those tasks are finished. Her view is insightful and empathetic.

McWade, Micki, M.S.W. *Getting Up, Getting Over, Getting On: A Twelve Step Guide to Divorce Recovery.* Beverly Hills, CA: Champion Press, 1999. If you like the 12-step model for recovery, you'll appreciate this book.

Vaughn, Diane. *Uncoupling: Turning Points in Intimate Relationships.* New York: Vintage, 1990. A fascinating sociological examination of how marriages actually come apart—who does the leaving, who gets left. I liked it because it didn't provide any bandages or superficial solutions. It makes clear that most such measures are, finally, ineffectual.

GROUP SUPPORT

Ariadne's Thread: Spa for the Soul. A healing getaway for divorcées. www.aspaforthesoul.com.

CODA, Co-dependents Anonymous. A 12-step group for those who weren't married to an alcoholic or addict but are or were addicted to a person and are having a hard time breaking free. www.codependents.org.

McWade, Micki, M.S.W. *A Divorce Group Leader's Guide*. Fredonia, WI: Champion Press, 2004. If you can't find a divorce support group, here's how to start your own.

The following are all sites with active communities where you can post your problems and get responses:

www.divorce360.com
www.divorcesource.com/wwwboard/bulletin
www.divorcesupport/about.com
www.firstwivesworld.com

PRACTICAL ADVICE: LEGAL, FINANCIAL, CAREER

Dailey, Nancy. *When Baby Boom Women Retire*. Praeger, 2000. Ammunition for your lawyer fighting for alimony. Dailey's research findings indicate that the inequity of wages between men and women combined with women's caregiving responsibilities penalize women in retirement. More info: www.drnancydailey.com.

Fishman Cohen, Carol, and Vivian Steir Rabin. *Back on the Career Track: A Guide for Stay at Home Moms Who Want to Return to Work*. New York: Warner Business Books, 2007. Lots of helpful advice for older women who have been out of the job market for a long time and want to revive former careers, or find new ones. www.backonthecareertrack.com/steps7.htm.

Herigstad, Sally, CPA. *Help! I Can't Pay My Bills: Surviving a Financial Crisis.* New York: St. Martin's Griffin, 2007. This was the only financial advice book I found that I could actually understand. Simple, clear, very helpful.

Mercer, Diana, J.D., and Marsha Kline Pruett, Ph.D., *Your Divorce Advisor: A Lawyer and a Psychologist Guide You Through the Legal and Emotional Landscape of Divorce.* New York: Fireside, 2001. Practical, direct guide for both the legal and emotional aspects of divorce and how they're interrelated. Extremely thorough and detailed.

Rosenwald Smith, Gayle, J.D., and Sally Abrahms. *What Every Woman Should Know About Divorce and Custody: Judges, Lawyers, and Therapists Share Winning Strategies on How to Keep the Kids, the Cash, and Your Sanity.* New York: Perigee, 2007. The subtitle says it all. A comprehensive insider's guide. You need to read this one.

Sember, Brette McWhorter, J.D. *The Complete Divorce Handbook: A Practical Guide.* New York: Sterling, 2009. Sember is a lawyer who looks at divorce from all angles—legal, social, psychological, and financial. This is a resource that speaks to everyone, from those just starting to contemplate breaking up a marriage, to those trying to renegotiate an unsatisfactory financial settlement.

————. *The Divorce Organizer & Planner.* New York: McGraw-Hill, 2004. This workbook streamlines the divorce process and helps you create a record of everything you need to organize, and prepare for the legal, emotional, and financial aspects of divorce.

Wild, Russell, and Susan Ellis. *The Unofficial Guide to Getting a Divorce.* New York: Wiley, 2005. Russell Wild, a journalist and financial planner, and Susan Ellis Wild, a lawyer, got divorced and then collaborated on this practical guide, which leads you through preparing for divorce, the process, legal issues, coping, sticky situations, and post-divorce financial and health care issues. Ya gotta admire them.

WEB SITES

www.aarp.org/revmort. Information about getting a reverse mortgage if you're over sixty-two.

www.abanet.org/legalservices/findlegalhelp/home.cfm. The American Bar Association has a Web site that provides information on obtaining pro bono or free legal help state by state.

www.divorceandfinance.org *and* www.idfa.com. Listings of divorce financial planners plus resources for divorce financial planning.

www.divorcesource.com. Information about every aspect of divorce.

www.prepaidlegal.com. Prepaid Legal costs twenty-five dollars to join and fourteen dollars a month; you get unlimited phone consultation with a divorce (or other) attorney. If you need local representation, the group will recommend a participating local divorce attorney who will give you a discount.

www.quintcareers.com. The site has a list of 169 questions that you can practice answering about your job background.

www.urbanext.uiuc.edu/ww1. Working Woman's Guide to Financial Security. Terrific financial planning resources for women, pre- and post-divorce.

www.womensmoney.com. Helpful site to figure out your future income needs, plus a lot of other financial information for women.

INFIDELITY

Druckerman, Pamela. *Lust in Translation: The Rules of Infidelity from Tokyo to Tennessee.* New York: Penguin, 2007. Find out how the French and other cultures deal with infidelity. We Americans are the most obsessed with therapeutic intervention, it seems. Lots of interesting and fun info.

Glass, Shirley P., and Jean Coppock Staeheli. *Not "Just Friends": Rebuilding Trust and Recovering Your Sanity After Infidelity.* New York: Free Press, 2004. The best book on the subject of "emotional" infidelity, which is more and more common these days.

Pittman, Frank. *Private Lies: Infidelity and the Betrayal of Intimacy.* New York: W. W. Norton, 1990. Pittman dares to take a stance against infidelity not based on spiritual or religious concepts, but on its effects on the psychological health of children and the destruction of the family. Very refreshing plus well-written, funny, easy reading.

DIVORCE AND GROWN CHILDREN

Fintushel (Oxenhandler), Noelle, and Nancy Hilliard, Ph.D., *A Grief Out of Season: When Your Parents Divorce in Your Adult Years.*

New York: Little, Brown, 1991. An intelligent, well-researched look at the trauma suffered by—and the possible courses of action open to—those whose parents divorce when they are adults.

Foster, Brooke Lea. *The Way They Were: Dealing with Your Parents' Divorce After a Lifetime of Marriage.* New York: Three Rivers, 2006. Challenges the prevailing myth that grown children are not affected by their parents' divorce. Foster tells her own story and uses the voices of other adult children of divorce to show how they can cope and heal.

DATING

Behrendt, Greg, Liz Tuccillo, and Lauren Monchik. *He's Just Not That Into You: The No-Excuses Truth to Understanding Guys.* New York: Simon Spotlight Entertainment, 2005. My girlfriend Roz gave this to me when she saw me agonizing about the guys who didn't call. No matter how old you are, you become a teenager again when dating.

Price, Joan. *Better Than I Ever Expected: Straight Talk About Sex After Sixty.* Emeryville, CA: Seal, 2006. Price found the great love of her life and the best sex after sixty, and she interviews lots of other women who had the same experience, including yours truly. Breezily written and fun to read.

Solomon, Alice. *Find the Love of Your Life After 50!* Writers Collective, 2003. Solomon, who calls herself a Gorgeous Grandma, takes an assertive stance about finding a mate after fifty, including following the "rules," as she outlines them. She's funny, sassy, and includes lots of quizzes.

STARTING OVER

Baar, Karen. *For My Next Act: Women Scripting Life After Fifty.* New York: St. Martin's Press, 2004. This book gives you the good news about life after fifty—how most women emerge from their fifties feeling better about themselves, with higher levels of satisfaction than women at all other stages of life.

Bauer-Maglin, Nan, and Alice Radosh, editors. *Women Confronting Retirement: A Nontraditional Guide.* Rutgers, NJ: Rutgers University Press, 2003. The voices of thirty-eight women from a wide range of professions, ages, and life situations as they confront the need to redefine who they are when they leave the workplace.

Davidson, Sara. *LEAP! What Will We Do With the Rest of Our Lives?* New York: Ballantine, 2008. Davidson interviewed people from across the country and from all walks of life, including such icons as Carly Simon, Tom Hayden, Tracy Kidder, Jane Fonda, Ram Dass, and Iman, as well as teachers, writers, psychologists, businesspeople, and spiritual leaders. The candid portraits are both inspiring and cautionary. A fun book.

Schacter-Shalomi, Zalman, and Ronald S. Miller. *From Age-ing to Sage-ing: A Profound New Vision of Growing Older.* Grand Central Publishing, 1997 An inspiring, spiritual approach to getting older through social activism, awareness, and mentoring.

Trafford, Abigail. *As Time Goes By: Boomerang Marriages, Serial Spouses, Throwback Couples, and Other Romantic Adventures in an Age Of Longevity.* New York: Basic Books, 2009. Trafford deftly narrates what it means to love and be loved in the decades after midlife—and she offers solutions to the most common problems that define this time of life.

————. *My Time: Making the Most of the Bonus Decades After Fifty.* New York: Basic Books, 2004. Accounts of people who had dramatic and uplifting life changes after fifty and before eighty.

RELATIONSHIP ADVICE
AND MARRIAGE COUNSELING

Emotionally Focused Therapy. EFT is a short term (eight to twenty sessions), structured approach to couples therapy formulated in the early 1980s. It claims an extremely high success rate. You can find therapists on www.eft.ca.

Gottman, John. *Why Marriages Succeed or Fail: And How You Can Make Yours Last.* New York: Simon and Schuster, 1995. An upbeat, easy-to-follow manual based on research into the dynamics of married couples. Gottman describes his studies as being akin to a CAT scan of a living relationship and asserts that he's been able to predict the future of marriages with an accuracy rate of better than 90 percent. To find Gottman therapists: www.gottman.com.

Hendrix, Harville. *Getting the Love You Want: A Guide for Couples.* Revised edition. New York: Holt, 2007. For seventeen years the author and his wife have been writing about how couples can express frustrated childhood needs constructively, instead of acting them out and poisoning any chance for happiness. This approach to marital communication is widely used across the country. To find Imago therapists: www.gettingtheloveyouwant.com.

Retrouvaille. Marriage-saving workshops run by the Catholic Church all over the country. Led by couples who have used Retrouvaille to save their own marriages, the workshops are nondenominational, inexpensive, and can be very helpful no matter what your religion. To find workshops in your area: www.retrouvaille.org.

Schnarch, David, Ph.D. *Passionate Marriage: Keeping Love and Intimacy Alive in Committed Relationships.* New York: Henry Holt, 1997. Schnarch believes that you can repair your marriage through what he calls the "sexual crucible," which integrates sexual and marital therapy. He also believes that we find the greatest sexual pleasure and emotional fulfillment in our middle and later years. To find Passionate Marriage therapists: www.passionatemarriage.com.

FUN AND INSPIRING
MEMOIR AND FICTION

Bauer-Maglin, Nan, editor. *Cut Loose: (Mostly) Older Women Talk About the End of (Mostly) Long-Term Relationships.* Rutgers, NJ: Rutgers University Press, 2006. A compilation of essays by older women who were dumped and write about it with unflinching honesty. There is also a section by experts that is extremely helpful and enlightening.

Ephron, Nora. *I Feel Bad About My Neck: And Other Thoughts on Being a Woman.* New York: Vintage, 2008. The inimitable Nora Ephron writes about being an aging woman in our looks-obsessed society. A fun read.

Finnamore, Suzanne. *Split: A Memoir of Divorce.* New York: Penguin, 2008. A brilliantly written memoir about being cheated on and dumped that is incredibly honest, funny, poetic, and totally avoids cliché.

Liberty, Anita. *How to Heal the Hurt by Hating.* New York: Villard, 2006. As she explains it: "My boyfriend Mitchell, whom I dated for three and a half years, left me for a woman named Heather. To get even, I have devoted my entire career to humiliating him in public." Truly hysterical.

Nestor, Theo Pauline. *How to Sleep Alone in a King-Sized Bed,* New York: Crown, 2008. A wonderful memoir of the author's divorce and an exploration of her own family's legacy of divorce.

Oxenhandler, Noelle. *The Wishing Year: A House, A Man, My Soul: A Memoir of Fulfilled Desire.* New York: Random House, 2008. After her divorce the author launched a year's experiment into wishing for what she really wanted. Both a scholarly exploration into wishing and a personal quest, this book is inspiring and a lot of fun to read.

Richards, Susan. *Chosen Forever: A Memoir.* New York: Soho Press, 2008. After writing her best seller *Chosen by a Horse*, Richards, fifty-five and long divorced, meets the great love of her life on her book tour. A delightful story of finding love late in life.

Shetterly, Caitlin, editor. *Fault Lines: Stories of Divorce.* New York: Berkley, 2001. A collection of fictional stories about divorce by famous authors including John Cheever and Alice Munro.

Swallow, Wendy. *Breaking Apart: A Memoir of Divorce.* New York: Hyperion, 2002. Swallow writes movingly about the shock of divorce, winding up in reduced circumstances, and having to share custody of her two young sons.

INDEX

activities, physical, 23–25, 110
affirmations, 106
age discrimination, 125–27
aging, 198–200, 224–29
alcohol, 29, 159, 194
alimony, 65, 76–79, 85, 86
aloneness, 88–89, 96, 97, 106,
    107, 110–11
anger (rage)
    antidotes to, 22
    bitterness due to ongoing,
        187–88
    brain chemistry contributing
        to, 5–6, 250–52
    of cheating husbands, 240–42
    childhood repression of, 49
    as child response to divorce,
        142, 152
    expressions of, 2, 6, 17, 30,
        261–62
    as fear reaction, 95
    forgiveness and, 22, 256, 257
    post-recovery triggers of,
        275–76
    during relationships, 15, 160
    rituals releasing, 272

balance of power, 172–76,
    177–78, 181–82
betrayal, 239–40, 242–43
bitterness, 187–88, 226, 243, 255
blame, 159, 185, 240–43,
    260–61
boyfriends of spouses,
    152–53, 232
brain chemistry studies, 5–6,
    250–52

change (transition), 159, 181,
    185–87, 197
child custody, 155
childhood experiences
    aloneness ability influenced
        by, 98–99
    relationship choices and,
        46–49, 56–57, 160–61, 180
children
    college financing as settlement
        provision, 84–85, 156
    co-parenting, 154–55, 247–48,
        262, 275
    divorce announcement advice,
        150–53
    divorce closure and, 81
    divorce effects on, 60, 137–45,
        153, 155, 247
    divorce postponement due to,
        148–49
    identity and childhood
        reevaluation of, 143, 144–
        45, 148–49
    infidelity and, 247–49
    introducing new boyfriends to,
        152–53, 232
    leaving home and parental
        neediness, 155–56
    lifestyle adjustments and
        spending time with, 33, 109
    parenting advice, 145, 146–47,
        149–50, 154, 155
    parents' assumptions about
        adult, 141–42, 156
    reconciliation efforts due to, 60
    relationship views of, 140,
        143, 147, 148

support and help with, 16
as support system, 12, 34,
147–49
child support, 83
closure, 80–81
collaborative divorces, 76
college tuition, 84–85, 156
confidence, 121–23, 195, 224–29
co-parenting, 154–55, 247–48,
262, 275
counseling, 7–10, 154. *See also*
marriage counseling
creativity, 93, 105
credit ratings, 116–17
crones, 97–98
crying, 8, 11–12, 100
cybersex, 222

dancing, 197, 229
dating
advice and warnings, 209,
219–24, 222–24, 231–33
"it" factor attraction and age,
224–29
overcoming fear of, 218
personal experiences, 209–14,
215–18
sex and, 205–6, 207–8,
211–13
shaman lovers, 214–15
success strategies, 229–31
deadlock, 173–76
death, fear of, 91, 178, 235
denial, 6, 23, 165
depression, 6, 17, 92, 93, 144,
208, 224, 252
divorce, overview
benefits of, 90, 107, 199,
253–54

cancer analogy, 187
crucial periods for, 54
major issues of, 81
statistics, xxiii, 2, 158, 159, 178

education, 85, 121, 129, 133,
197–98, 202
elderly care, 157
employment
age discrimination and,
125–27
benefits of, 120
career research and search,
121–25, 127–34
challenges facing older women,
121
education and training for,
121, 133
meaningful, 125, 192–93,
200–201
social security benefits and,
135
escapism, 25–29, 196
exercise, 23–25, 199

fear, 87–92, 95–97, 112, 115,
174, 195
feminism, 76–77, 97, 106, 239
finances. *See also* employment
alimony, 65, 76–79, 86, 117
assets disclosure and forensic
accounting, 81–83, 85
equitable distribution laws,
63–64
fear of destitution, 112, 115
financial planning, 79, 116, 118
income changes of older,
divorced women, 64–65, 77,
112–13

planning ahead, 67–68
post-divorce lifestyle
    adjustments and strategies,
    113–20
prenuptial agreements, 157
reverse mortgages, 134–35
settlement change
    provisions, 83
social security benefits, 135
web site resources, 67
forgiveness
    core message of, 255
    definition, 257
    as human nature, 255–56
    as option *versus* requirement,
        256–59
    personal experiences of,
        264–73
    rage and, 22
    self-, 260–64
freeze-and-hide syndrome, 92–94
friends and friendship
    as dating networks, 229–30
    between ex-spouses, 149–50,
        264–69
    as recovery strategy, 93, 104
    shared social networks and
        losing, 104–5
    social communities for, 107–8
    as support system, 12–16,
        14, 109

girlfriends of spouses, 236, 247,
    248–49, 254
grief, 1–3, 5–8, 11–12, 101, 253
guilt, 4, 66, 68, 141, 145, 241–42

holidays, 109, 151
homicide, 252

houses and housing. *See also*
    living alone
    environmental harmony
        practices, 105–6
    post-divorce solutions, 118–20
    reverse mortgages, 134–35
    second mortgages, 68
    as settlement property, 75–76,
        79, 85
humor, 13–14, 18–20

income. *See* employment; finances
infidelity
    age and, 182
    blame, 159, 240–43
    children and, 141, 143, 152,
        156–57, 247–49
    coping and recovery from, 234,
        243, 253–54
    as divorce cause, 159
    divorce laws and, 235
    French practice of, 246
    integrity and ethics,
        237–40, 243
    marriage counseling and, 39
    as other woman, 236
    personal stories and lessons of,
        243–47
    during previous marriages,
        23, 166
    reactions to, 235–36, 242,
        250–53
    societal views of, 234–35,
        236–37
insurance, health, 75, 85
integrity, 165–67, 237–39
Internet dating. *See* dating
intimacy, 169–72

job search. *See* employment
journaling, 18, 22
Judaism, 239, 258, 272
juvenile delinquency, 153, 154

laws, divorce, 69–70, 235
lawyers
    alimony and economic
        negotiations, 78
    collaborative divorce and, 76
    as divorcées, 84
    free or low-cost alternatives to,
        70–72, 74
    premature closure warnings,
        80–81
    preparation and self-reliance
        with, 68–70, 72
    selection of, 72–74
living alone. *See also* loneliness
    benefits of, 90, 107
    childhood experiences
        influencing, 98–100
    cultivating solitude, 102–4
    fear of, 87–92
    financial independence,
        113–18
    friendships, singles *versus*
        couples, 104–5
    initial disorientation and
        adjustment, 93–94
    reality of, 94–95
    as relief, 93, 100
    stereotypes of older, single
        women, 96–98
    strategies for, 93, 105–11
loneliness
    aloneness *versus*, 88–89
    childhood experiences and
        coping with, 98–99

dealing with, 100–102
    fear of, 88
    grief *versus*, 101
    intensity and disorientation of,
        93–94
    during marriage, 54, 100
    rage as response to fear of,
        95–96
    tribal theories and, 92–93
love, 6, 215–17, 250–52

marriage. *See also* marriage
        counseling; marriage
        deconstruction
    children of divorced parents'
        views on, 140
    divorce statistics and length
        of, 159
    foundation for happy, 52
    as legal partnership,
        77–78, 113
    religious views on, 239
    second, and divorce rates, 158
    societal expectations
        and, 160
marriage counseling
    approaches, programs and
        workshops, 42–59
    counselor selection process,
        39–42
    good *versus* typical
        experiences, 37–39
    overview, 35–36
    relationship details indicating
        reconciliation potential, 39
    success statistics, 39–40
marriage deconstruction
    age group considerations,
        181–82

initial attraction assessments,
160–63
integrity, 165–67
intimacy, 169–72
power balance, 172–76, 177–78
purpose of, 158–59
self-analysis questions,
180–81
self-reflection and
responsibility, 22–23
sex life, 167–69
wrong person, marrying the,
163–65
mediation, 74–76
midlife crises, 54, 64, 176–77,
181–82, 236–37

negotiation skills, 66, 78, 80
networking, 124, 229–30
no-fault divorces, 63

outbursts, 30

parental influences, 46–49,
56–57, 98–99, 104, 160
pets, 32–33, 106–7
Phoenix Process, 10, 188–91,
273–74
post-traumatic stress disorder
(PTSD), 92
prenuptial agreements, 157
psychic readings, 29–30

rage. See anger
reconciliation, 35–37. See also
marriage counseling
recovery
age groups and strategies for,
33–34

friendship as strategy for,
93, 104
from infidelity, 234, 243,
253–54
leavers versus left, 3–4
process of, 272–76
timelines for, 6–7, 275
reinvention
age groups ideas, 200–202
aging and physical self,
198–200
as benefit of divorce, 10, 183
destiny fulfillment, 191–94
emotional growth toward,
187–91
self-esteem restoration
strategies, 195–98
transition stages, 185–86
wife syndrome versus authentic
identity, 184–85
rejection, 250–52
relief, as reaction, 93, 100
religion, 239, 257–58
remarriage, 157
remorsefulness, 258–59
retail therapy, 28
retirement, 82, 86, 182
revenge, 17–22, 30, 253–54, 256

security, as illusion, 192
self-esteem, 161, 180, 185, 195,
227–28
settlement proceedings
age group considerations and
provisions, 83–86
alimony, 65, 76–79
divorce law knowledge and
preparation, 69–70
document signing, 82

financial disclosure, 81–83
financial preparation and
planning, 67–68
future change provisions,
83–84
health insurance provisions,
75, 85
house award and costs, 75–76,
79, 85
legal assistance, 68–74
mediation, 74–76
negotiation skills, 66, 78, 80
possessions negotiations, 80
timing and premature closure,
80–81
women and, 66
sex. *See also* infidelity
cybersex, 222
dating and, 205–6, 207–8,
211–14
marriage deconstruction
analysis of, 167–69, 170–71
promiscuity and casual sex,
29, 208, 222–23
shaman lovers, 214–15
shame, 33, 96
shock, 3, 4, 138, 141, 142, 156
shopping, 28
Social Security, 135
solitude, 102–4, 106
soul mates, 169
spinsters, 96

spirituality, 102–3, 193
stalking, 252
step-parents, 153, 249
suicide, 6, 10, 252
support systems
children as, 12, 34, 144,
147–49
communities and groups,
107–8
counselors, 7–10
divorce support groups, 31–32
friendship types as, 12–16
of leavers, 3–4
pets, 32–33
vulnerability expressions and,
11–12
website resources for, 22, 108

teenagers, 84, 110, 153–54, 155,
248
tribal theory, 90–91, 92–93, 97,
261
truces, 149–50

volunteering, 31, 93, 107, 109,
132–33

weight loss, 23–24, 199, 227
"wife" syndrome and identity,
184–85
writing, as therapy, 17–22, 253

ACKNOWLEDGMENTS

Getting through the end of a long marriage while maintaining your sanity is not possible without the help of girlfriends. I couldn't have made it without mine. Thanks many times over to Wendy Wynberg; Nancy Zeldis; Loni Bosnos; Patti Manfrates; Roz Marcus; Minda Zetlin; Joan Miller; Avigail Lansmann. I hope I haven't left anyone out.

I will be eternally grateful to the therapists who got me through the worst of my post-divorce angst and helped my daughter get through it as well: Kali Rosenblum expertly and compassionately guided me through the post-separation wilderness; psychologist Denise Morett said the words that saved my life when I most needed to hear them; my daughter's therapist and director of her special ed program, Alice VanWagner, rescues both of us on an ongoing basis and should be a candidate for sainthood.

Thank you to my wonderful family, especially my mom, Freda—although she is gone, I know she is always standing beside me cheering me on—and her namesake, my adorable, brilliant daughter Freda, who I know will someday also move on from the trauma of divorce. I was constantly supported by my beautiful, inspiring foster daughter Tina Fox, who makes me feel I really am a good mother.

In divorce there are always two sides of the family, who may or may not be speaking. I want to let my niece Erica know that I will always love her even though our families may be estranged. I also want Freda's stepmother to know that despite our differences I am grateful to her for taking such good care of my daughter.

To my lawyer Dan Gartenstein, an advocate with a heart, thanks for keeping me out of trouble and charging me a lot less than you could have.

To the wonderful members of the Woodstock Jewish Congregation, I appreciated all your kind words and hugs—especially Regina Waterhouse, Carol Fox Prescott, Mary Sarsheen, Tsurah August—and of course Rabbi Jonathan Kligler for his words of wisdom.

Thank you to Harry, Bob, and Jamie, the guys I dated who brought me back to life as a woman: I won't include your last names because your current wives/girlfriends might not appreciate it.

Kudos to the town of Woodstock, New York, for being a uniquely welcoming place for writers, artists, and other oddballs like me.

On the literary side I want to acknowledge all the members of the ASJA and Freelance Success forums who were so generous with their encouragement, advice, and support, and the occasional criticism that made me think. There are too many of you to list—but I want to especially thank Randy Dotinga, who came up with the clever title for this book, and Daylle Deanna Schwartz for her encouraging words.

To Laurie Harper, my ever-supportive agent, who brainstormed with me on the idea for this book, and helped me revise the proposal until it worked. Thanks for being my biggest fan.

Thank you to my editor, Mary Norris, who did a meticulous editing job, and stepped in to help when I felt totally overwhelmed.

To Christine Petrozzo, my able and talented assistant, who kept me on track and contributed a lot to this book, including some great interviews.

Thanks to Gini Scott and her service www.publishersagents.com, which helped me sell the book.

I will forever be grateful to Jim Walters, my wise former therapist, without whose encouragement I would never have become a writer in the first place.

Advance praise for *He's History, You're Not*

"Divorce is the loss of a relationship and the death of dreams. It is also a beginning with new hope and possibility. Reading *He's History, You're Not* is like having a friend on your side to help you let go of the past, get through the turmoil, and turn to a better future."

—Abigail Trafford, author of *Crazy Time* and *As Time Goes By: Boomerang Marriages, Serial Spouses, Throwback Couples, and Other Romantic Adventures in an Age of Longevity*

"Erica Manfred wants to be your best girlfriend, the one who stands by your side every step of the way through the tsunami of divorce. And, with this book, she succeeds. But not only is she a best girlfriend, she's a smart girlfriend offering great advice on emotional, legal, financial, and spiritual matters, thoroughly researched and referenced for those who want to dig deeper—and for later, when it's time to move on, she offers advice on Internet dating as well. Best of all, Manfred herself has walked every inch of the divorce plank and with disarming honesty lets us see her own successes and failures on the road back to sanity. A must read for anyone contemplating a divorce or going through one."

—Susan Richards, author of *Chosen Forever*

"Erica Manfred's *He's History, You're Not* is for every woman who suffers the anguish of a ruptured relationship. Having survived and surmounted the pain of her own divorce, Manfred is every reader's 'wise friend,' sharing her own story and the fund of knowledge she accrued along the way so the rest of us need never feel 'alone' or believe we can't survive. For we can; and we do, as Manfred teaches us, inevitably emerge the stronger for it."

—Florence Falk, psychotherapist, and author of *On My Own: The Art of Being a Woman Alone*

"*He's History, You're Not* is like sitting down with an older sister who has already gone through a divorce and can guide you around the pitfalls. Manfred offers a unique, and desperately needed, take on divorce for mature women. Her advice is money-smart, wise, and on target. A straight talking, clear-eyed, and savvy guide, this is required reading for the over-forty divorcee."

—Brette Sember, J.D., author of *The Complete Divorce Handbook* and *The Divorce Organizer & Planner*

"Erica Manfred turned a bad situation into great lessons for other women going through midlife divorce. Her honesty and her ability to find the humor in her experiences make this book a fun yet constructive read."

—Daylle Deanna Schwartz, author of *Nice Girls Can Finish First*

"Erica Manfred's book is exactly what it sets out to be: the warm, witty, gritty, kind, and very knowing friend who's forged ahead, through a forbidding place, and blazed the trail before you. It's packed with information, beautifully organized, and full of funny, poignant, and inspiring stories. It is, in the truest sense, a *companion volume*, the book you'll want to keep beside you as you forge your own new life."

—Noelle (Fintushel) Oxenhandler, author of
The Wishing Year and coauthor of *A Grief Out of Season:
When Your Parents Divorce in Your Adult Years*

"*He's History, You're Not* needed to be written at least a decade ago (or, at least, before my own divorce happened). It's a fun(!), fresh, and practical approach to surviving the big break-up—a must read for anyone over forty, at any stage of the divorce process, whether about to be divorced, just divorced, long divorced, or even just thinking about divorce (wives of certain prominent politicians, take note). Manfred's first-hand tale is compelling not only for its details, but also for the very specific and practical advice she hands out. As an attorney of more than twenty-five years, I will be handing out copies of Manfred's book along with a pack of tissues to all of my female divorce clients. And, maybe to the male clients, too, since many of the tips would work for either gender."

—Susan Ellis Wild, coauthor of *The Unofficial Guide to Getting a Divorce*

"This is one of the few divorce books that addresses the fact that divorce has a different meaning at every age. Manfred is so candid about her own divorce as 'a woman of a certain age' that readers are sure to feel they've found a wise friend to see them through the trauma of divorce and help them discover their postdivorce selves. I wish I'd had this book when I went through my divorce."

—Theo Pauline Nestor, author of *How to Sleep Alone in a King-Size Bed*

"Divorce is different for women in their forties, fifties, and sixties, and Erica Manfred addresses those special concerns head-on, from grieving to finances to dating and sex. Manfred spills her guts, disclosing even embarrassing experiences with emotional nakedness. Her tips are invaluable, and her candor will make you feel she's your best friend sharing her mistakes so you don't have to make them. Through it all, she even manages to be laugh-out-loud funny!"

—Joan Price, author of
Better Than I Ever Expected: Straight Talk About Sex After Sixty